YORKSHIRE
RIPPER THE SECRET MURDERS

YORKSHIRE
RIPPER THE SECRET MURDERS

**THE TRUE STORY OF HOW PETER SUTCLIFFE'S TERRIBLE REIGN
OF TERROR CLAIMED AT LEAST TWENTY-TWO MORE LIVES**

CHRIS CLARK
AND TIM TATE

JOHN BLAKE

Published by John Blake Publishing Ltd,
3 Bramber Court, 2 Bramber Road,
London W14 9PB, England

www.johnblakebooks.com

www.facebook.com/johnblakebooks
twitter.com/jblakebooks

This edition published in 2015

ISBN: 978 1 78418 418 6

All rights reserved. No part of this publication may be reproduced, stored in a retrieval system, or transmitted in any form or by any means, without the prior permission in writing of the publisher, nor be otherwise circulated in any form of binding or cover other than that in which it is published and without a similar condition including this condition being imposed on the subsequent purchaser.

British Library Cataloguing-in-Publication Data:

A catalogue record for this book is available from the British Library.

Design by www.envydesign.co.uk

Printed in Great Britain by CPI Group (UK) Ltd

1 3 5 7 9 10 8 6 4 2

© Text copyright Chris Clark and Tim Tate 2015

The right of Chris Clark and Tim Tate to be identified as the authors of this work has been asserted by them in accordance with the Copyright, Designs and Patents Act 1988.

Papers used by John Blake Publishing are natural, recyclable products made from wood grown in sustainable forests. The manufacturing processes conform to the environmental regulations of the country of origin.

Every attempt has been made to contact the relevant copyright-holders, but some were unobtainable. We would be grateful if the appropriate people could contact us.

To Jeanne. Thank you for enduring my long absences,
for your loyalty and encouragement and most of all for
believing in me. You are the wind beneath my wings.

CHRIS CLARK

For my children, born in the heartland of the Yorkshire
Ripper but who grew up, thankfully, free of his shadow.
And for Mia, whose support makes everything possible.

TIM TATE

In this truck is a man
Whose latent genius, if
Unleashed, would rock the
Nation, whose dynamic energy
Would overpower those
Around him. Better let him sleep?

Handwritten poem found in the cab of Peter Sutcliffe's lorry
2 January 1981

We feel it highly improbable the crimes in respect of
which Sutcliffe has been charged and convicted
are the only ones attributable to him.

Sir Lawrence Byford: Report into the police handling
of the Yorkshire Ripper case.
December 1981

CONTENTS

AUTHORS' FOREWORDS

31 December 1978

It started snowing at Nottingham. It would not stop until the end of May.

The M1 was quiet that New Year's Eve, a combination of the weather and the season. A cheap in-car cassette player belted out the hits: Tom Robinson's '2-4-6-8 Motorway', 'Rat Trap' by The Boomtown Rats and – inevitably, given my destination – Kate Bush's extraordinary 'Wuthering Heights'. Even at full, distorted volume it struggled against the straining engine of my overladen Mini.

I had been a journalist – a *reporter*, as we were taught to term ourselves back then – for less than a year, learning the trade on local weekly newspapers in the comfortable Surrey commuter belt. But now I was heading north, for a new job in what every newspaperman knew was the traditional heartland of good stories: Yorkshire.

And not *just* Yorkshire, and not just *any* good stories. I was bound for – and, under the industry's strict apprentice scheme, *bound to* – a paper in the epicentre of the area and the story that was then beginning to grip the nation. I was to join the local newspaper in Keighley – the place where a vicious killer had apparently struck his first blows in what had been dubbed the Yorkshire Ripper murders.

The phrase had first been used ten months earlier. In early February 1978, the body of Helen Rytka, an eighteen-year-old prostitute, had been found in a timber yard in Huddersfield. She had suffered severe head injuries – the result of being hit from behind with a hammer; she had also been stabbed thirteen times, causing savage wounds to her lungs, heart, liver and stomach.

Helen Rytka was, according to West Yorkshire Police, the likely eighth victim of the same serial killer. The severity and brutality of the injuries each had suffered – and the fact that most were prostitutes – recalled the crimes of Victorian London's Jack the Ripper, and for more than two years the tabloid press had referred to 'Ripper-style' killings. From Rytka's murder onwards this would be abandoned in favour of a shorter and pithier description: the man being sought was henceforth 'The Yorkshire Ripper'.

The hunt for Britain's newest serial killer exploded from being merely a regional story to dominating the front pages of national papers and television news headlines. The shocking and ritualistic nature of the Ripper murders was recounted extensively and feverishly; and while almost all the victims appeared then to be prostitutes, press coverage began to refer to a climate of fear affecting all women in the county – 'respectable ladies' as well as those who worked the streets.

For a young reporter with ambitions, Yorkshire was unquestionably the place to be.

A few miles south of Leeds – scene of four presumed Ripper murders – the M1 branches off to join the M62; foot pressed hard to the floor, I urged the overburdened little car up the exit slope and on towards Bradford (the location for two more).

Even under a softening blanket of snow, Bradford appeared grim: a shabby city grown out of its mill-town roots and falling on increasingly desperate times. A hundred years of pollution and grime clung to the millstone grit of row after row of terraced houses. Some places reek so deeply of poverty that their stench seeps in even through the closed windows of a speeding car. The Mini laboured on, struggling to shrug off the meanness of the city and to cope with the growing piles of soot-blackened slush and snow.

From Bradford the road wound up through the Aire Valley, past the once-proud villas of Manningham Lane – now down-at-heel and an edge-marker for the city's red-light area – towards Shipley and Bingley, and then on to the small town of Keighley, surrounded by the moors and memories of its literary luminaries, the Brontë sisters. *Wuthering Heights*, indeed.

I would spend the next four years working for newspapers in West Yorkshire – first weekly, then the regional daily, the *Yorkshire Post*. In those four years the callous blight of Thatcherism would take an unforgiving toll on an already struggling region: unemployment, poverty and desperation were its constant companions.

And fear, too. The Yorkshire Ripper would strike again and again, beating the life out of five more women, gouging and stabbing their stunned bodies in recession-hit back alleys across the county, and leaving yet others for dead. At least five of his murder victims were middle class and with no connection to the local vice trade.

Now terror was no longer a press exaggeration: families urged their women either to stay indoors at night or, if they must venture out, to do so in pairs. Darkness comes early in the northern winter: by mid-afternoon there was, in those Ripper years, a palpable tension in the streets.

That fear was heightened by the seeming powerlessness of West Yorkshire Police's Ripper Squad to catch their quarry. The largest manhunt in British criminal history was played out very publicly – in newspapers, on television and radio, day in and day out. Poster campaigns, public appeals, telephone hotlines: nothing brought the detectives closer to the serial killer stalking Yorkshire's streets.

And then it was over.

On 3 January 1981 – exactly three years and three days since I had arrived in Yorkshire – police issued the good news: a man they believed to be the Ripper was in custody.

Television news played footage of senior detectives smiling and relaxing for the first time. The time for fear was over: now it was time for anger. Crowds, baying for blood and revenge, crowded round police stations and flocked to the magistrate's court where Peter William Sutcliffe – a thirty-four-year-old lorry driver from Bradford – was first arraigned.

Under English law, after someone is charged almost nothing

about the alleged criminal can be published: the principle of 'innocent until proven guilty' – the emphasis being on 'proven' – is enshrined in statutes aimed at ensuring a jury is not prejudiced by bad publicity against the person facing trial before them.

If the public – fed a television diet of American police procedurals where no such law applies – was frustrated, journalists took the opportunity to spend the months before trial uncovering the life story of Peter Sutcliffe. Chequebooks were flourished; wads of cash flashed. Anyone with a story to tell – and who could be bought – was signed up on the spot. Those with the most precious commodity of all – photographs – could claim the highest price.

But if the nation's press was hard at work on the *who* – the man behind Britain's longest run of serial killings – who was at work on the *why*? Who would explain what drove this apparently happily married man to such savage butchery of women? We contented ourselves with the assurance that all would be revealed at his trial. Off the record, police officers hinted at psychiatric reports that would uncover the Yorkshire Ripper's motivation. We settled down for a lengthy wait: no one expected the trial to take place until much later in the year.

We were wrong. And in almost every respect. Because Peter Sutcliffe's trial began remarkably quickly – less than four months from the date of his capture. And rather than a full and exhaustive examination, the prosecution had decided on much shorter and much more cursory proceedings.

Instead of a trial for murder, the Yorkshire Ripper was to be allowed to plead guilty to the lesser charge of manslaughter, on the grounds of mental illness.

It was an extraordinary decision – and one that the

prosecution, led by the government's most senior law officer, would soon be forced ignominiously to abandon. The country wanted – it needed – a trial, and a trial it would have, lasting four long weeks.

And yet, despite this, much remained hidden. Evidence that should have been seen or heard was suppressed. The truth about Peter William Sutcliffe, and the true number of his victims, was locked away in the files and archives of West Yorkshire Police, hidden from public view and understanding.

The result was not simply a failure adequately to inform the public. It would cause – largely unseen – investigations into a long series of other, unsolved murders to be curtailed or abandoned.

The suppression of what West Yorkshire Police knew – or at least should have known – about Peter Sutcliffe and his motives for murder ensured that these killings still remain unsolved today.

This is no academic exercise, no mere bureaucratic failing. The families of at least twenty-two murdered women have been cheated of their right to know how and why their loved ones died; the pain of living with that may diminish over time, but it never fades completely away. Five other women survived his attacks: their plight, too, has never been officially acknowledged. And there are even two cases in which men were the victims – one who died and one who lives to this day with the legacy of his injuries.

Worse still, the police blunders and subsequent suppression of evidence ensured that three entirely innocent men were imprisoned for murders committed by the Yorkshire Ripper. They lost the best parts of their adult lives, locked up and forgotten in stinking cells for more than two decades each.

AUTHORS' FOREWORDS

This book is the story not just of those long-cold killings, of the forgotten families and of three terrible miscarriages of justice. It is also the story of how an instinct of institutional self-protection has enabled the truth about Peter Sutcliffe to be hidden for more than thirty years.

That truth challenges much of what we have come to know about one of Britain's most terrible serial killers. It suggests that even the most fundamental element of his story – the very term 'The Yorkshire Ripper' – is dangerously wrong.

That this truth can now be told is attributable to one remarkable ex-policeman. His name is Chris Clark.

Tim Tate, June 2015

I joined the police force to make a difference.

My first real job was that of a gardener. Not just any gardener, just as my boss was not any ordinary employer. Between 1964 and 1966, I worked at Sandringham House, an enormous country pile set in 20,000 acres of beautiful Norfolk countryside. My job was to tend the kitchen gardens on behalf of the owner: she was Her Majesty the Queen.

But I knew I wanted to do something more, something different – something that involved service to the public rather than its head of state. And so, on Thursday, 10 March 1966, I found myself boarding the train at King's Lynn for the fifty-mile journey to Norwich. There, in the city's Shirehall magistrate's court, I was to be sworn in as an officer of the Norfolk Constabulary.

When the ceremony was over I was Constable 409, Clark,

C: 'A citizen locally appointed but having authority under the Crown for the protection of life and property, the maintenance of order, the prevention and detection of crime and the prosecution of offenders against the Peace.'

I then collected my warrant card, uniform and the tools of my new trade: one set of handcuffs, a whistle and a truncheon.

After a thirteen-week training course in Oxfordshire I was ready to pound the beat as a probationary constable. I was sent to an urban district on the fringes of Norwich, which at that time had its own separate police force.

I was then twenty years old, rather shy and distinctly introverted. But the job – as all coppers call it – was no place for shrinking violets. By the mid-1960s, crime was growing and changing fast. The immediate post-war years had seen an explosion in robberies – many of them carried out with the glut of weapons brought home from the fight against Hitler – in cities up and down the country. But throughout the 1940s and 1950s there was still strong respect for the law and particularly for those who upheld it: attacks on policemen were rare and shocking.

Shortly after I began patrolling my beat – often at night, always alone, unarmed (of course) and with no means of communication other than the traditional whistle and any public telephone that happened to be nearby – the police and the country itself received a wake-up call.

The summer of 1966 had, by and large, been a good one: England was swinging (not that we saw much of this in Norfolk) and the national football team had just won the World Cup. But within a fortnight the news would be dominated by what became known as the Massacre of Braybrook Street.

Harry Roberts – a thirty-year-old petty criminal who had

learned his trade as a child black marketeer during the war, before learning how to kill during two years' National Service – shot dead three unarmed police officers in broad daylight in a residential street in London's Shepherd's Bush. He and his accomplices then went on the run: using his military training, Roberts evaded capture for almost three months.

If any one crime symbolised the transformation coming over Britain, it was the cold-blooded murders of those three police officers. The world we had known was changing – and not for the better.

By the time I'd finished, the police force itself had changed. Like other forces up and down the country, the old city, county and borough constabularies were merged into new and amalgamated organisations. This was, I think, the beginning of the end for much that had been traditional: the bobby on the beat was losing out to the patrol car. And the hierarchy was changing, too: the bosses and management we had worked under were solid ex-World War Two veterans who had grafted their way to the top and had both real experience and the ability to deal with their staff in a fatherly way that got the best out of them.

Gradually, they were squeezed out by high-flyers who came into the job with higher education qualifications – no bad thing, of course – but more worryingly with old-school ties and membership of secretive masonic lodges.

But there was, at least, one change for the better. It was during this time that divisional intelligence officers – collators, as they became known – were introduced, and I was instrumental in setting up the office for the King's Lynn district. From then until 1991, I worked in the criminal intelligence section –

looking to use information to outsmart and outmanoeuvre the professional criminal.

It didn't stop me also fulfilling other duties – some of which returned me to my first place of employment. Between 1969 and 1981, I regularly undertook royalty protection duties at Sandringham. This was the period when 'The Troubles' – as the IRA's war against the British state was politely known – were at their height. Despite the growing threats of bombings and attempted assassinations, my colleagues and I patrolled the perimeter of the house, unarmed except for solid lumps of *lignum vitae* wood – our trusty truncheons. We had only our eyes and ears, and precious little in the way of equipment to warn our control room should we detect any unauthorised approach to the royal residence. It seems a long, long way from today's royal protection squads, with their automatic weapons, body armour and sophisticated communication systems.

I might have grown up on the job and lost a bit of the innocence and shyness of my first years as a copper, but I was never one to push myself forward for promotion. While the police force changed around me, becoming ever more political and ever less concerned with the needs of the public, I kept my head down and got on with the job of safeguarding life and property. I didn't bother with exams, happy to remain a constable for my entire career.

But intelligence work fascinated me. When, in 1987, I took over the full-time post of local intelligence officer for King's Lynn division of Norfolk, I studied the new science of crime pattern analysis; very quickly I realised that organised criminals didn't restrict themselves to our turf but also operated freely in neighbouring divisions and counties. It may sound obvious now, but back then policing was still very parochial, and for all the new university-educated men coming in to run the force, there was still a widespread assumption that local villains would helpfully confine themselves to our arbitrary divisional borders.

I was able – and, more importantly, willing – to investigate the reality. Crime and criminals were increasingly mobile. And so I forged links with the local intelligence officers for the surrounding divisions. From there it was a short step to extending our informal information network out to Lincolnshire, Cambridgeshire and Suffolk, as well as the regional intelligence and crime squads for the east of England.

Writing this now, almost thirty years later, it all seems terribly obvious. But at the time it was revolutionary: there was then no National Criminal Intelligence Service (that wouldn't be set up until 1992) and police forces across the country tended to view each other with suspicion, rivalry and sometimes outright hostility. The idea of sharing information was often anathema: detectives who might be separated geographically by no more than a few miles refused to pass on intelligence to their opposite numbers.

It was, quite simply, madness. And it would play a part in the terrible fiasco of the Yorkshire Ripper murders.

In 1994, I finally retired. I hung up my uniform and truncheon, handed back my warrant card. Almost thirty years on the job had, it's fair to say, taken their toll. I was mentally and physically exhausted, suffering from work-induced stress and my first marriage had imploded under the strain.

But retiring proved the making of me, and it would lead to this book.

I met my second wife, Jeanne, in 2002. It turned out that, decades earlier, while still a youngster, she had survived an attempted abduction. This crime had never been solved and had left deep scars. Together we began studying the evidence, piecing together clues: it would lead to a breakthrough, which, perhaps one day, will see the man responsible (a convicted child killer) brought to justice.

But that investigation also threw up the details of an astonishing number of unsolved murders. There were – there are – dozens of killings, dating back more than fifty years. The sheer number astonished me: how could there be such a catalogue of long-cold cases? Who was trying to solve them today?

The answer shocked me even more than the numbers of them. No one.

Retired coppers who reinvestigate cold cases have become something of a cliché: switch on any TV channel, search around the internet, and you'll find any number of us turning our long-honed skills to solving everything from the original Jack the Ripper crimes to the conspiracies surrounding 9/11. It's a cliché I'm happy to adopt – so happy, in fact, that I've formally registered myself as The Armchair Detective.

But the more I looked at the dozens of cold cases, the more my intelligence background and training kicked in and shouted at me. There were *patterns* – clear, definable, evident repetitions – that stood out in many of them. What's more, those patterns (which are, to a police intelligence officer, as telling as fingerprints) reminded me of someone: the Yorkshire Ripper.

When I began I had no idea what my investigations would involve. Years of digging and dead ends, Freedom of Information Act applications and refusals: these have been my constant companions for the past three years.

But I have also met and talked to the families of these

long-cold murder victims. For them, the pain of not knowing how, why and at whose hand their loved ones died is almost unbearable. And because I know – or at least have reached a solid, responsible, policeman's conclusion – who killed their sisters, mothers or brothers I have a duty to them to speak up.

And I have also met one of the men who spent decades in prison for a crime he did not commit – a murder that every single piece of evidence suggests was carried out by the Yorkshire Ripper. That, too, imposes a duty to speak out.

This book is the result.

Chris Clark, June 2015

INTRODUCTION

Friday, 22 May 1981: 4.30 p.m.
Central Criminal Court, London

Peter William Sutcliffe, the jury have found you guilty of thirteen charges of murder. If I may say so, murder of a very cowardly nature. For each was a woman. It was murder by getting behind her and beating her on the head with a hammer from behind.

It is difficult to find words that are adequate in my judgement to describe the brutality and gravity of these offences and I say at once I am not going to pause to seek those words. I am prepared to let the catalogue of crimes speak for itself.

Mr Justice Boreham, the sixty-two-year-old judge who had presided over the month-long trial of Peter Sutcliffe, warmed to his task of sentencing the man who had brought terror to the people of Yorkshire.

It is a population which to my knowledge does not lack fortitude. But I am left in no doubt that women from a wide area were in the deepest fear, and I have no doubts too that that fear spilled over to their menfolk on their account.

I have no doubt that you are a very dangerous man indeed. The sentence for murder is laid down by the law and is immutable. It is a sentence that you be imprisoned for life.

I shall recommend to the Home Secretary that the minimum period that should elapse before he orders your release on licence shall be thirty years. That is a long period, an unusually long period in my judgement, but I believe you are an unusually dangerous man. I express my hope that when I have said life imprisonment, it will precisely mean that. For reasons that I have already discussed with your counsel in your presence I do not believe that I can make that as a recommendation in statute.

So far as the other seven counts of attempted murder are concerned, those, too, will carry sentences of life imprisonment.

You may go.

The Yorkshire Ripper was led down the steps from the court, to the holding cells below. Within hours he would be inducted into Britain's crumbling Victorian penal system, to begin his twenty life sentences in Parkhurst Prison.

On that late spring afternoon, three other men – convicted

killers all – were several years into their sentences for the brutal murders of young, defenceless women. Stephen Downing, Andrew Evans and Anthony Steel were, by then, used to the routine of prison life; used to the unique stench of their confinement – a sour combination of sweat, ingrained dirt and stale cigarette smoke.

They were used, too, to the sapping boredom of their days, and the frequent bouts of violence that provided welcome excitement and unwelcome fear in equal measure.

They did not know each other, but they had two things in common. Each was innocent of the crime for which he had been convicted. And each was paying the price for murders committed by the man then held under close guard in the cells under the Old Bailey.

They, too, were victims of the Yorkshire Ripper.

ONE

R. VS SUTCLIFFE

Wednesday, 29 April 1981: 9.30 a.m.
Court One, Central Criminal Court, London

They had begun queuing the night before. The narrow street in front of the Old Bailey was crowded with people hoping for a glimpse of the Yorkshire Ripper or – for the lucky few – a seat in the public gallery.

That section of Britain's most famous criminal court held just thirty seats. By the next morning, more than 300 men and women were lined up outside. For most of them, the only reward they would receive for their patience came at 9.34 a.m., when an armoured police van – flanked by two squad cars, sirens screaming and blue lights flashing – sped past into the secure receiving area.

Press passes had been issued some days earlier. National and provincial newspapers, radio and television all sent reporters and star columnists, producers and on-screen correspondents; outside the court foreign journalists who had not been allocated a place offered up to £1,000 to buy the passes of those who had.

Public interest in the case was all-consuming and every major paper had set aside vast numbers of column inches for the next day's editions. But they were not planning on traditional court reports: there was no expectation of verbatim accounts of thrust and parry by prosecution and defence.

The media had been quietly briefed that, far from being 'the trial of the century', what would play out that morning would be little more than a formality. The prosecution in *Regina vs Sutcliffe* had accepted a claim by the defence team that their client was, essentially, mad. He would plead guilty not to serial murder but to thirteen counts of manslaughter on the grounds of diminished responsibility – though he simultaneously agreed to plead guilty to the seven counts of attempted murder covering his attacks on the women who had survived – and the Crown would graciously assent.

It was – though neither side would use the term – a distinctly un-British bit of shabby plea-bargaining. The defence knew that psychiatric reports all suggested that Peter Sutcliffe was suffering from paranoid schizophrenia, and thus met the legal threshold for diminished responsibility. The Crown would later claim that it agreed to admission of lesser offences – and with it the certainty of a short and detail-free hearing – to spare the families of his victims 'many days of extensive press coverage and detailed knowledge of the horrifying injuries'.

Quite what business the prosecution had suppressing this information was never challenged. But the proposed deal would have had one other effect, whether intended or not: it would have protected from public sight some of the more glaring failures of West Yorkshire Police throughout its five-year manhunt.

And so when, shortly after 11 a.m., Peter Sutcliffe stood up in the dock to answer the charges, no jury was present – a clear signal that this was not to be a conventional murder trial.

The court usher read out each of the thirteen counts of murder, followed by the seven charges of attempted murder. In a quiet, high-pitched voice, with the distinctive flat vowels of Bradford, Sutcliffe stumbled over his responses so frequently that the entire performance lasted seven minutes. For the thirteen women who had died at his hands he pleaded: 'Not guilty to murder but guilty to manslaughter on the grounds of diminished responsibility.'

Sir Michael Havers, as Attorney General both the most senior lawyer in England and simultaneously a government minister, rose to address the court. He solemnly advised the judge that the Crown accepted Sutcliffe's pleas. He did so on the basis of reports by four psychiatrists who had interviewed the Yorkshire Ripper.

I have met with them to discuss their reports with the greatest care and anxiety and at great length. The general consensus of the doctors is that this is a case of diminished responsibility, the illness being paranoiac schizophrenia.

The script, at this point, called for the judge to acquiesce, the jury to be dismissed (before it had even seen the accused) and for a two-day recital of psychiatric evidence. The script, however, did not take account of Mr Justice Boreham. The judge's reply caught Havers on the hop.

I have very grave anxieties about Sutcliffe and his pleas. I would like you to explain in far greater detail than usual any decision that you are going to make about the acceptance of these pleas.

For the next two hours, the press and public gallery was treated to the bizarre spectacle of the Attorney General – the man charged with leading the prosecution – assuming instead the role of de facto defence counsel. Evidently nonplussed, Havers set out the reasons why the Crown was prepared to accept the pleas of diminished responsibility: he detailed Sutcliffe's conversations with the psychiatrists, their reports and the Ripper's statements to them that he had been ordered by God to clean the streets of prostitutes. The defence – which would, in any conventional trial, have been responsible for introducing this mitigating evidence – sat quietly while the Crown did the job for it.

At the end of the extraordinary morning session, Havers summarised his argument succinctly: 'This', he solemnly insisted, 'is a case of diminished responsibility.'

If the Crown believed it could get away with such a clearly shabby plea bargain, it had evidently failed to do its homework.

Mr Justice Boreham, a veteran of the criminal bar, had a well-earned reputation for the legal niceties – and for frowning on informal deals between prosecution and defence. Six years before he presided over the Ripper trial, he had made this position admirably clear when, at the start of a trial for rape, the prosecution announced it had agreed to accept a defence plea to the lesser charge of unlawful sexual intercourse. Boreham had rejected the proposed deal, telling the prosecutor: 'It is for me to see that justice is done, and the Crown should consider very carefully where its duty lies.'

As Havers resumed his seat in Court One, apparently confident that his argument – and his status as the government's most senior law officer – had done the trick, Boreham was about to remind him exactly where his responsibility ended and that of the judge began.

The matter that troubles me is not the medical opinions, because there is a consensus. But it seems to me that all of these opinions – and I say this without criticism – all these opinions are based simply on what this defendant has told the doctors, nothing more.

Moreover what he has told the doctors conflicts substantially with what he told the police on the morning of arrest. I use the word 'conflict' advisedly. In statements to the police he expressed a desire to kill all women.

If that is right – and here I really need your help – is that not a matter which ought to be tested? Where lies the evidence which gives these doctors the factual basis for these pleas? It is a matter for the defendant to establish. It is a matter for a jury. We have in a sense conducted a trial which has satisfied us. It seems to me it would be more appropriate if this case were dealt with by a jury.

The ensuing ninety-minute lunch adjournment must have been distinctly frenetic. When the court resumed, Sir Michael Havers performed what tabloid journalists call 'a reverse ferret'. He abandoned the Crown's previous acceptance that Peter Sutcliffe was mad, and announced instead that the prosecution was

5

ready and able to prove the exact opposite. The defence was much less ready: Sutcliffe's lead barrister, James Chadwin QC, pleaded for time to prepare his case. After some discussion, Mr Justice Boreham agreed: the trial of the Yorkshire Ripper – a full trial this time – would now begin six days later.

* * *

Tuesday, 5 May 1981: 9.45 a.m.
Central Criminal Court, London

They had queued, once again, since the previous afternoon. Monday, 4 May was a bank holiday, enabling would-be spectators to travel from all over the country in the hope of catching a glimpse of the Ripper. Newspapers reported the claims of a retired butcher from Harrogate that he and his wife had attended every one of Peter Sutcliffe's remand hearings, while an 'Essex mother' proudly announced that she and her teenage son planned to be there 'every day, if we can get in'.

The pavement outside the Old Bailey was covered in tents and sleeping bags, leading *The Times* to sniff about 'a motley rabble … that could have come straight from a Newgate hanging with only a quick change of costume'.

In the event, these representatives of the unruly lower orders (as the lofty men of *The Times* evidently saw them) were unlikely to be granted their wishes. The rather less patrician *Guardian* later reported that the public gallery and VIP benches inside Court One were permanently occupied by those of a higher income group.

A succession of well-groomed middle-aged women with Harrods carrier bags and winter suntans sat there with their daughters or best friends from 10.30 in the morning until the curtain fell at four [in the] afternoon.

There were free seats for the manager of the hotel where the Yorkshire police were staying, for MPs, councillors, sundry lawyers with their children, the Arsenal goalkeeper Pat Jennings and for three men who were commended in another case for tackling a bank robber.

Those privileged spectators could feast their eyes on a long oak table in the well of the court: on it was arrayed the collection of Peter Sutcliffe's 'killing tackle'. Seven ball-peen hammers, a claw hammer, a hacksaw, a long and wickedly thin kitchen knife, an assortment of carving knives and screwdrivers, a cobbler's knife and a short stretch of rope. All had yellow labels attached to them; all were recovered from Sutcliffe's possession – the tools of his trade in murder.

There was, though only the police, prosecution and defence knew it, a singular omission from this grisly tableau – a vital piece of the Yorkshire Ripper's killing kit, seized from him at the same time as the other exhibits laid out on the table. Its absence would have a devastating impact on future investigations into Peter Sutcliffe's crimes, and the continuing incarceration of three entirely innocent men. It also spoke volumes about the honesty of the entire Ripper trial.

At 9.45 a.m., the clerk of the court rose from his place beneath the judge's oak and leather chair and called for silence. In the ensuing quiet the sound of Sutcliffe and four burly warders climbing the wooden stairs into the dock echoed around the room.

Sutcliffe was dressed in a grey suit with an open-necked pale-blue shirt. On his feet were what farmers in West Yorkshire called 'dealer boots' – high-sided, laceless and made of tan leather.

For a man who, according to his barrister, was suffering from an acute mental illness, Peter Sutcliffe appeared remarkably alert and astute. As the process of picking a jury progressed, he twice moved to the front of the dock and instructed his counsel to reject candidates.

When the jury of six men and six women was finally sworn in, the clerk of the court read out the indictment. Sutcliffe was charged with the murders of thirteen women, starting with Wilma McCann in October 1975 and ending with Jacqueline Hill in November 1980 – and the attempted murder of seven others. And then Sir Michael Havers rose to make the opening speech on behalf of the prosecution.

Havers was both an obvious and an interesting choice to present the Crown's case: under England's antique rules of jurisprudence it was quite usual for the Attorney General – a politician and member of the government – to adopt the role of chief prosecutor in high-profile cases, and Havers had done so on several previous occasions.

But it was precisely those previous trials that should have been the cause for concern. Havers had represented the Crown in two of the most notable miscarriages of justice in British judicial history: the trial and appeal of the Guildford Four and also of the Maguire family (known as the Maguire Seven) – all of whom were wrongfully convicted and who collectively served a total of 113 years in prison.

In the case of the Guildford Four, the Director of Public

Prosecutions, for whom Havers was acting, was found to have suppressed evidence that supported two of the men's claims of innocence. Papers were found in the prosecution's files, marked 'Not to be shown to the defence'. Despite the fact that these documents clearly showed that the men had alibis, Havers had taunted one of them in court, sneering at him that he had no alibi. The sorry business showed a shameful and cynical disregard for both the truth and justice – and Havers was at its shabby heart.

Almost from his first words in the Ripper trial, Havers drew yet more controversy: in his introductory speech he seemed to suggest that some of Sutcliffe's victims were less deserving of sympathy than others: 'Some were prostitutes, but perhaps the saddest part of the case is that some were not. The last six attacks were on totally respectable women.' Within hours women demonstrated outside the Old Bailey with placards accusing Havers of 'condoning the murder of prostitutes'.

But was it murder? That was the question Havers began setting out for the jury. The evidence of fact showed that Peter Sutcliffe had carried out a series of calculated, premeditated and sadistic murders. But what drove him to do so? Havers told the court that there was medical evidence indicating Sutcliffe suffered from paranoid schizophrenia: all four doctors who had examined him since his arrest were agreed on the diagnosis. In one of these examinations the Yorkshire Ripper had told a psychiatrist about his motive for the killings. 'He said, in short, that he had messages from God to kill prostitutes and that what he was doing was a divine mission.'

If true, Havers explained, this could amount to 'an abnormality of the mind which, in the view of the doctors, substantially impairs his mental responsibility for his acts, namely murder'.

But the doctors' opinions were just that – opinions. What's more, they were based entirely on Peter Sutcliffe's own version of events – an account that had changed significantly between his confession to the police and his meetings with the psychiatrists.

Mindful of Mr Justice Boreham's instruction that the jury alone could decide whether the claim of insanity was true, Havers set out the question they should bear in mind throughout the evidence that would be set before them.

> The reason for this trial is simple. There is a marked, significant difference between the version which Sutcliffe gave to the police and the version he gave to the doctors. You will have to consider whether the doctors might, in fact, have been deceived by this man; whether he sought to pull the wool over their eyes, or whether the doctors are just plain wrong. You will have to decide whether as a clever, callous murderer he has deliberately set out to provide a cock and bull story to avoid conviction for murder.

What Havers did not explain – and what would be suppressed throughout the trial – was that the police and prosecutors had strong evidence of the Yorkshire Ripper's real motive. That evidence remained locked up in the filing cabinets of West Yorkshire Police, and would remain so long into the distant future. By this deliberate omission, the true extent of Peter Sutcliffe's murderous reign of terror would be hidden: the killings of at least twenty-two women, the attempted murder of five more and two attacks on men – one fatal – would all be left unsolved. Worse still, three innocent men would rot for decades behind bars for crimes they did not commit.

Instead, the prosecution began with a lengthy exposition detailing each of the thirteen murders and seven attempted murders. In doing so, Havers made extensive use of Peter Sutcliffe's own confession statement to police – a document so extensive that it had taken almost sixteen laborious hours to record on handwritten forms. The confession was unequivocally untruthful – at least in so far as Sutcliffe only admitted responsibility for twelve of the twenty attacks for which he was now being tried: but it did provide the Crown with an easy way to lay out its case.

What the twenty cases also revealed was the Yorkshire Ripper's modus operandi. For police investigating serial killers, an established MO amounts to a personal signature – a trademark by which his crimes can be recognised and defined. It can include the method of attack, the implements used, reoccurring locations, dates and times: fitted together, it can reveal a pattern of habitual or repeated behaviour.

What emerged from the catalogue of slaughter and attacks Havers presented to the jury was something even more telling: Peter Sutcliffe deliberately altered the constituent elements of his MO, regularly changing its pattern by dropping some parts of the ritual or introducing new ones. West Yorkshire Police failed to spot this and, as a result, failed to see all of the elements of the Ripper's MO. This was one reason the manhunt had dragged on for five long years: it was also the reason why detectives allowed themselves to be misled by their quarry when they finally caught him.

But as Havers laid out the facts of the twenty cases for the jury – the shocking and gruesome details of Sutcliffe's reign of terror – the whole picture should have been clear to see.

The first identified victim had been thirty-six-year-old Anna Patricia Rogulskyj, a slim blonde Irish woman who had moved to Keighley at the age of fifteen. She had found work at Woolworths in the town centre; at the same place she had also met her future husband, Roman, part of Keighley's unexpectedly large Ukrainian community. The pair had married in 1957 and divorced in 1973.

Anna then took up with another local man, Geoffrey Hughes. On Friday, 4 July 1975, the couple had quarrelled and Anna travelled to Bradford to drown her sorrows at a nightclub. She hitched a ride back to Keighley around midnight: she was distinctly inebriated. When she got home she discovered that Geoff had packed up his belongings and left.

Anna poured herself a stiff drink, put her favourite record on the stereo and became increasingly maudlin. Around 2 a.m., she decided her boyfriend must have gone back to his own house, and set off to find him.

The two main streets in Keighley – North Street and Cavendish Street – form two sides of a triangle containing most of the shops, clubs and, in 1975, the town's cinema. Anna turned off North Street and into Alice Street behind the Ritz Picture House; from here it was a few strides to one of the maze of little cobbled streets containing Geoff's terraced cottage.

Keighley did not have a red-light district – the town was too small and too near the known prostitution area in Bradford to have established one of its own. But like most grimy and impoverished working-class places, there were a handful of prostitutes to be found: Peter Sutcliffe had heard about them and had visited the town on several previous occasions. That Saturday morning he was back.

As Anna Rogulskyj tottered over the cobbled streets she heard a man's voice call out from a darkened doorway; he asked if she 'fancied it'. Anna was no prostitute and never had been: she briskly replied, 'Not on your life', and quickened her pace until she reached Geoff's house. Despite pounding on the front door, yelling and finally smashing a window with her shoe, she could get no answer; she turned round and headed back home.

As she passed through the alleyway behind the cinema she heard the same voice asking the same question as before: did she 'fancy it'? Anna had barely rebuffed and got past him when she was hit three times on the back of the head with a ball-peen hammer. She dropped like a stone, unconscious after the first blow.

As her blood seeped out on to the cobbles, Sutcliffe stood over her. He pulled down her panties, pulled up her blouse and began to slash her exposed stomach with a knife. He was about to finish her off by stabbing her in the stomach, when a neighbour, disturbed by the noise, called out and asked what was happening.

Sutcliffe called back, calmly reassuring the man that there was no problem and that all was well. He rearranged Anna's clothing then strode briskly away, leaving his victim bleeding profusely and barely alive. Anna Rogulskyj was found at 2.20 a.m. and rushed to hospital: only twelve hours of emergency surgery saved her life.

In his police statement, Peter Sutcliffe readily admitted that he had intended to kill Anna and that he had set out equipped with the hammer specifically to do so. He also let slip something that should have alerted the detectives: he told them that he knew Anna 'had a funny name'. Since there had been only the briefest of words between them that night, he had to have previously spoken with her.

The attack on Anna Rogulskyj provided the first clear elements of the Yorkshire Ripper's MO: he had knowledge of his victim and was sufficiently confident to make initial sexual approaches to her before smashing her skull from behind with a hammer. He then pulled up her clothing before mutilating the body, and intended to finish with the act of killing.

That MO was to be repeated six weeks later. On Friday, 15 August 1975, Sutcliffe went out drinking with his friend, Trevor Birdsall. They visited several pubs before ending up in the Royal Oak in the town centre. In the bar Sutcliffe told Birdsall that he thought the pub was full of prostitutes.

Olive Smelt was forty-six, an office cleaner and a happily married mother of three. Most Fridays she would venture out into Halifax for a few drinks with friends; she was emphatically not a prostitute. That evening she arrived in the Royal Oak a few minutes before closing time and ordered a sweet Copper Beech sherry. She chatted with the bar staff and arranged a lift from the town centre to the fish and chip shop near her home: here she planned to buy a late supper to share with her husband.

Across the pub, Sutcliffe pointed at Olive and muttered to Birdsall: 'I bet she's on the game.' He repeated a similar remark to Olive's face when he pushed past her to get to the toilet: she brusquely disabused him of the notion.

At around 11.30 p.m., Olive was dropped off in a lay-by near the fish and chip shop and just a short walk from her home. Sutcliffe and Birdsall were driving along the same road: 'That is a prostitute we saw in the public house,' Sutcliffe told his friend, before abruptly stopping the car, grabbing a hammer from beside the seat and disappearing down an alleyway.

He caught up with Olive Smelt at 11.45 and began talking to her. 'Weather's letting us down, isn't it?' As she walked past, he struck her twice on the back of the head with the hammer; then, as she lay face down and unconscious on the rough cobbles, he pulled up her skirt and exposed her buttocks.

He pulled a knife out from his clothing and slashed at the bottom of her back: two deep and ugly wounds – one twelve inches long – opened up and began bleeding profusely. But before he could do anything else he saw the headlights of a car coming down the road towards him: he fled back to the safety of his own vehicle and drove off into the summer night.

After recounting the details of these two attempted murders, Sir Michael Havers moved on to the first of the Ripper's successful killings. Once again he laid out the clear MO.

The body of twenty-eight-year-old Wilma McCann, apparently a part-time prostitute, was found at 7.41 on the morning of Thursday, 30 October 1975. She was lying face up on a sloping grass embankment on Prince Philip Playing Fields, off Scott Hall Road in Leeds. Her dark-blue bolero jacket and pink blouse had been torn open, her flimsy pink bra pushed up exposing her breasts. Below the waist her white flared trousers had been pulled down around her knees, but her panties were still in place.

Wilma had been hit twice on the back of the head with a hammer and had been stabbed fifteen times with a knife – once in the throat, five times beneath her breast and nine times around her belly button.

Havers read to the jury parts of Sutcliffe's confession statements. In the first he had claimed to have innocently given Wilma a lift as she hitched home from a night out in Leeds, only to be surprised and disgusted when she suggested he pay her for sex. This, he claimed, led him to lose control and impulsively kill her. In a subsequent clarification he admitted that he had deliberately gone in search of a prostitute with the specific intention of killing her.

But there were two telling details that Havers didn't reveal to the jury. Both related to the condition of Wilma McCann's body – and pointed clearly to Sutcliffe's real motive for murder.

Wilma had been found on her back, her lifeless face staring at the early morning sky. But the physics of the attack on her – beginning with a blow to the back of her head, delivered from behind – meant that she could not have fallen that way. She had, therefore, been moved: her killer had turned her over. This, of itself, was revealing: it indicated an element of ritual – an action that was, to the killer, important.

But it was the second detail that was even more telling: despite the evidently frenzied ripping of her clothes, a post-mortem showed that there was no semen inside Wilma's body. This had led the detectives to believe the murder was not sexually motivated. But forensic tests had revealed the presence of sperm elsewhere: the back of Wilma's trousers and panties tested positive for semen.

In October 1975, criminal profiling had not yet been invented: the first attempts at what would – eventually – become a recognised science did not begin for another four years, and only in the United States. But with the benefit of hindsight the two unspoken details about Wilma McCann's body are vital clues as to the methodology of her killer. They suggest that after smashing in the back of her skull he masturbated over her as she lay dying, then, after he had climaxed, turned her over and mutilated her corpse. It would not be the last time he left such a signature.

Next, Sir Michael Havers turned to the murder of forty-two-year-old Emily Jackson on the night of Tuesday, 20 January 1976. Like Wilma McCann, Mrs Jackson had been a part-time prostitute who worked the rough red-light district of Chapeltown in north-east Leeds. She too had engaged in conversation with Sutcliffe before being attacked with a hammer and stabbed fifty-two times with a screwdriver. Once again there was clear evidence that he had turned her body over and moved it.

Almost twelve hours passed between the murder and Emily's body being found, in a narrow passageway between derelict buildings. These two factors – the elapsed time and the rough ground – would make it impossible to know whether Sutcliffe had masturbated over her.

There should have been no such doubt about his next victim. In the early hours of Sunday, 9 May 1976, Sutcliffe attacked Marcella Claxton, a twenty-year-old prostitute, as she walked from a party in Chapeltown to her home in nearby Roundhay.

Once again, Sutcliffe had struck up a conversation by offering his victim a lift. On the way he suggested paying for sex and drove into Roundhay Park: he landed eight or nine blows to the back of her head with a hammer. As she lay moaning and – to all intents and purposes – dying, she recalled seeing Sutcliffe masturbating. He then drove off at high speed. But Marcella Claxton didn't die: she staggered to a phone box and dialled 999. As she waited for an ambulance to arrive she saw

Sutcliffe's car driving round and round the park: she realised he was looking for her, trying to establish whether or not he had killed her.

Not only was Marcella Claxton able to give a remarkably accurate description of her attacker but her evidence that he had masturbated over what he presumed to be her dying body should have been a clear signal to detectives that the man they were looking for had a sexual motive for murder. Instead, the police discounted almost everything she told them, refusing even to include her in the growing list of Ripper attacks. It was only when Peter Sutcliffe confessed to her attempted murder that she was formally acknowledged as his fifth victim.

Over the next two days, Sir Michael Havers ground on through the grisly details of the Ripper attacks. He outlined the circumstances of the killings of Irene Richardson, Patricia Atkinson, Jayne MacDonald, Jean Jordan, Yvonne Pearson, Helen Rytka, Vera Millward, Josephine Whitaker, Barbara Leach, Marguerite Walls and Jacqueline Hill. And he showed the similarities between these and the attempted murders of Anna Rogulskyj, Olive Smelt, Marcella Claxton, Maureen Long, Marilyn Moore, Upadhya Bandara and Theresa Sykes.

His purpose was not to prove that Peter Sutcliffe had carried out these crimes – that was accepted by the defence: instead, he was setting out the circumstances of each to establish that the man in the dock was bad, not mad.

As the evidence mounted, a clear pattern of common elements in the Ripper's MO emerged: there were ten separate components. The most common – present in almost all the murders and most of the attempts – were the conversation between attacker and victim, leading to the initial attack with a hammer; stabbing with a knife or a screwdriver; and the turning, moving or covering of victims' bodies. But there were other repeated elements, too: added to the 'tick-list' of methodology they formed a revealing picture.

On four of his victims – Emily Jackson, Jean Jordan, Yvonne Pearson and Marguerite Walls – Sutcliffe left evidence to show that he had stamped or stood on their bodies. With two – Marguerite Walls (again) and Upadhya Bandara – he had used a ligature to strangle them after hitting them with a hammer. These attacks occurred very late in his reign of terror and indicated that his MO was either mutable or (as he would later claim) had been deliberately changed to throw police off the scent.

The final two components of this checklist of common methods were the most problematic. Despite the evident frenzy of Sutcliffe's attacks – stabbing victims repeatedly, sometimes through the same entry point more than once – he had always used an implement to inflict the wounds. But the body of Josephine Whitaker, a nineteen-year-old bank clerk murdered on Wednesday, 4 April 1979 in Halifax, displayed evidence that she had been bitten her on her left breast. Whoever left the bite mark had a gap between their two upper front teeth: Peter Sutcliffe had exactly this dental configuration.

Biting and bite marks usually indicate a sexual element. So too did other wounds on Josephine Whitaker's body: again uniquely in the grim catalogue of his other victims, Sutcliffe had repeatedly inserted a screwdriver into the teenager's vagina. This alone was highly suggestive of a sexual motive in her murder, and since the prosecution's case centred on demolishing the Ripper's claims of receiving instructions from God to kill (which would qualify him as insane) it would become a key battleground throughout the trial.

Sutcliffe insisted he had not bitten Josephine Whitaker's breast and consistently denied any sexual motivation for the attacks. He admitted having sexual intercourse with the dying body of Helen Rytka – again, highly suggestive that he associated sex with death – but claimed he did so because there were other prostitutes and clients nearby and mounting Helen was the only way to keep her quiet.

Oddly, given the need to attack the Ripper's insanity defence, Sir Michael Havers spent little or no time exploring the final component of his MO in the twenty cases: the evidence that he had masturbated over two of his victims, Wilma McCann and Marcella Claxton. This should have been a strong indication that – in those attacks at least – Sutcliffe was sexually aroused in the presence of death (or presumed death). Nor did the physical evidence in the other cases rule this out. In seven of them Sutcliffe was disturbed during the attacks, and fled to avoid discovery, often leaving his victims still alive. And on the occasions when he was able to complete the act of killing uninterrupted, the circumstances in which the bodies lay for many hours or even days on waste ground meant that searching for semen samples in the vicinity was a non-starter.

Instead, Havers went after the four doctors who had diagnosed Sutcliffe as a paranoid schizophrenic. Their evidence and cross-examination would be crucial to understanding what drove the Yorkshire Ripper to kill.

TWO

MAD –
OR BAD?

The laws governing pleas of insanity in criminal trials date back to Norman times. Madness (in its widest sense) was then not seen as a defence to a charge, but as a special circumstance: juries habitually found mentally deranged individuals guilty, but then referred the case to the King for an inevitable pardon.

As English law developed over the ensuing centuries, the role of judges increased as the constitutional power of the monarch was reined in. In 1724, judges in the case of Edward 'Crazy Ned' Arnold issued a landmark ruling that enshrined the humanitarian principle giving protection to someone so mentally ill that he could not have realised that what he was doing was wrong. The test, the judges ruled, must be 'whether the accused is totally deprived of his understanding and memory and knew what he was doing no more than a wild beast or a brute, or an infant'.

21

A century later, this judge's rule of thumb was enshrined in English common law – where it has remained ever since – as the M'Naghten Rules. They arose from an 1843 trial in which Daniel M'Naghten (pronounced *MacNaughton*) was acquitted of murdering the secretary of the then prime minister, Sir Robert Peel.

After the case, the House of Lords instructed a panel of judges to come up with an agreed codification of the law. The result was a formal pronouncement that:

> to establish a defence on the ground of insanity, it must be clearly proved that, at the time of the committing of the act, the party accused was labouring under such a defect of reason, from disease of the mind, as not to know the nature and quality of the act he was doing; or, if he did know it, that he did not know he was doing what was wrong.

If this test was (deliberately) subjective, the M'Naghten Rules were absolutely clear on one thing: that it was the defence's responsibility to prove the accused was mad, not the Crown's to disprove it. Yet on the second day of *R. vs Sutcliffe*, it was the prosecution who asked permission to introduce psychiatric evidence supporting the Ripper's plea of insanity.

It was an odd move – and one that troubled Mr Justice Boreham. Surely, he asked both sets of barristers, this evidence should be put forward by the defence? Why was the prosecution seeking to do so – especially since it had not even begun to present its own witnesses? The only answer he received was that both prosecution and defence agreed that it was 'convenient' for the psychiatric evidence to be put before the jury first: it smacked of continuing collusion between the two theoretically opposing sides.

The first psychiatrist to examine Peter Sutcliffe was Dr Hugo Milne. Their first meeting had been on 14 January 1981, twelve days after Sutcliffe was arrested and charged. Milne had then undertaken ten further interviews with the Ripper while he was on remand in Armley Gaol.

Dr Milne was highly experienced in homicide, having previously analysed 200 other murderers, and he had produced for the court a thirty-five-page report detailing his conclusions on Sutcliffe. Its contents and tone were remarkably sympathetic, and the prosecution read them out to the jury.

> I have had the opportunity of spending many hours with the accused and there is little doubt that he is friendly and open in his manner and at no time did he withhold information.

Dr Milne's report stressed that, due to the details of the attacks, he had been concerned to discover what lay behind them and, specifically, if there had been any sexual motivation. This had been the recurring theme of his sessions with Peter Sutcliffe, supplemented by meetings with his wife, Sonia; by their conclusion he had formed a definite view.

> I found that there was no suggestion that the accused is in any way sexually deviant, or that his wife is sexually deviant.

Dr Milne had explored with Sutcliffe the psychiatric history of his family. None of Sutcliffe's five brothers and sisters had suffered from any mental illness, but in 1972 Sonia Sutcliffe had been diagnosed with schizophrenia and had spent twenty-two days in a Bradford psychiatric hospital. This, perhaps, contributed to the tensions in her relationship with Peter, problems that continued after their marriage in 1974.

> She readily admits that she had been at times temperamental and difficult, and freely admits that she had teased and provoked her husband, who said himself that the marriage had its ups and downs. He told me that she was over-excited, highly strung, unstable and obsessed with cleanliness. If he wanted to read a newspaper she would shout at him, swipe him and, as a result, he would hold her but never hit her.

Peter Sutcliffe also confided to the psychiatrist that Sonia had sometimes shouted at him to such an extent that he was embarrassed, as he thought that the neighbours would hear her.

But by 1976, Sonia had recovered from her illness and described her marriage as a happy one. Her husband, however, was more equivocal in his assessment. He told Dr Milne that the couple had an intense relationship – sometimes very loving, at other times permeated by anger.

> It is interesting to note that he has had episodes at home typical of an anxiety or panic attack. This may obviously relate to his concern at the time he was offending.

Nonetheless, the Yorkshire Ripper had been at pains to stress that sexual relations with his wife were extremely satisfactory.

Why then, Dr Milne had asked him, did he and his wife have no children? Sutcliffe had explained that they both preferred material possessions to the prospect of a family.

If the seeds of Peter Sutcliffe's grim crimes did not lie in the marital home – much less, apparently, in the marriage bed – the psychiatrist had instead reached back into the Ripper's upbringing and early adult life. First, his report discussed Sutcliffe's childhood.

> The mother became involved with a policeman and as a result the happy marriage was destroyed and the father became unfaithful with the woman with whom he is now living ... It is also apparent that he was very much fonder of his mother than his father.

But neither this, nor Sutcliffe's devout Catholic upbringing, offered any clues as to the origins of his desire to kill. Instead, according to what the Ripper told the psychiatrist, the genesis of his offending lay in a cemetery.

In 1964, at the age of eighteen, he had begun work as a gravedigger in Bingley. The following year, he had ridden his motorbike into a telegraph pole and knocked himself briefly unconscious. From that moment on, the Ripper said, he had suffered from 'severe bouts of morbid depression and hallucinations. My mind goes into a haze and I don't know what was right or wrong, or I was acting rationally or not.' Then, while he was working in the Catholic section of the cemetery, he had experienced symptoms of what Dr Milne decided was a long-standing paranoid schizophrenic illness.

He described when he was working he heard a mumbling voice, looked up and saw nobody, got out of the grave and thought he was imagining what he was hearing.

It appeared to be coming from the top of the cross. It was an echoing voice, vague and distant, and it repeated itself some two or three times, and it was direct from the stone itself and I have never forgotten it.

Sutcliffe examined the inscription on the gravestone, but since it was in Polish he did not understand it. Despite this, he told the psychiatrist, he interpreted the foreign words as if they were English. One was 'jego', a Polish pronoun meaning 'his'; Sutcliffe claimed to have thought it could mean 'Jesus'. He also thought another inscription on the gravestone might mean 'We be echo'.

'I decided', Dr Milne's report quoted the Ripper as explaining, 'it was some kind of message from God … It had a really strange effect. I felt I was privileged to hear it. I went back to the stone several times but I never heard it again. I had quite a lot of messages. I have had all kinds of words and messages since.'

In 1966, Sutcliffe met and began courting Sonia Szurma. Their relationship blossomed until, one day in 1969, he claimed to have discovered that his girlfriend had been seen with another man. Sutcliffe went to find and confront her, and, according to Dr Milne's report, the couple had a row.

He could not imagine she had been unfaithful to him … [and] walked off from Sonia in an angry and resentful frame of mind.

Later that same day, according to the story Sutcliffe told the psychiatrist, he spotted a prostitute soliciting in the street. He picked her up and drove her to a house where they were to have sex for the price of £5. But Sutcliffe had only a £10 note, so the girl directed him to a garage where he could get change. But here, according to the report:

> He had threatening remarks made to him by some man and the girl laughed at him. He became extremely angry and left. From this moment on he became consumed with hatred for prostitutes ... He was convinced from that moment on that prostitutes were hateful people.

It would, according to this version of events, take another six years before Sutcliffe acted on this growing hatred. In 1975, he had been told by workmates that there was 'a plague of prostitutes in Keighley'. Based on that remark alone he went to Keighley to find them: the attack on Anna Rogulskyj (not, of course, a prostitute) was the result.

> I had a hatred for prostitutes. I don't know what to think. It was a pathological hatred. I was seized in a grip, difficult to explain, occasionally getting depressed at times with splitting headaches. Sometimes I didn't want to go on living. I didn't tell people because it would pass off.

At some point this loathing coalesced with the voices Sutcliffe was hearing – some of them from God, others apparently not religiously derived – and he became convinced he had been given a divine mission to rid the streets of prostitutes.

When I have been on this sequence of kills I have heard, 'God giveth and God taketh life' and 'God works in mysterious ways' and odd comments as normal conversation to kill and wipe out all the people called scum who cannot justify themselves in society.

Despite the extensive (and indeed intensive) series of interviews, Dr Milne was unable to give a precise date on which Sutcliffe first became convinced he was carrying out God's instructions. The best he could suggest was that it was 'a possibility' that the murder of Irene Richardson marked the point at which Sutcliffe believed God was controlling his behaviour.

The sole evidence for this was that, after killing Wilma McCann and Emily Jackson, Sutcliffe had fled from the murder scene in panic. By contrast, after bludgeoning and stabbing Irene Richardson to death he had carefully replaced her clothes and boots; this suggested a man behaving in a controlled way, rather than a man in panic.

When Dr Milne asked Sutcliffe if he felt he had the protection of God, the Ripper had replied that at the times of the attacks he was confident he was chosen to do it and it was his calling and he didn't have any qualms about it. When recalling the murder of Jean Jordan he also said that he remembered reading an article in a church magazine, in which a priest inveighed against prostitutes in Moss Side, Manchester.

This was my message. It was certainly a message. I remember reading it and the priest saying it and that is why I went. It was given to me in print that time and then the voices came.

This illustrated, according to Dr Milne's report, Sutcliffe's genuine belief that messages had been passed to him in various ways from God. And it was, the psychiatrist averred, typical of a classic schizophrenic illness.

It was only later, when Sutcliffe realised a victim had not been a prostitute, that he experienced any doubts.

> I have tried to fight it. I have been frightened of it. I have been unsuccessful and I wondered whether it was God when I killed an innocent person.

Remarkably, Sutcliffe's distinction between a prostitute ('scum') and a' non-prostitute ('an innocent person') did not appear to have been challenged in Dr Milne's report. Instead, the psychiatrist allowed the Ripper to ruminate on the 'dreadful misgivings' he suffered when – after killing Josephine Whitaker, an 'innocent person' – he wondered if it was not God's voice he had heard, but the Devil's.

He explained that he had been in 'a terrible state' for an entire year after the killing of Barbara Leach: the report noted exactly Sutcliffe's unusually terse statement. 'Didn't kill. Mental anguish.' But after murdering Barbara Leach, Sutcliffe also described being completely under the control of the voice: 'I had lost the battle, God had won the battle.' What was more, God had apparently sought to reassure his murderous disciple.

> The voice told me Whitaker and Leach were prostitutes. God knew best … God wouldn't have punished them. Prostitutes are not innocent. God couldn't make a mistake.

Nor, he confided in the psychiatrist, had he deliberately mutilated his victims:

> Rather than mutilate them, I leave them exposed to show them up because there is no reason to mutilate. It's only a matter of killing them.

That this did not in any way tally with the facts was apparently a further indication of mental illness. Moreover, although Dr Milne's report stated that he could find absolutely no reason why Sutcliffe had stabbed his victims through the same hole on repeated occasions – including inserting and reinserting a screwdriver into Josephine Whitaker's vagina – he was confident that there was no specific sexual symbolism to the act.

The report then moved on to the changing pattern of Sutcliffe's MO. He had told Dr Milne that he had used a rope to garrotte Upadhya Bandara and Marguerite Walls because he was 'getting angry with the media because they were calling him the Ripper'. Remarkably, this seemingly nonsensical explanation passed without comment: Dr Milne simply recorded as fact that Sutcliffe 'wished to show that he was not the Ripper and used the rope. He didn't like it because it took longer and was unpleasant.'

It appeared that every inherent contradiction in Sutcliffe's story had not only simply been accepted by the psychiatrist, but also that the glaringly obvious inconsistencies were taken as evidence of his insanity. Thus, despite the Ripper's self-proclaimed divine mission to rid the streets of prostitutes, his killing of women who were quite obviously not streetwalkers was supportive of his claims of madness. Questioned about the Marguerite Walls murder, Sutcliffe had told Dr Milne:

I was on my way to Leeds primed with weapons for the mission. She lifted her leg up, put it down and then lifted it up again. She looked like a prostitute and was walking at a snail's pace. I killed her with no doubt. The voice shouted 'Filthy prostitute'. It wasn't like my voice, it was filthy and angry. Not like me. I don't get angry. I knew it was me who had done what I had done with my own hands, and when I get into the depression this happens.

Similarly, when asked about the Jacqueline Hill killing, Sutcliffe had said:

She turned round and looked as if she was adjusting her skirt or her stocking, and this suggested that it was the behaviour of a prostitute. God invested me with the means of killing. He has got me out of trouble and I am in God's hands. He misled police and perhaps God was involved in the tapes so the police would be misled.

Dr Milne's psychiatric report concluded that Sutcliffe's comments illustrated two aspects of schizophrenic illness. Firstly, his conviction that innocent women were prostitutes. Secondly, his inability to control what he was doing physically, even though he knew what he was doing was wrong.

Ultimately, Dr Milne's report accepted and endorsed Sutcliffe's self-diagnosis and rejected the more obvious motive for murder – sex.

He completely denies that he was using the assaults to help in the sexual situation. There is no suggestion that he is a sadistic, sexual deviant. I am convinced that the killings were not sexual in any way and the stabbings which were a feature of the assaults had no sexual component.

The Ripper, then, was mad, not bad. And the evidence for asserting this had been introduced by the prosecution: it severely undermined the ensuing six days of the Crown's case – six days in which the Attorney General introduced witness after witness with testimony intended to prove the exact opposite.

The author of the remarkable psychiatric assessment would not make a personal appearance in the trial until Tuesday, 12 May 1981. When Dr Hugo Milne did enter the witness box, to testify for the defence, the bizarrely topsy-turvy nature of proceedings continued. Over the course of his evidence the psychiatrist would concede that all the most vital parts of his report might well be wrong – but that its conclusions were correct.

He began by asserting that throughout his sessions with Sutcliffe he had been 'very much on my guard' that the Ripper might try to deceive him by feigning mental illness.

There was no evidence whatever to say he was simulating. I had been looking for this all the time, and I cannot accept that, in the sequence his symptoms were made known to me, that he could have been simulating ... I do not believe that the accused is, in fact, simulating mental illness. He is suffering from schizophrenia of a paranoid type.

From the outset, Dr Milne found his evidence challenged not just by the prosecution (which, after all, had originally been happy to accept it) but also by the judge himself. And Mr Justice Boreham was evidently unimpressed.

He began by asking the psychiatrist to explain how exactly he defined the symptoms of paranoid schizophrenia. The doctor reached for an analogy to explain what was, apparently, a complex answer.

> The great difficulty is that what the individual says is very often the symptom is in fact the sign of underlying schizophrenic disorder. If a man says that he is the king of Siam when it is patently obvious he is an ordinary office clerk, the symptom he presents is 'I am the king of Siam'. But the disorder would be that he has grandiosity.

Sutcliffe's defence counsel, James Chadwin QC, stepped in to assist: could there be other symptoms – other than those deliberately told by a patient to a doctor – which helped formulate a diagnosis? If so, what would they be? The psychiatrist's response was somewhat nebulous.

> The way he might behave as if he was suspicious of other people's behaviour. The way he may misinterpret people's behaviour and the way he may react to what he believes.

Mr Justice Boreham promptly cut through Dr Milne's apparent vagueness: his statement went to the heart of all the psychiatric evidence the court would hear.

It sounds as if you are saying that you are very much dependent upon what you are told and, rather as we in these courts, you have to test its accuracy.

Over the next two and a half days, Dr Milne would have the accuracy of his diagnosis tested to destruction. He began by outlining the symptoms of madness presented by the Yorkshire Ripper: these included suspicion and an uncontrollable impulse to kill prostitutes. This, the psychiatrist pronounced, was such an extreme preoccupation that it moved into the realms of delusion.

I am referring to his phrases that have come out in court here about prostitutes being the scum of the earth, and being responsible for all sorts of problems to the extent that he could not see beyond that idea.

Dr Milne said that during their prison interviews Sutcliffe had told him: 'I know it is wrong to kill. If you've got a good reason, it's justified and all right.' When asked if he felt justified in killing, Sutcliffe had replied:

Yes, I have no doubt whatsoever. I was not as rational then as now but if there were women around now it would not take long to get those thoughts again. I'm glad to be here because of the innocent people. I am not glad really because of the trouble and the family. The prostitutes are still there, even more on the streets now, they say. The mission is only partly fulfilled.

There was a glaring hole in this argument – and one that the Ripper, if not the psychiatrist, had evidently spotted. Of the thirteen women he killed, just eight were prostitutes; of the seven women he admitted attempting to murder, that figure was just two.

The prosecution, too, had noticed. Sir Michael Havers turned Dr Milne's cross-examination over to his junior, Harry Ognall QC; the barrister was about to fatally skewer the psychiatrist on his own testimony.

Ognall began by getting Dr Milne to admit that if the Ripper had a desire to kill all women – prostitutes or not – then his self-proclaimed divine mission could not be genuine evidence of mental illness. Then he moved in for the kill, prompting Milne to repeat his diagnosis that the attacks were not sexually motivated.

In simple terms, although his victims were female and it might be thought he might be a sexual killer, I am not of the opinion that he is primarily a sexual killer.

The ensuing cross-examination was cold-eyed and merciless. So crucial was it to the jury's eventual verdict – and so central are its implications to the murders detailed in later chapters – that it is worth setting out, verbatim.

OGNALL: If we can discern here a sexual element, that tends markedly to go against the divine mission theory, do you agree?
MILNE: Yes.

Mr Ognall then picked up from the exhibits table the screwdriver with which Sutcliffe had inflicted the fatal wounds on Josephine Whitaker. He presented it to the psychiatrist and asked:

OGNALL: How on earth are we to reconcile the pathologist's evidence of three stab wounds deep in the vagina with what you said? There is no doubt that this wicked agent [the screwdriver] was introduced with almost no injury to the external part of the vagina. I suggest that indicates the most fiendish cruelty, deliberately done for sexual satisfaction. Do you agree?

MILNE: It may be a most vicious and foul thing to do, but not necessarily for sexual satisfaction. Mutilation of the genitalia for sadistic satisfaction would have to be repetitive and there is no evidence, as far as I know, that this man has attacked any of the other victims in this way. There is no other evidence that he has in any way despoiled them or carried out any unnatural acts with them during the killing.

In fact, as Harry Ognall would shortly expose, Dr Milne knew perfectly well that there had been evidence of Sutcliffe 'despoiling' his victims and carrying out 'unnatural acts'; it was simply that the psychiatrist had declined to see any sexual significance in them, preferring instead to believe Sutcliffe's assurance that they were no more than 'accidental'.

Once again Mr Justice Boreham interrupted, asking the psychiatrist: if Ognall was correct, would he still stand by the observations made in his report? Dr Milne began to backpedal, acknowledging that it did not seem as accurate as it should be, and that he would withdraw the observation that inserting a screwdriver repeatedly into the wound he had made in Josephine Whitaker's vagina was accidental. Then, when pressed by the QC what else the screwdriver attack could be but sexual, Dr Milne admitted: 'It may well have been sexual.'

> *OGNALL:* What else could it have been? I will have an answer.
>
> *MILNE:* I do not think it could have been anything else other than sexual.
>
> *OGNALL:* Did Peter Sutcliffe tell you there was no sexual element in the attacks?
>
> *MILNE:* Yes.
>
> *OGNALL:* Well, that doesn't seem to be right, does it?
>
> *MILNE:* No.
>
> *OGNALL:* He deceived you. Why did he do that?
>
> *MILNE:* Perhaps he might have been very reluctant to talk about this because of what people might think of him.

Harry Ognall was incredulous: his voice dripping with sarcasm, he forced the psychiatrist to reflect on his answer.

> *OGNALL:* He had admitted thirteen killings and seven attempted killings. But he thought he might be worse thought of, because he stabbed one of them in the vagina? Is that a considered reply?
>
> *MILNE:* It is a considered reply. He has said he never ever wanted to be seen as a sexual killer.
>
> *OGNALL:* I expect he has never wanted to be seen as a sexual killer because, if he puts himself forward as a

sexual killer, the divine mission goes out of the window. That's why, isn't it?

MILNE: It could be.

OGNALL: If you were to find a number of instances of sexual molestation, the more instances you find, the more it would erode the validity of the diagnosis?

MILNE: It would lead to erosion, yes.

The QC then reminded Dr Milne that Sutcliffe had exposed, and then stabbed, Jacqueline Hill's breasts. He had told the police that he did it because: 'It's just something that comes over me.'

OGNALL: Unless I'm very naive, that betrays a specific, clear sexual element in his killing.

MILNE: If you interpret it in that way, it does suggest that there may be a possible sexual component.

And what about Emily Jackson? After killing her, Sutcliffe had pushed a yard-long piece of wood against her vagina; he had also admitted to the police that he had pulled her clothes up: 'In order to satisfy some kind of sexual revenge as, on reflection, I had done with Wilma McCann.'

MILNE: If in fact you believe what he said, then it obviously could imply a sexual component.

Ognall moved on to Sutcliffe's own description of the murder of Helen Rytka: hitting her with a hammer, having sex with her, stabbing her, and taking her clothes off. When he had sex with her after hitting her with the hammer, according to his police statement: 'She just lay there limp and didn't put much into it.'

> *OGNALL:* Normal?
>
> *MILNE:* Not normal, no.
>
> *OGNALL:* Could you think of anything more obscenely abnormal than his behaviour with that unfortunate girl?
>
> *MILNE:* I entirely agree with you, but I still think that this was a use of sexual behaviour for entirely the wrong reason – to avoid detection, quieten her and get away.
>
> *OGNALL:* Why did he have to have intercourse with her to keep her quiet? I don't suppose he could have just put his hand over her mouth?
>
> *MILNE:* As he himself said, this was what the girl expected.
>
> *OGNALL:* Look, Dr Milne, he is having intercourse with a woman who has been cruelly attacked and is near death. I ask you again – no underlying sexual component?
>
> *MILNE:* A sexual component, yes.

Relentlessly, Harry Ognall pursued his witness. Did not the murder of Marguerite Walls also have a sexual component, in that Sutcliffe had left fingernail scratches at the entrance to her vagina? Surely there was an underlying sexual component in that case?

> *MILNE:* You may possibly be right.
>
> *OGNALL:* I put it to you that the injuries to these women betray quite clear sexual components in the attacks. Do you agree?
>
> *MILNE:* Yes.

By the time he left the witness box, Hugo Milne was significantly wounded. He had managed simultaneously to recant much of his evidence that the Ripper was not a sexual killer, while grimly clinging on to his belief in Sutcliffe's self-proclaimed motivation – the mysterious voice of God (or the Devil) instructing him to kill.

Milne had also been forced to admit – as would the three other psychiatrists who gave evidence after him – that the sole basis for his diagnosis was what Sutcliffe himself had said: other than the Ripper's own, plainly self-serving statements there was not a shred of corroborative evidence of mental illness.

> I think it is a very straightforward decision to make. Is this man pretending to be mad, and has duped me and my colleagues, or am I, from my clinical examination, right in saying that he is a paranoid schizophrenic? As far as I can see in this particular case, either he is a competent actor, or I am an inefficient psychiatrist.

If Peter Sutcliffe was, as the psychiatrists insisted, to be believed about hearing voices instructing him to kill, there remained the problem of why he had made no mention of this in his police statements. These extraordinarily lengthy documents are packed with detail about the offences he confessed to; they also clearly show that Sutcliffe professed a hatred for prostitutes. But of the divine voice and mission there is no mention.

There was also the fact that he had, during the early part of his marriage, had the opportunity to observe at close quarters the symptoms of Sonia Sutcliffe's quite genuine schizophrenic episode.

Together these two pieces of evidence should have raised suspicions about the reliability of what Sutcliffe presented to the doctors. While there was some doubt as to whether the psychiatrists had known the contents of his police statements – for reasons never explained the prosecution only laid out its case to them the day before they gave evidence – Sonia Sutcliffe's illness was no secret.

But there was a further piece of information that neither Dr Milne nor any of his colleagues had known when conducting their extensive interviews with Sutcliffe. It was the report of a statement he had made to his wife during one of her regular visits to Armley Gaol, and it gave a very clear indication that he was faking madness.

John Leach was one of the wardens who supervised the Ripper twenty-four hours a day in the prison's hospital wing. His duties included monitoring and writing down conversations between the Sutcliffes. On 8 January 1981, he recorded what Peter Sutcliffe told his wife.

I am going to do a long time in prison, thirty years or more, unless I can convince people in here I am mad, and maybe then [I will serve] ten years in the loony bin.

Like much of the prosecution's most damning evidence of the Ripper's motive, this was not revealed to those professionals charged with assessing his state of mind. It was only introduced to the trial after Mr Justice Boreham threw out the tawdry agreement between the Crown and the defence, requiring the crucial questions of sanity and motive to be decided by the jury.

The six men and six women retired to consider their verdict

at 10.21 on Friday, 22 May 1981. Five hours later, they returned to the courtroom to say that they could not reach a unanimous decision.

The judge advised them that he would accept a majority verdict: forty-seven minutes later, the panel returned with a 10–2 finding of guilt. Mr Justice Boreham duly imposed the mandatory sentence of life in prison for each of the murders, and one each for the seven attempts.

The verdict, while undoubtedly popular with the British public, infuriated Dr Hugo Milne. Eighteen months after his diagnosis was so visibly criticised and rejected he gave an interview attacking the entire process of the Ripper's trial.

The whole trial was a charade for public opinion. As a doctor I found it hard to understand how the Crown, who had tested and accepted the medical evidence, could then discard that evidence and say it was idiotic and cross-examine their own experts on that basis.

The man couldn't be hung, which was what everyone was screaming and shouting about, so he had to be found guilty of something. We're talking here about majority public opinion, not what you might call 'thinking opinion'.

By the time he gave that interview, Dr Milne had visited Peter Sutcliffe in Parkhurst Prison – the high-security Category A jail that housed Britain's most dangerous (sane) killers. He had been open-minded enough initially to accept that Sutcliffe had perhaps indeed pulled the wool over his educated eyes, but when he sat down once again with the Ripper he observed exactly the same symptoms that had informed his original diagnosis.

Sutcliffe had, for example, told Parkhurst's doctors that the ghost of Emily Jackson visited him in his cell: he said he could see her and even smell her perfume. That there was nothing but Sutcliffe's own word for this occurrence – just as the psychiatrists had relied exclusively on his own statements prior to the trial – did not affect Dr Milne's renewed conviction that the Ripper was mad.

> There was no evidence to suggest he was malingering at any time that I saw him. You couldn't possibly malinger for such a long time.

That same autumn, two other psychiatrists added their voices to Dr Milne's views: they recommended that Sutcliffe should be transferred to a secure mental hospital for treatment, not punishment.

It would be a further year and a half – eighteen months in which the Ripper would be attacked and severely injured in Parkhurst, and in which Sonia Sutcliffe pleaded for him to be declared mad, not bad – before they got their way. In March 1984, Peter Sutcliffe was quietly shipped to Broadmoor, to be held there indefinitely under Section 47 of the new (1983) Mental Health Act. He could – and did – pronounce with some justification that he was not 'responsible' for the murders and attempted murders: it was all the fault of the voices instructing him to kill.

Aside from the public's undoubted desire for retribution – to see the Yorkshire Ripper rot in prison for his crimes rather than live in the relative comfort of a secure psychiatric hospital – there was a very real reason why all of this mattered. If Peter

Sutcliffe was bad, not mad, then the question of his motives was important. If, as the prosecution had belatedly insisted (and the jury had accepted), he was driven by a sexual desire to murder, then a long list of other unsolved murders and attempted murders needed to be re-examined.

In fact, the police and prosecution had known from the day of his arrest that Peter Sutcliffe was a sex-killer. They had known because they recovered from him a crucial piece of physical evidence.

After agreeing and signing his lengthy police statement, painstakingly handwritten over sixteen gruelling hours, the Ripper was escorted into the CID office at Dewsbury police station by Detective Sergeant Des O'Boyle. He ordered his captive to empty his pockets and strip off so that every item of clothing could be logged into evidence before being taken away for forensic examination.

As Sutcliffe began to remove his clothing, O'Boyle searched his coat. The bottom of the pockets had been cut to enable the Ripper to conceal his weapons deep inside the lining. As he checked these cavities, the detective found a pair of underpants: he showed them to Sutcliffe, who confirmed they were his.

Then, as the Ripper dropped his trousers, the reason for the underpants being in his pocket became clear: in place of them, he was wearing an upside-down V-neck sweater, his legs pushed through the sleeves, and the V of the neck arranged so that his genitals were exposed. It was a bizarre sight: O'Boyle told Sutcliffe to remove the odd attire and pass it over. He examined it carefully and found that padding had been sewn into the area of the sleeves that would cover Sutcliffe's knees.

DS O'Boyle duly bagged and tagged the adapted 'underwear':

many years later, in an interview with journalist Michael Bilton, he remembered being convinced that the garment was plainly designed to enable Sutcliffe quickly to expose his genitals during an attack.

> That's why his underpants are in his coat pocket, because he has changed when he has gone out ... He would have gone out with his underpants on when he left home. At some stage he has taken his underpants off and put on this other item.
>
> The reason it was padded around the knees was for one reason – and it wasn't so he could drive a bloody car. It was so that he could kneel on them, and if he is kneeling down cushioning his knees, the only thing he is going to be doing is dealing with a corpse.

The police already knew from the murder of Wilma McCann and the attack on Marcella Claxton what Peter Sutcliffe did when he knelt over a dying body: he masturbated. The bizarre jersey-cum-underpants had been adapted to make his posture more comfortable and to allow him to expose his genitals in the shortest possible time.

It was clear and very physical evidence that the Yorkshire Ripper's true motivation was sexual: that he derived pleasure from ejaculating over, or beside, the women he had attacked.

Yet this singular piece of evidence was the one major item missing from the oak exhibits table in the well of Court Number One of the Old Bailey. It – and the clear story it told – had been hidden away in a filing cabinet and would not be uncovered for more than a quarter of a century. It would not be the last evidence about the Yorkshire Ripper concealed by West Yorkshire Police. A major and concerted cover-up was about to begin, and at its heart was the truth about at least twenty-two other murders.

THREE

ERRORS OF JUDGEMENT AND COVER-UPS

On Tuesday, 19 January 1982, the Secretary of State for the Home Department – more usually known as the Home Secretary – rose to address a sombre and silent House of Commons. Willie Whitelaw, a true-blue Tory and Prime Minister Margaret Thatcher's 'go-to' man in times of crisis, was sixty-four: he had been in charge of what is traditionally the most difficult of all government offices since her landslide election victory and – true to departmental form – had already slipped on significant political banana skins.

That afternoon he faced one more.

With permission, Mr Speaker, I should like to make a statement on the review of the Yorkshire Ripper case carried out, at my request, by Mr Lawrence Byford, one of Her Majesty's Inspectors of Constabulary.

I asked him to report on any lessons which might be

learnt from the conduct of the investigation and which should be made known to police forces generally. Mr Byford was assisted in his review by the external advisory team set up in November 1980. He was also able to take account of views put to him about this tragic case by relatives of the victims, who greatly appreciated the opportunity to voice their misgivings.

I have now received and considered Mr Byford's report and I am extremely grateful to him for it. I should like to let the House know of its main conclusions and recommendations. A more detailed summary has been placed in the Library.

It is apparent from the report that there were major errors of judgement by the police and some inefficiencies in the conduct of the operation at various levels ... With hindsight, it is now clear that if the errors and inefficiencies had not occurred Sutcliffe would have been identified as a prime suspect sooner than he was.

Mr Byford's report concludes that there is little doubt that he should have been arrested earlier, on the facts associated with his various police interviews.

I would remind the House that the Ripper case gave rise to the largest criminal investigation ever conducted in this country, imposing a great strain on all concerned. It would have been surprising if in this unprecedented situation there were no mistakes. What we now have to do is to respond constructively to the considerable experience gained in the course of it in order to ensure that future investigations of crimes such as this are carried out as effectively and quickly as possible.

Hidden among the standard boilerplate of parliamentary language were two crucial pieces of misdirection. The first concerned the 'detailed summary' Whitelaw promised would be placed in the House of Commons Library (the antique, but obligatory, Westminster version of publication); the second was the apparently unequivocal allegation that police had made serious mistakes – 'errors of judgement' that had allowed Sutcliffe to carry on killing. Both statements were, in their own way, true, but both managed to avoid telling the whole story.

* * *

Her Majesty's Inspectorate of Constabulary is one of the less prominent and frequently misunderstood agencies of the British state. It is – deliberately – not a government agency: since its origins in the 1856 County and Borough Police Act, HMIC has been independent of Westminster. Its Inspectors – all retired very senior police officers – are appointed by the Crown. Although the Chief Inspector presents an annual report to Parliament, he is not technically accountable to either the House of Commons or 10 Downing Street.

This constitutional independence is important: since HMIC's job is to assess the efficacy of the country's forty-three separate police forces, its remit is primarily one of serving the interests of the public, not those of the government of the day.

On Tuesday, 26 May 1981, four days after Peter Sutcliffe was convicted at the Old Bailey, the Home Secretary had asked HMIC to undertake an inquiry into the handling of the Ripper case by West Yorkshire Police. Lawrence Byford, local Inspector for the north-east – which included West Yorkshire – was tasked with the job.

Byford was a trained lawyer who, after World War Two, had joined the old West Riding Constabulary and worked his way to the top of the force before joining HMIC: he therefore knew Sutcliffe's killing ground personally. Nor was Whitelaw's summons his first involvement with the Ripper case. After the murder of Jacqueline Hill in November 1980, the Home Secretary had appointed him to review and reorganise the operations of the Ripper Squad.

Politically connected and tactically astute, Byford quickly spotted that the senior West Yorkshire Police management was not capable of running Britain's biggest manhunt: he sidelined the Chief Constable, Ronald Gregory, and brought in a new team to run the inquiry. Now, with Sutcliffe safely behind bars, Byford set about investigating what had gone wrong.

His was neither the first nor the only inquiry. On the day Sutcliffe was jailed, Ronald Gregory had ordered his Assistant Chief Constable, Colin Sampson, to undertake an internal investigation. Sampson also finished first, submitting his 200-page report to Gregory less than five months later.

Gregory promptly blocked its publication, citing Sampson's conclusion that there were several unsolved murders and attacks that could have been the work of the Ripper and which required further investigation. The Chief Constable did not, however, state this reason publicly: it would not be the last time that evidence pointing to Peter Sutcliffe as the killer of other women would be suppressed.

Internal government papers, released many years later, show that Home Secretary Willie Whitelaw had laid down a very clear remit for Lawrence Byford's report. A letter from his private secretary, Colin Walters, dated 28 May 1981, laid it out.

> During the course of the trial at the Old Bailey, which was concluded last week, a number of shortcomings were revealed in the massive and protracted police investigation which eventually led to Sutcliffe's arrest ...
>
> Although it is easy to criticise with the benefit of hindsight, the West Yorkshire Police have not come well out of the trial and the subsequent publicity ...
>
> In the circumstances, it was to be expected that there would be criticism of the police and pressure for a public inquiry into their conduct of the investigation.
>
> Interest in the case seems to have died down since the week-end, but may well be resumed when Parliament reassembles next week. It would be possible for the Home Secretary to institute a formal inquiry under Section 32 of the Police Act 1964, as has been done in the case of Lord Scarman's inquiry into the Brixton riot.
>
> The Home Secretary has, however, concluded that this form of public inquiry – which would inevitably be in the nature of an inquest into the way in which the police handled the investigation – would serve little useful purpose.
>
> What is important now is not so much to criticise the police as to ensure that the proper lessons are drawn from this case and made available to the police service generally to assist in future investigations ...

Yet when Whitelaw got to his feet in the House of Commons

the following January, he devoted a substantial proportion of his pre-drafted speech to highlighting the 'errors of judgement' by West Yorkshire Police, which Byford's report had uncovered. None was more crucial than its reaction to letters and tapes[1] sent – anonymously – by a man with a Geordie accent who had declared that he was the Ripper. The senior detectives had been convinced that these were genuine; as a result they had ruled out any evidence pointing to suspects who did not come from the north-east.

A serious error was the excessive credence given to the letters and tape from a man claiming responsibility for the series of murders and signing himself 'Jack the Ripper'. The available evidence did not justify the conclusion that the author was the killer.

Another serious handicap to the investigation was the ineffectiveness of the major incident room. This should have been the effective nerve centre of the whole police operation but it became overloaded with unprocessed information with the result that vital connections between certain related pieces of information were overlooked.

Turning to specific details, the Home Secretary's speech took the police to task for failing to examine closely enough evidence from a succession of victims who had survived attacks bearing the Ripper's trademarks. In particular, these victims had helped to create photofits of their attacker.

---

[1] It was not until many years later, in January 2006, that John Humble, an unemployed and alcoholic Sunderland man, was sentenced to eight years in prison for sending the series of letters and a tape in which he claimed to be the Yorkshire Ripper. He had no connection with the crimes and the communications were a tragic hoax.

Insufficient attention was given to the significant common elements in photofit impressions obtained from surviving victims of hammer assaults or assaults involving serious head injuries on unaccompanied women.

Worse, the systemic failures in the management of the Ripper inquiry had allowed Peter Sutcliffe to slip through the net.

Sutcliffe was interviewed by the police in connection with the Ripper investigation on nine occasions between 1975 and his arrest in January 1981. The attitudes of interviewing officers were in some cases conditioned by the credence given to the letters and tape, and in some interviews the officers concerned were simply not positive enough in their approach. Often they were inadequately briefed before the interviews, principally as a result of the ineffectiveness of the Major Incident Room.

The vast majority of officers involved in the case worked diligently and conscientiously throughout the Ripper investigation.

Whitelaw then outlined a series of very practical proposals to improve major investigations. But if he thought – as had been his stated intention – that this would be the focus of subsequent attention, he badly misjudged both the mood of the House and of the country. One after another, MPs stood up to attack West Yorkshire Police, and in particular its Chief Constable, Ronald Gregory. Jonathan Aitken led the charge for the Tories.

> Does my right honourable friend expect any senior police
> officers in West Yorkshire to resign or to be moved as a
> result of the report, and if not, why not?

For Labour, Geoffrey Lofthouse demanded that the Home
Secretary put a ban on any of the senior Ripper detectives from
being considered for future promotion, while his colleague on
the opposition benches, Martin Flannery, called for Whitelaw
to impose rather more immediate punishment.

> Would he finally accept it from me that if some major
> heads in West Yorkshire do not roll as a result of this ...
> there will be grave disquiet throughout the whole of West
> and South Yorkshire?

Whitelaw responded to all of these calls with his trademark
emollient regret. It had, he conceded, been a terrible business
and one that exposed major flaws in policing, but it was
important now to look to the future, not the past.

There were a small handful of MPs who spotted a significant
flaw in the Home Secretary's statement. Labour's Ken Woolmer,
who represented a Leeds constituency, summed it up.

> Is he [Whitelaw] aware that anything less than the very
> fullest publication of the report will not satisfy the public
> of West Yorkshire?

Once again, Whitelaw appeared regretful. He could not publish
the Byford Report itself because conventionally such documents,
commissioned by the Home Secretary from an Inspector of

Constabulary, would 'enjoy the normal confidentiality which such reports have always had'.

It was a trademark Whitelaw performance: soothing, placatory and polite, and one which – whether by convenient accident or careful design – had the effect of focusing public attention on West Yorkshire Police rather than on a publicly paid-for inquiry report he did not want to publish.

There were, that January in 1982, thirteen compelling reasons why the Byford Report needed to be fully published. They would remain compelling for the next twenty-five years in which the report was protected from public view.

And they remain compelling today, eight years after a redacted version of the report was finally released. Because each of those thirteen 'reasons' was an unsolved murder or attempted murder; every one bore the hallmarks of Peter Sutcliffe, and Byford recommended that each should be investigated urgently. This was the big secret of the Byford Report that the Home Secretary was determined to protect – and which, to this day, remains under governmental lock and key.

Predictably, the news coverage that followed the Home Secretary's statement to the House focused on the failures of West Yorkshire Police. There was little or no attention paid to the decision to keep secret Byford's report and – because of its suppression – no journalistic effort to link the Ripper with other unsolved murders.

Byford was not alone in reaching the conclusion that Peter Sutcliffe had many more victims than those whose names had been put to him in court. The internal West Yorkshire Police Sampson Inquiry flagged up the fact that there were several unsolved murders and attacks – each with elements of the Ripper's known MO – in the force area.

Yet, even when a summary of the Sampson Report was released the following summer – a retributive strike by the West Yorkshire Police Committee against Chief Constable Ronald Gregory and caused by his decision to sell his memoirs to the *Mail on Sunday* for £40,000 – the issue of other possible Ripper attacks passed unnoticed in the press. The public focus remained resolutely on the failures of the Ripper Squad and its management.

But away from the public gaze, police forces across the country began to contact West Yorkshire. Each had unsolved attacks – often murders – that bore some resemblance to Sutcliffe's known MO; each wanted permission to interview the Ripper in prison.

The niceties of British law enforcement generally place the 'ownership' of an individual offender with one police force: it controls access to him long after he has been imprisoned. For obvious reasons, Peter Sutcliffe was 'owned' by West Yorkshire Police.

Rather than facilitate a succession of individual forces trailing down to speak to the Ripper, in 1983 West Yorkshire Police set up a new team to investigate the list of unsolved murders and attacks. At its head was Assistant Chief Constable Keith Hellawell. What he discovered strongly suggested that Sutcliffe's reign of terror had started not in 1975 with Anna Rogulskyj but at least nine years earlier, in 1966.

When we first pulled everything together there were in the region of seventy-eight murders and attempted murders that either we or other forces believed Sutcliffe might have committed.

All the information we had on them was catalogued and we looked at factors which might eliminate Sutcliffe from them. For example we knew from his driver's logs where he was when the crime was committed and for some of them we found that he was in a different part of the country.

When Hellawell's team had finished this sifting exercise he was left with a list of twenty-two murders and attacks that bore the hallmarks of the Ripper's MO – and in places where the detectives could place him at the relevant time. It was a shocking catalogue of unsolved crimes, and one that Hellawell was convinced had been committed by Peter Sutcliffe.

But it wasn't just the scale of this catalogue of offending that proved surprising: the files detailed killings or vicious attacks on men as well as women. What's more, from the outset, the victims were predominantly not prostitutes: they were mostly nurses, students and hitch-hikers. Nor were they confined to Yorkshire or the north of England: the crimes had been committed across the length and breadth of the country.

Who were these unknown women and men? What had happened to the investigations into their cases? And why had Sutcliffe never been identified as the man responsible?

For the next ten years, Keith Hellawell would attempt to answer these questions. He would meet repeatedly with the Yorkshire Ripper and attempt to persuade him to confess. It was an extraordinary, draining and – ultimately – very expensive exercise, paid for by British taxpayers. Yet it was kept strictly secret and, with two solitary exceptions, the victims have never been acknowledged, much less publicly identified.

There is a reason for this deliberate and protracted cover-up. And it lies in the truth about Peter Sutcliffe – truth that remains hidden to this day.

FOUR

THE GRAVEDIGGER

In any given year, there are between 550 and 700 murders committed in Britain. In the vast majority of cases the victim knows – and quite probably lives close to – his or her killer; this is the primary reason why most murderers are caught, and caught quickly.

But there is a stubborn – and growing – rump of homicides that have never been solved. Some date back more than a century, to the original Jack the Ripper killings in London's East End, but there is scarcely a police force area – and certainly not a single decade – without a sad scattering of unavenged dead bodies.

In total, there are – depending on how records are interpreted – at least 1,100 of these long-cold cases. And those records are a mess: there is no central database, much less any nationwide analysis of what they might imply. Each police force keeps – and often guards jealously – its roll call of the unsolved. Academic researchers and journalists alike can only petition individual forces with requests under the Freedom of Information Act; all too often these are rebuffed on the grounds of time and cost.

But persistent digging has produced some results, and there are indications that some decades have left more unsolved murders than others.

The 1960s and 1970s, in particular, stand out because by and large these were some of the country's most peaceful post-war years and their legacy of unexplained homicides is statistically unusual.

In the five months following Peter Sutcliffe's conviction at the Old Bailey, Assistant Chief Constable Colin Sampson discovered from the scattered (and often incomplete) records of the once independent local forces across West Yorkshire a series of these 'ghosts in the machine'. The exact number has never been released; instead, an executive summary of his findings was published. It included this brief and stark statement:

A number of attacks on women since 1966 in West Yorkshire remain undetected. Sutcliffe has now been interviewed about these and other cases which occurred elsewhere in the country, but has denied responsibility.

Aside from its imprecision, there were several serious flaws in Sampson's summary pronouncement. The most glaringly obvious was the terse statement – evidently intended to close the door on future investigations – that the Yorkshire Ripper denied committing the unsolved murders. West Yorkshire Police knew from Sutcliffe's evasive and wily confessions that he admitted responsibility for a murderous attack only when he saw no other possibility. As his trial had revealed, the confession in which the police had placed so much faith excluded several of the murders or attempts for which he was ultimately convicted.

They also knew – because a jury had rejected the shabby attempt at a plea bargain – that Sutcliffe had deliberately feigned mental illness to avoid being convicted of murder. That he refused to admit responsibility for other long-cold cases should have been neither surprising nor a reason to stop investigating.

Within West Yorkshire Police there were dedicated detectives who wanted to do exactly that. Often against the instinct of their senior officers – and in an atmosphere that was both recriminatory and poisonous – they started to do what the force had so signally failed to do when Peter Sutcliffe was arrested and confessed to being the Yorkshire Ripper. They began properly investigating the Ripper's early life.

* * *

The town of Bingley has been on official maps of England since Saxon times. The Domesday Book of 1086 listed it under the name 'Bingheleia' and recorded its size as 'four carucate [a measure of ploughed land] to be taxed'. The manuscript goes on to dismiss the settlement as 'waste'.

By medieval times, Bingley had become a feudal manor extending for several miles along the bank of the river Aire between the (then) hamlets of Keighley and Cottingley. Poll tax returns show that in 1379 it boasted 130 households with a total likely population of 500 adults – twice the contemporary size of either of the two neighbouring towns of Bradford and Leeds.

The Industrial Revolution of the late eighteenth and early

nineteenth centuries brought prosperity and grime in equal measure. Mills were built, canals dug and locks constructed, connecting all the towns of the Aire Valley with the growing wool-trading centre of Bradford. Slowly but inexorably, Bingley became overshadowed by 'Worstedopolis', as its increasingly affluent neighbour became known.

By 1857, when the Victorian novelist Mrs Gaskell travelled through the town, en route to a memorable meeting with Charlotte Brontë further up the valley in Haworth, the grinding poverty and exploitation of the poor that were the true faces of the Industrial Revolution had evidently taken a heavy toll on Bingley's population.

> The remarkable degree of self-sufficiency they possess gives them an air of independence apt to repel a stranger … Their accost is curt; their accent and tone of speech blunt and harsh. A stranger can hardly ask a question without receiving some crusty reply if, indeed, he receive any at all.
>
> Sometimes the sour rudeness amounts to positive insult. Yet if the 'foreigner' takes all this churlishness good-humouredly, or as a matter of course, and makes good any claim upon their latent kindliness and hospitality, they are faithful and generous and thoroughly to be relied upon.

Almost ninety years later, on Sunday, 2 June 1946, Peter William Sutcliffe was born in a small stone cottage tucked into the hillside along Ferncliffe Road, one of the steepest of several precipitous streets rising westward out of Bingley town centre.

The summer of 1946 was unseasonably dull and wet, with cold air depressions punctuated by frequent thunderstorms. It was a far cry from the scenes of wild rejoicing on VE Day, just a year previously. Then the whole country had set aside several weeks to commemorate Britain's triumph over Nazi Germany and Winston Churchill – the nation's wartime leader – opened the first of what would be a succession of fêtes and street parties to celebrate Hitler's defeat, and to salute all those who had played their part in it.

Peter's father, John, was one of them. He had, in truth, had a relatively easy war, mostly stationed on Gibraltar, where he had used his undoubted singing and acting talents to cheer up rather more frontline troops who passed through the colony en route to battle.

In his pre-war life, John Sutcliffe had been an apprentice at the Co-Op bakery in Bingley. He had courted a young local girl, Kathleen Coonan, and – despite the war intervening – had married her while on leave in 1945. Peter was the couple's first child.

Kathleen Sutcliffe had been brought up as (and remained) a devout Catholic. Although John was (and would equally remain) Church of England, he was forced to abide by one of the unchallengeable tenets of his wife's religion. There would be no contraception employed in the Sutcliffe household; unsurprisingly, within a few short months of Peter Sutcliffe's arrival, Kathleen announced she was once again pregnant.

Thomas Sutcliffe was born in September 1947, but died three days after his arrival in the little cottage on Ferncliffe Road. Peter had been sent to stay with his maternal grandmother in the weeks leading up to the birth; by the time he returned home, his baby brother had been quietly and unceremoniously buried in a common grave at Bingley Cemetery.

Whether because of this or due to the arrival – in fairly short order – of a succession of five siblings, Peter Sutcliffe grew up a quiet and nervous child. He read voraciously, avoided sport (a preoccupation for all self-respecting men and boys in Yorkshire) and was deeply self-conscious about his relative shortness (no more than five feet eight inches) and his slight frame. He clung to his mother and was seen, in the local dismissive language, as 'nesh' – soft, weak and unmasculine.

Although his school reports were unremarkable and his academic performance seemingly mediocre, Peter was plainly bright. John Sutcliffe let himself imagine that his eldest son would sit the eleven-plus – the exam that separated the wheat of potential grammar-school boys from the chaff who would be sent to a local secondary modern (the precursor of comprehensive education). But the teachers at St Joseph's Roman Catholic Primary School disabused him of the notion: if Peter went to the grammar school he would be in full-time education until at least sixteen, and more likely eighteen. There were several younger children in the Sutcliffe family, and in the teachers' view, John and Kathleen needed the boy to bring home wages long before then. In September 1957, Peter Sutcliffe was sent to Cottingley Manor Roman Catholic Secondary Modern.

His adolescent academic career was no more distinguished than his earlier years had been. He remained shy, awkward and nervous – not helped by a light, high voice and a pronounced stammer that led to repeated bullying. When he left Cottingley in 1961, at the age of fifteen, Peter had no significant qualifications and only a handful of friends – all exclusively male.

It wasn't that girls didn't find him attractive. The teenage Peter Sutcliffe had dark, swarthy good looks and – thanks to a course of home bodybuilding – his short frame had become wiry and well muscled. But he was ill at ease in female company and came across as somehow disconcerting – not exactly threatening, but equally not someone with whom an adolescent girl felt comfortable.

The Sutcliffes had, by 1961, moved to a council house to accommodate the growing family. Number 57 Cornwall Road, Bingley, was a standard brick-built post-war box on an estate that clung to a steep hillside on the edge of the town.

John Sutcliffe was working as a weaver at a local mill and, on leaving school, his eldest son joined him. But within weeks, Peter quit and took up an apprenticeship at the Brierley and Fairbank engineering works. It wouldn't take long for him to walk out on this job, the long haul of learning his trade apparently too tedious to be contemplated.

The family house was both crowded and, by the end of the year, tense. In the early hours of Christmas Day 1961, John Sutcliffe was arrested and charged with burgling a neighbouring property. Two weeks later, the *Bingley Guardian* carried a report of his conviction and sentence at the local magistrate's court.

Thirty-nine year-old weaver John William Sutcliffe admitted stealing foodstuffs valued at 19 shillings 7½d and was conditionally discharged for twelve months on payment of costs.

He was on his way home from a Christmas Eve party which lasted until 4.30 a.m. on Christmas Day. Some young people in another room were having a party which was just about breaking up.

On hearing a light switch in the kitchen they went to investigate just in time to see Sutcliffe, whom they recognised, making a dash for the door. Some youths chased him down the road, caught him and sent for the police. As he ran Sutcliffe left a trail of packets of raisins, sweets etc., behind him, which he had stuffed into his pockets.

He was genuinely sorry for the theft because the complainants were distant relatives of his, and hitherto he had a perfectly clean record.

It would not be the last time the police had cause to visit 57 Cornwall Road.

The house was also no stranger to sexual tension. Girls from the estate visited, often enjoying surreptitious liaisons there with Peter's friends. His father, too, was known to publicly flirt with the youngsters, playing and seeming to touch them in jest – despite Kathleen's presence. But Peter himself showed no inclination to indulge in anything more physical than an occasional awkward attempt at chatting up.

If, as the poet Philip Larkin once claimed, 'sexual intercourse began in 1963', it showed every sign of having bypassed Peter Sutcliffe. At the age of nineteen – as the Age of Aquarius and the era of permissiveness began – he displayed little interest in girls. Aside from an unswerving closeness to his mother, his twin passions were motorbikes (later cars) and drinking with his friends. One of them, Eric Robinson, would later tell reporters:

He was very backward at coming forward with girls other than his sisters. If we were in a pub and a couple of girls came in who Peter liked the look of he would mention it, but he never seemed to have it in him to go and talk to them. I got the impression that he thought that chatting up girls was somehow distasteful.

I often wonder if it was anything to do with the fact that when we were back at the Sutcliffes' house at night his father, on occasions, would openly flatter his sisters' friends and pretend to fondle them: he would reckon to mess with them. There was no harm done, but it seemed to make Peter uncomfortable. He was always much closer to his mother ...

In a more enlightened age – and in a place less grimly macho (homosexuality would not be made legal for another four years) – it might have occurred to Sutcliffe's friends to wonder if he was gay. Certainly, an incident involving his friend, Steve Close, the following year seemed to hint at something other than conventional heterosexual desires.

We were on holiday together on a caravan site in the Lake District and one night we were pretty drunk. We were both down to our underpants, getting ready to turn in, when I made some sort of remark about sex. Peter picked up a knife and jumped on me shouting, 'I'm going to cut your dick off, you bastard!'

I'm a big bloke, but he was like a mad thing and I just couldn't stop him. He seemed possessed of some sort of super strength. It was only when he slashed my private parts that he calmed down. He went pale and said, 'Sorry, Steve – I'd better get you to hospital.' It took several stitches to stop the bleeding.

Close worked with Sutcliffe at the new job he had begun that year: both were gravediggers at Bingley Cemetery. It was a place and an occupation that would come to dominate his life.

> Bingley Cemetery is one of the most popular places of resort, and is justly accounted one of the prettiest and most attractive places of the kind in England.

This glowing, if slightly bizarre, endorsement in a 1904 guidebook waxed lyrical about the extent and variety of flora to be found in the graveyard.

> The mezereons, lilacs, roses and flowerbeds present in season a fine and varied show. But to lovers of botanical treasures, the extensive range of rockery, which bears hundreds of curious and beautiful Alpine plants, will prove the chief attraction.

The book's enthusiastic author, a local historian of Bingley, might more honestly have mentioned that in the long northern winter months the cemetery was one of the coldest places in the area.

But neither the bitter wind whipping viciously down the Aire Valley nor the macabre occupation seemed to affect the eighteen-year-old Peter Sutcliffe. He joined the staff in the summer of 1964 at the standard wage of £7 for a forty-four-hour week. He was not unduly impressed by the money and was, according to his workmates, happy to earn extra cash by washing down dead bodies in the chapel of rest. He received 5 shillings per cadaver.

All the cemetery workers were men: most were young and

plainly did not see the job as a long-term career, merely a first staging post on their road to adult working life. Sutcliffe, though, was different: from the outset he demonstrated an unhealthy fascination with corpses, and his behaviour was at times disturbing. Laurie Ashton, who worked with Sutcliffe as a gravedigger, would later recall a succession of bizarre incidents.

One night we had been out boozing, and had certainly had a few drinks, when Peter mentioned that he had the key to the morgue. He said there were two 'ripe ones' in there and suggested we should go and have a look at them. He seemed quite disappointed when we turned down his offer.

On another occasion he was reopening a grave at the cemetery and I saw him chasing some grammar-school girls with an old skull. I thought that was a bit much but Peter was very amused …

He certainly had a morbid interest in death and all things connected with it. He told me that bodies from accidents and those which had been opened up for post-mortems were the ones he liked best. He had to wash them down and clean up the scalpels, knives and remains after autopsies. He used to go on and on about all the gory details.

Ashton was not alone in his assessment. Other co-workers recalled the aftermath of a funeral when all the mourners had departed and Sutcliffe jumped down into the grave, removed the lid of the coffin and began rooting around inside. A few hours later, drinking in a local pub, he took a handful of rings from his pocket: he had pulled them from the fingers of the corpse.

Sutcliffe and his friends spent most of their free time in pubs. In that, they were hardly uncommon, but even leaving aside his obsessive talk about death and bodies, Sutcliffe's behaviour stood out. Eric Robinson, one of his regular drinking companions, later remembered:

> His eyes would be everywhere and he didn't seem to miss anything. In fact he would notice things that you didn't. Like if a girl was with a bloke and not taking any notice of him, Peter would draw it to our attention.

But other than watching, Sutcliffe showed no discernible sexual or romantic interest in women. Throughout 1964, he frequently slept over at a house shared by his best friend, Keith Sugden, with a number of young women.

> Peter used to stay a couple of nights a week. There were about five women in the house and there was plenty going on at the time. But Peter never latched on to any of the women: he just didn't bother.
>
> I remember that we came down one morning into the kitchen and there was a girl lying starkers across the kitchen table, asking, 'Who wants me for breakfast?' Peter turned her down.

During the early years of their friendship, Keith Sugden married his long-term girlfriend, Doreen. Her family, too, would have cause to remember Sutcliffe's strange and disturbing attitude to women. One night, Mrs Sugden's younger sister Colleen – then no more than ten years old – was staying over at 57 Cornwall

Road. Standing at the top of the staircase, she was suddenly picked up from behind and thrown down to the bottom. Fortunately uninjured, she looked back up to the landing to see Peter Sutcliffe.

> Peter was standing there, staring down at me with those funny dark eyes. He had that silly, sickly, giggly grin on his face that was so familiar. He never said a word.

It was 1965: Peter Sutcliffe was nineteen years old with a growing reputation as someone to be treated with caution – a young man who revelled in telling stories about death and bodies, and in whose presence women felt oddly uncomfortable.

He had also, by then, come to the notice of the police. His first brush with the law had occurred two years earlier when he was summonsed to Keighley magistrate's court for driving unaccompanied while holding only a provisional licence, and for failing to display L-plates. It was the first of eleven separate motoring convictions he would clock up in the coming years – an indication, perhaps, of his growing contempt for the law.

But his first serious conviction came on 17 May 1965. Two months earlier, he had been caught in the act of attempting to break into cars parked along Bingley's Main Street. He was arrested, bailed and, when he appeared before the town's magistrates that May morning, he was fined £5 and ordered to pay costs of £2 7s 6d.

This conviction generated – as was the procedure of the times – two separate official records. The first was held in the criminal record office maintained by West Riding Constabulary – the precursor of today's West Yorkshire Police. The second was sent to New Scotland Yard in London, where it was duly filed in the Central Criminal Record Office. Young Peter Sutcliffe was beginning to make a name for himself as a teenage delinquent.

In 1966, 22 April fell on a Friday. By tradition, workers in mills and factories throughout Bingley sent a junior employee out to their nearest fish and chip shop to bring back sizeable orders for the 12 noon lunch break. By 11.30 a.m., a large queue had formed outside the town centre chippie on Wellington Street.

A hundred yards down the road and at that very moment, Fred Craven was murdered.

Bingley was a small town, in many ways still as insular as Mrs Gaskell had observed a hundred years earlier. It retained a sense of community that ensured most people knew each other, at least by sight. They certainly knew and recognised Fred Craven – not least because a congenital spinal disability meant that for all his sixty-six years he had never grown above four feet seven inches tall.

Mr Craven had spent the first twelve years of his life in a plaster cast. His family's doctors had predicted that he would not live past the age of twenty-one, but the frail young man was evidently made of sterner stuff than the medics realised. He not only survived, but also went on to set himself up in business as a 'commission agent' – a bookie who provided a personalised service for punters wishing to bet on horse races.

Fred Craven's life was a testament to his inner strength and determination. He came from a tough Yorkshire family – both his father and his brother were celebrated rugby league players with a fierce local reputation. In addition to his spinal disability and short stature, he had also suffered from a serious problem with the bones in his right hand: an operation to remove one of them left him unable to write, so he painfully taught himself to use his left hand instead.

He had married and become a father to four children, but when his eldest was just fourteen, their mother had left home. Thereafter, Fred Craven brought up his son and three young daughters single-handed.

There was no racing on the calendar that Friday in April and normally Mr Craven would not have made the journey into town. But that morning he decided briefly to drop in at his work to collect a few business papers. He unlocked the door to his small office, situated above an antiques shop on Wellington Road, at a little before 11.30 a.m. and made a short phone call.

Two men had followed him that morning. Inside the office, one smashed him over the back of his head with what police would describe as 'a blunt instrument', before kicking him in the chest and smashing his ribs. The robbers then made off with his imitation crocodile-skin wallet containing round £200. Ten minutes later, a relative found Fred Craven's lifeless little body in a pool of blood behind his office door.

The robbery-murder was evidently an opportunist crime. Fred Craven had not been following any particular routine that morning – making it unlikely that his killers had planned the raid – and that made it more likely that they were local men. Detectives' enquiries yielded descriptions of the two suspects: they were both, in the police jargon of the time, 'artisan types' – in other words, working men. One was around forty years old, perhaps five feet four inches tall, unshaven, wearing a dark jacket and a cloth cap; his companion was described as no more than twenty, slim, five feet five inches tall and dressed in a dark jacket, light-coloured trousers and – most distinctively – a 'Donovan cap'. This was a popular item of the day: Donovan – the Scottish folk-singer-cum-pop-star – was approaching the zenith of his fame and his denim cap was something of a trademark.

Within two days, police led by Detective Superintendent George Oldfield and Detective Sergeant Dick Holland – both of whom, a decade later, would be running the Yorkshire Ripper inquiry – turned up at 57 Cornwall Road. They arrested Michael Sutcliffe, Peter's sixteen-year-old brother, who was gaining a reputation as something of a tearaway and was known to wear a Donovan cap. They held him for forty-eight hours before establishing that, at the time of the murder, he was in the queue outside the fish and chip shop, collecting the orders for his workmates at a local joinery.

What Oldfield and his team didn't know was that the more likely suspect lived in the same house. Peter Sutcliffe also owned and regularly wore the distinctive cap; he also fitted very closely the description of the second robber.

Perhaps on its own this would not have been enough to take him in for questioning (even had the detectives realised the similarity). But there were other factors that, in the eyes of Fred Craven's relatives, put Peter in the frame. He, like his younger brother, definitely knew the bookmaker. Not only did Fred Craven live less than a hundred yards away on the same street, but Sutcliffe had also repeatedly pestered Craven's daughter, Jennifer, to go out with him. She had repeatedly rebuffed his clumsy advances.

And so the trail went cold. The murder of Fred Craven, a hard-working and well-liked Bingley bookmaker and devoted father, was consigned to the files of West Riding Constabulary as an unsolved crime. It would be fifteen years before anyone thought to connect it with the Yorkshire Ripper.

Crime in the small towns and villages that run along the Aire Valley was, in the mid-1960s, local and low-key. In an era of near-full employment and before drugs undermined communities from within, offences of serious violence – let alone murder – were rare. Which made the events of Wednesday, 22 March 1967 all the more remarkable.

John Tomey was twenty-seven. A slightly built young man with strong prescription spectacles, he earned his living as a taxi driver in and around Leeds. Late that March evening he picked up a fare in the city centre. His passenger was younger than him, in his early twenties at most, and was wearing a zipped beige-coloured jacket, jeans and a green and white college scarf. Mr Tomey assumed he was a student.

The young man first asked to be taken to Bradford; then he changed his mind and told the driver to head for Bingley. As they approached the town, Mr Tomey stopped under a street lamp and showed his fare the rate card; he got a clear look at the man's face and observed that he had dark hair, a moustache and a beard. His accent was clearly local and his behaviour, too, was memorable.

> I noticed him in the back getting very agitated. He told me he hadn't got any money but said he had an aunt at Nelson who would pay the fare.

Nelson was more than twenty miles away over the border in Lancashire – a solid hour's driving. Today, few if any taxi drivers would agree to take an evidently penniless passenger such a distance on the vague promise of being paid by a relative. But the 1960s were a more innocent, more trusting time. John Tomey drove on.

The road passed through Keighley and on up the winding, steep hills towards Brontë country and the moors that separate Yorkshire from Lancashire. This was well outside Mr Tomey's normal routes and before long he was lost. On a lonely and deserted stretch of road running across Cockhill Moor he decided to consult his map.

> I had been looking for somewhere to turn round but there were grey stone walls on either side of the road. Eventually I managed to find an opening and did a U-turn. I didn't know where I was, so I stopped there and reached over to the glove compartment to pull out the map.

As he bent forward, his passenger suddenly attacked him from the rear seat. He smashed a ball-peen hammer several times into the back of Mr Tomey's skull, knocking him briefly unconscious. As he came to, he saw that his attacker had got out of the taxi and was pulling at the locked driver's door. When this wouldn't open, the man swung his hammer again and again at the window, smashing it into tiny pieces.

Dazed and bleeding heavily, Mr Tomey somehow managed to gun the engine and drive away. He found the nearest cottage, staggered up to its front door and asked the evidently shocked owner to call the police.

John Tomey would spend several days hospitalised in Keighley. Doctors discovered that his skull had been severely fractured and the weapon had left deep, crescent-shaped lacerations. He would never again drive his taxi: the physical and mental after-effects of what was unquestionably an attempted murder left him unable to work for the vast majority of his life. Nor would he ever marry or have a family.

Two murderous attacks in an otherwise peaceful area: both similar in their methods and less than a year apart. Two converging descriptions, also, of the suspect: a young man – in his early twenties at most – and likely to be local. Not a tall man, no more than five feet five, and one who wore a full beard and moustache. Yet the attempt on John Tomey's life, like the killing of Fred Craven eleven months earlier, was never solved. It, too, was left as a mystery; like the bookmaker's murder, it would be 1981 before anyone connected it with Peter Sutcliffe.

By the time of the attack on John Tomey, three important events had converged in Sutcliffe's life. He had passed his driving test and bought the first of a series of vehicles; he had met a young Bingley man who would become his longest-lasting and closest friend; and he had begun to date his first – and last – girlfriend.

Getting his driving licence had enabled Sutcliffe to purchase the first of what would become a succession of second-hand vehicles. It also enabled him to indulge a secret – and growing – taste for prostitutes. His friends noticed that the young man who had seemed so disinterested in women now talked about streetwalkers almost compulsively. Nor was it only talk: during a drinking session one night in the Ferrands Arms in the centre of Bingley, he asked Keith Sugden to come with him to the toilet. In front of the urinals, Sutcliffe unzipped his flies and calmly asked Sugden to examine his penis. It was not a pretty sight.

It looked a mess and it certainly seemed as though he had contracted venereal disease. I told him the best thing he could do was to go to St Luke's Hospital in Bradford [which had a VD clinic] and get it sorted out. I was staggered really because I had never seen Peter Sutcliffe bother with girls.

It seems likely that Sutcliffe had caught a sexually transmitted infection from a prostitute on one of his regular trawls of the local red-light districts; if so, it must be open to question whether she survived. Disturbingly, there remain unsolved cases of missing or murdered sex workers in the 1960s – but the police papers on them are long gone.

Certainly, Sutcliffe was, by this time, no stranger to the streets where prostitutes operated – sometimes alone but on occasions with a local youth, three years his junior.

Trevor Birdsall was eighteen and had met Peter Sutcliffe in one of the pubs along Bingley's Main Street that served as second homes to both young men. They shared a fondness for hand-pulled Tetley's Bitter, a near-obsession with cars – and a deeply unpleasant habit of trawling the red-light districts of Bradford and Leeds. Together Sutcliffe and Birdsall forged a kerb-crawling partnership – albeit one in which the younger man appears to have been little more than a driver and confidant.

Like every other industrial and commercial city, ever since the Industrial Revolution the sprawling conurbations of Leeds and Bradford have had sizeable and constantly shifting loose communities of prostitutes. Always marginalised, economically desperate and deeply vulnerable, they have historically been the victims not simply of the men who paid to abuse their bodies but also of laws that were explicitly designed to punish them rather than those who demanded their services.

In 1824, the Vagrancy Act created the offence of being a 'common prostitute', punishable by one month's imprisonment with hard labour. Two decades later, the Town Police Clauses Act of 1847 forbade prostitutes to 'assemble at any place of public resort'. These two pieces of legislation were followed in the mid-nineteenth century by the Contagious Diseases Acts, which subjected prostitutes to compulsory (and highly painful) medical checks for infection and provided for the imprisonment of any woman found to be carrying a disease until such time as she might be deemed cured.

Since supply – in the form of women sufficiently desperate to rent their bodies – merely catered for an unceasing demand, these laws targeting only women were unsurprisingly unsuccessful. By the time Britain had been through two world wars, demand for sexual services was on an almost constant upward curve: inevitably, perhaps (since it was almost exclusively a male preserve), Parliament introduced a further discriminatory law – the Street Offences Act of 1959. This made it an offence 'for a common prostitute to loiter or solicit in a street or public place for the purpose of prostitution'. To be condemned as a common prostitute required two separate cautions by police for soliciting.

In the still thriving wool heartlands of West Yorkshire, the overlapping and (often) rival forces mounted periodic clean-up drives: vice squads would descend on streets where prostitutes were known to work, issue the necessary cautions and 'encourage' the women to move on to a patch in another force area. It was not a strategy designed or destined to win the fragile confidence of this already vulnerable population.

In Bradford, the industrial centre for the worsted trade, the once affluent district of Manningham slowly descended into a de facto red-light district. In Leeds, where wool magnates operated the commercial side of the industry, the equally forlorn suburb of Chapeltown became home to several hundred working women.

Peter Sutcliffe, often accompanied by Trevor Birdsall, quartered and patrolled the streets of both. They drove up and down Lumb Lane in Bradford and Spencer Place in Leeds, obsessively observing the poor and desperate women who eked out a brutal living, £5 a time.

They did so despite the fact that Sutcliffe had met and begun courting his first ever girlfriend. Her name was Sonia Szurma: for the next fifteen years she would be his closest companion – and yet would be utterly unaware that he was the Yorkshire Ripper.

FIVE

LOVE AND DEATH

They met on Valentine's Day, 1967. Sonia Szurma was sixteen, a schoolgirl studying for her first exams and under the legal age for drinking. Nonetheless, she made the four-mile journey from her home in Clayton to the Royal Standard on Manningham Lane, on the other side of Bradford. The pub was one of Peter Sutcliffe's regular haunts: that evening their paths crossed.

She had been christened Oksana, the second daughter of Ukrainian refugees who had escaped from behind the Iron Curtain. Bohdan Szurma had been born in Poland in 1912 and had fled the country in September 1939, after the German and Russian occupation. He later became a physical education teacher, first in Ukraine and then in Czechoslovakia. When, in 1947, Soviet tanks entered Prague as Moscow tightened its post-war grip on Eastern Europe, Bohdan and his wife, Maria, fled to Britain. Here they were first housed in a displaced persons camp near York, then given the keys to a council-owned semi in Tanton Crescent, Clayton.

Their first child, Marianne, was born shortly after their arrival. Oksana was delivered in a Bradford hospital on 10 August 1947. Bohdan – by all accounts a severe and ascetic father – got a low-paying job as a wool-comb box-minder in a local mill, but appears to have made little effort to fit into the parochial and sometimes claustrophobic working-class community. His most noticeable concession to his surroundings was to change his younger daughter's name to Sonia just before she started at the local primary school.

The two Szurma daughters were very different. To her father's evident satisfaction, Marianne excelled at school, passing exams with flying colours en route to the Royal College of Music in London. Although she earned a place at the local grammar school, Sonia found academic work harder: in the summer of 1967 – when she had been dating Sutcliffe for four months – she managed to pass just six CSEs (a lower educational qualification than the then standard O levels).

Both she and her parents had hoped for better. The plan was for Sonia to go on to teacher training college, but CSEs wouldn't get her a place, so she transferred to Bradford technical college to study for the prized O levels. Her success in passing them would – though neither she nor her family could have known it – play a crucial role in Peter Sutcliffe's future killings.

The Szurma family's initial reaction to Sutcliffe can't have been positive. While he was – outwardly at least – polite and unassuming, he was both five years older than Sonia and still in a (quite literally) dead-end job at Bingley Cemetery. But the relationship continued and, before 1967 was out, they were very clearly a couple.

They didn't, of course, live together: even for families less conservative than the Szurmas, 'living over the brush' (or 'in sin') was not to be contemplated. Sonia stayed with her parents in Tanton Crescent, while Peter continued to live in Cornwall Road, six miles out of Bradford, in Bingley.

Nor did they spend all their free time together: Sutcliffe regularly went out drinking with his old friends – and maintained his night-time patrols of the red-light districts of Bradford and Leeds.

* * *

They found Mary Judge on waste ground beneath the railway arches opposite Leeds Parish Church. She was naked, her clothes scattered over the derelict ground. Her body showed signs of a savage attack: it appeared that she had been bent over a wall before her attacker smashed in the back of her head with either a brick or a hammer. The damage was so severe that visual identification was impossible. It was Monday, 26 February 1968 – just over a year since Peter Sutcliffe had begun courting Sonia Szurma.

A murder room was established at the headquarters of Leeds City Police. Here detectives sifted through the few clues until a fingerprint check finally revealed the victim's identity. Mary Judge was forty-three and had convictions for prostitution. Though the sparse local news reports described her as 'Mrs', there was no trace of a husband or family. Instead, for the previous seven years, the dead woman had shared the home of an elderly man who employed her as a housekeeper.

James Morton, a frail seventy-five-year-old, had no idea that Mary Judge was moonlighting as a part-time prostitute. She only went out one evening a week – Monday – and he thought she was lonely with few friends in the area.

The reality of that Monday – Mary Judge's last – was probably typical of her narrow and unhappy life. In the morning she had followed her usual routine, placing a one-shilling bet on a horse race. In the evening she set out for the city centre pubs wearing a red-and-black-check coat over a white blouse and dark-blue skirt.

Police enquiries revealed that the last sighting of Mrs Judge was at 10.10 p.m. outside the Regent Hotel on Kirkgate in Leeds city centre. Neither the hotel nor the street was a known haunt of prostitutes, though some women did work nearby in the then run-down and shabby area of The Calls. It is not known whether Mary Judge was seeking clients that Monday evening, but within minutes of being spotted outside the pub she was beaten to death a few hundred yards away, beneath the railway arches backing on to the Parish Church. The church verger, John Dunhill, was close enough to hear the attack and able to give detectives a reliable timeframe.

About ten past ten I was just going from my house to the vestry when I heard sounds of banging over towards the railway arches. It was just banging – no screaming – and I did not take a great deal of notice because there is always some noise coming from the road and that bit of land.

But the most crucial evidence came from an unlikely eyewitness. At 10.18 p.m., a small boy – never named – was in a railway carriage rattling its way into Leeds city centre. As the train passed within fifty yards of the arches, he was staring out of the window: he saw a slim, youngish man with long dark hair attacking a woman who then fell to the ground.

It was the most fleeting of glimpses but it added to the pictures being built up by Leeds detectives. And most importantly of all it provided them with a basic description of the killer.

The man leading the investigation was Detective Superintendent Dennis Hoban, then head of Leeds City Police CID and locally renowned for his skill in catching criminals. He had worked his patch for more than thirty years with skill and great diligence: the *Yorkshire Evening Post* and other local papers tended to refer to him as 'The Crime Buster in a Sheepskin Coat' and he had earned commendations from judges and magistrates, as well as once being named Citizen of the Year in Leeds.

Hoban knew from experience that the murder of Mary Judge was unlike most of the (relatively few) killings that took place on his patch. The evident savagery of the attack suggested that the man responsible would almost certainly strike and kill again. Within just six years, Hoban would stare down at the lifeless body of Wilma McCann on Prince Philip Playing Fields on the other side of Leeds – the first in the official catalogue of murders by the Yorkshire Ripper.

Mary Judge's case was never solved. She was destined to remain one of the ghosts in police files. And she would not be alone.

It is less than ninety miles from Bradford (or Leeds) to Nottingham. In 1968, the M1 – Britain's first motorway – was extended to link Leeds with the rest of the country, dramatically cutting journey times between West Yorkshire and the East Midlands. Getting to Nottingham from the heartlands of the wool cities would have taken little more than two hours.

On the evening of Monday, 4 August 1969, a young woman was celebrating her twenty-first birthday at her parents' home. Shortly after 11 p.m., Lucy Tinslop set off for Nottingham city centre. At 11.30 p.m., screams were heard coming from St Mary's Rest Garden in Bath Street – a quiet former cemetery donated to the city by its Victorian benefactor, Samuel Fox, to bury the victims of a major outbreak of cholera.

When police found Lucy Tinslop's body, they discovered that she had been strangled – then, as now, not the most common method of murder. But her other injuries were even more shocking and rare: Lucy's killer had ripped open her abdomen and stabbed her more than twenty times in the vagina.

What happened next is something of a mystery. Less than a year before Lucy Tinslop was murdered, Nottingham City Police had ceased to exist: under the nationwide 1968 major reorganisation of police forces, it had merged with the historic county force to form a new Nottinghamshire Combined Constabulary. Three years later, there would be another upheaval with the abolition of the Combined Constabulary and the creation of Nottinghamshire Police.

No records remain of any investigation into what became known locally as the 'Birthday Girl Murder' in the Rest Garden that August night in 1968. Today, Nottinghamshire Police does not hold any documents about the investigation or even a copy of Lucy's post-mortem. What is certain is that no one was ever arrested or prosecuted for the killing of Lucy Tinslop.

Could Peter Sutcliffe have been her attacker? Certainly,

the scant remaining records indicate that the killer's MO matched very closely the way in which the Yorkshire Ripper dispatched his victims: strangulation, disembowelling and – most tellingly of all – the repeated stabbing of her vagina. And Sutcliffe was most certainly mobile at this time: his growing criminal record for driving offences indicates that he either owned or had access to vehicles and was using them to travel in search of victims.

But the official account of his vicious career would seem – at first glance – to rule him out. According to this history, he would not commit his first murder for another six years, when he battered Wilma McCann to death and stabbed her repeatedly in the chest, neck and abdomen.

This authorised version of history is wrong, however: as far back as August 1969 – and then again shortly after he was arrested in 1981 – West Yorkshire Police knew that Peter Sutcliffe had admitted to at least one attack in the late 1960s.

Just after 10 a.m. on Thursday, 22 January 1981, Sutcliffe – in the presence of his solicitor – told detectives that in 1969 he had gone out looking for prostitutes. He claimed, in his sworn statement, that this began when he suspected Sonia of having an affair with a local ice-cream salesman: according to his self-serving (and in many places factually wrong) account, this led him to seek revenge on her by having sex with a streetwalker.

> I was wanting to level the score and I thought by just picking her up I wouldn't have reason to judge Sonia [for] going with this man.

But according to Sutcliffe, after handing over a £10 note, he had changed his mind and sought to get his money back. The prostitute refused.

> It left me feeling bitter towards them [prostitutes] especially when there was a sequel to this with the same person a few weeks later in the Old Crown pub in Bradford ... I approached her and said I hadn't forgotten and she could still give me it back.
>
> She flatly refused and started joking about it in a loud voice to someone else who was with her. After this I left the pub feeling humiliated and outraged and embarrassed and I felt a hatred for her and her kind ...

As a result, at some point in August 1969, he had also attacked another prostitute, leaving her for dead. He was out with Trevor Birdsall on one of the pair's regular patrols of Bradford's red-light district. As they sat in Birdsall's Austin Mini Van, munching on fish and chips and watching prostitutes work the streets around Manningham Park, they saw a woman staggering along the pavement, evidently very drunk. Sutcliffe suddenly got out of the vehicle and walked briskly up the adjacent St Paul's Road. He returned ten minutes later, out of breath, telling Birdsall to drive off – and quickly. Birdsall asked what he had been doing: Sutcliffe said he had followed 'an old cow' to a house and then hit her on the back of the head with a stone he had stuffed into a sock. As they drove towards Bingley, he opened the window, removed a sock from his pocket and shook its contents out of the speeding van.[2]

---

[2] Despite hearing this evident confession to a serious crime, Trevor Birdsall did not turn his friend in to police. He would not contact detectives until 26 November 1980 – a week after the Ripper's last acknowledged murder.

The woman Sutcliffe attacked survived: she had also – by chance – noted the registration plate of the Austin Mini Van. The next day, police questioned Birdsall, who suggested they speak to Sutcliffe. When they did so, he admitted hitting the woman, but claimed that it had happened in the course of a drunken argument. The woman herself – she has never been named – was at the time married to a man serving a prison sentence; she didn't want him to discover that she was making money as a prostitute, so she declined to press charges and the police weren't inclined to pursue the case. In the macho culture of the time, assaults on a 'brass' or 'tom' were less worthy of attention than on 'innocent' women: the police issued Sutcliffe with a simple caution.

But even a caution should have been recorded properly in police files. One of the many changes brought about by the wholesale reorganisation of forces in 1968 was the introduction of a central intelligence collator. This new position replaced the previous system in which each of the ten local forces in the region (each based on a historic borough) maintained its own criminal intelligence files, and was designed to ensure that the records of criminals known to one force would be collected in a central location and available to detectives anywhere in the county. A caution is a criminal record, since the offender has to admit an offence before a caution can be issued, and Sutcliffe's attack on the prostitute should have been formally recorded on a card index at force HQ. But even more importantly, the central collator was tasked with linking together patterns of criminal behaviour – MOs, for short – from these records. If the collator was doing his (or her) job correctly, Sutcliffe's highly unusual MO should have been noted on his intelligence file.

That this was important – crucial, in fact – was emphasised by an incident the following month.

On Tuesday, 30 September 1969, Peter Sutcliffe was back in the Manningham area. He was alone this time, but had in his possession two items of hardware: a long-bladed knife and a ball-peen hammer.

In the early hours, a beat bobby patrolling the red-light district spotted a man sitting, crouched down, in an old Morris Minor car with its lights off but the engine running: unsurprisingly, he was suspicious and began walking towards the vehicle. The driver sat up and drove off at high speed.

The policeman called the suspicious incident in to the local control room and patrols began to search the area. They found the car half a mile away, parked up by a kerb: there was no one inside, but the engine was running.

Peter Sutcliffe was then discovered crouched behind a privet hedge with a hammer in his hand. Asked to explain himself – and in particular why he was out in the red-light district clutching a hammer – Sutcliffe claimed that a hubcap had flown off his front wheel and he was trying to find it. The hammer, apparently, was to help him refit the hubcap, should he manage to find it.

The police didn't believe a word of this evidently feeble excuse. Sutcliffe was arrested, taken in for questioning and photographed as a criminal suspect. Unusually, he was not searched and the long-bladed knife remained undiscovered. Nonetheless, several hours later, he was charged with a criminal offence.

Peter Sutcliffe arrest photo, 1969.

By all police procedures – then as now – the offence should have been possession of an offensive weapon: the hammer. Equally, the caution issued to Sutcliffe just three weeks earlier for the stone-in-the-sock attack in the same red-light district should have flagged up that this was a potentially dangerous offender with a known and recent record for assaulting a prostitute.

For reasons that have never been explained, no connection was made: evidently unaware of his caution, the police charged Sutcliffe with the relatively minor offence of 'going equipped for stealing'. One month later, he appeared before Bradford City magistrates and was fined £25, to be paid off at the rate of £2 per week.

It was a golden opportunity lost: the police should have linked both attacks and highlighted Peter Sutcliffe's known MO in the central collator's files and copied to the force intelligence system at Wakefield, as well as the Central Criminal Record Office at New Scotland Yard, which maintained an intelligence-based method index. Had this been done that autumn of 1969, it would have highlighted similarities in the still unsolved attacks on Fred Craven, John Tomey and Mary Judge. It should also have been a vital 'red flag', highlighting Sutcliffe as a suspect whenever a similar MO was used in the future.

Instead, his card in West Yorkshire collator's office simply recorded his conviction as 'going equipped for stealing'. There was no mention of the hammer and no cross-reference to the stone-in-the-sock attack. As a result, it joined thousands of others, languishing unnoticed in the overstuffed and user-unfriendly intelligence files at Wakefield; it would ultimately be completely lost through a weeding process, which binned intelligence no longer regarded as 'relevant'.

By contrast, the duplicate card held in the Metropolitan Police Criminal Record Office at New Scotland Yard did record the crucial detail of the hammer. There would come a time when this should have provided detectives in London with a vital clue as to the identity of a savage killer operating on their patch. But like their counterparts in the north, the Met's officers would somehow overlook Sutcliffe.

Who – or more precisely what – was Peter Sutcliffe at this point in his life? As the 1960s – a decade of optimism and relative prosperity – gave way to the looming bitterness, poverty and industrial strife of the 1970s, Sutcliffe's personal world was also changing.

He had by then been fired from his job at the cemetery: a lengthy charge sheet of bad timekeeping and insubordination had finally exhausted his managers' patience. Instead, at the age of twenty-four, he was picking up labouring jobs and casual work – just enough to put a few pounds in his pocket until he spent them in the pubs and working men's clubs around Bingley and Bradford.

He also bought up a succession of old cars, tinkering with their engines and selling them on for a modest profit. It was hardly a financially rewarding career path, and for a young man who had been courting for almost four years, nowhere near enough to think about settling down to married life.

His relationship with Sonia was clearly a serious one. Her alleged relationship with the Italian ice-cream salesman had been put behind them and Sonia now spent time at the Sutcliffe family home in Cornwall Road. After a period of initial shyness, she had also begun to enjoy nights out as a foursome with Sutcliffe, his sister Maureen and her boyfriend.

In public, she now seemed to dominate him – both willing and able to control her boyfriend's excitable moods with little more than a stern look or terse word. She also gradually weaned him off his taste for country and western music and clothing, introducing him to the rather more rarefied atmosphere of classical music concerts.

But the couple were far from inseparable, and Sutcliffe continued to spend night after night trolling the red-light districts of Bradford and Leeds. And he wasn't just window shopping.

Robin Holland – then Maureen's boyfriend, soon to be her husband – later recalled going out drinking with Sutcliffe in Bradford.

> I've been with him in a pub in Lumb Lane [then the heart of Bradford's prostitute area] and known Peter get up and go out with a girl for five or ten minutes and then come back and sit down with a silly grin on his face. I stopped going out with him in the end: I couldn't stand the hypocrisy.

It wasn't just the knowledge that Sutcliffe was apparently cheating on Sonia during these drinking sessions: what sickened Mr Holland was the way talk always seemed to revolve around infidelity when he, Maureen, Sutcliffe and Sonia went out together as a foursome.

Peter always had plenty to say for himself. The favourite topic of conversation – more a sermon, really – was men who two-timed their wives. He used to call them 'beasts'.

The rest of the family seemed to think that Peter was a saint, sort of the perfect son. But I knew he wasn't. I had regularly gone out drinking with him in pubs in the red-light districts and his main topic of conversation had been sex and prostitutes. He regularly boasted about prostitutes he had been with, so when he used to be on his hind legs, going on about unfaithful married men I used to sit there thinking 'you hypocrite'.

Was Peter Sutcliffe, the future Yorkshire Ripper, then paying for sex with a class of women whom he would later profess to despise to the point of murdering them? Or, as the new decade dawned, was there another explanation for his disappearances and bluster? Had the ten years in which he had turned from an adolescent into an adult, and in which he had probably killed two people and attacked two others, marked him with a twisted obsession with death, a pathology that would determine the course of the next decade – both for him and for his future victims?

SIX

THE SICK AND THE DEAD

For something so ubiquitous that it has become almost a cliché in today's popular culture of Hollywood films and books, the phrase 'serial killer' is a remarkably recent invention.

The first time it appeared in print – in *The Meaning of Murder* by British author John Brophy – was 1966: the same year that Fred Craven was murdered in his first-floor bookie's office in Bingley. But the term was little noticed and it would take until the early 1980s for an American criminologist to define precisely what it meant.

Robert Ressler was a soldier in the US Army who became an FBI special agent in 1970. A decade later, he was recruited to the Bureau's Behavioral Science Unit at Quantico, Virginia: here he organised interviews with thirty-six men who had been imprisoned for multiple homicides, with the aim of finding common links between their backgrounds and motivation. Soon the research was sufficiently advanced for the US Justice

Department to come up with a reliable definition of serial killings: 'a series of two or more murders, committed as separate events, usually, but not always, by one offender acting alone'.

On this simple standard, Peter Sutcliffe was, by the start of the 1970s, already a serial killer. He had – by his own subsequent admission – tried to kill two women, and the very clear similarities between these attacks and the murders of Fred Craven, Mary Judge and Lucy Tinslop (as well as the attempt on John Tomey) strongly suggest that his pathology was well advanced.

Ressler went on to conduct more interviews and to refine his research. He was able to identify two distinct categories of serial killers: the Organised and the Disorganised. He determined that an organised offender typically planned each murder, choosing a stranger as a victim and then engaging in limited conversation. Subsequent examination of the crime scene usually showed that the killer had attempted to control it – often by rearranging aspects of the tableau and taking away with him the tools he had used to commit the crime; the victim, too, displayed evidence of this deliberate control, typically having suffered other violent acts than those that caused death.

By contrast, a disorganised offender was more opportunistic, the killing itself being a spontaneous act with very little conversation having preceded the sudden and fatal violence.

There were, Ressler discovered, also marked differences between the personalities and backgrounds of the two types of killer. An organised offender was likely to be of good intelligence, have some social skills, and would typically have consumed alcohol before carrying out the crime.

The disorganised killer showed only average intelligence, was socially immature, and rarely used alcohol. In medical terms, the disorganised serial murderer was much more likely than his counterpart to have a psychosis – a definable mental illness involving a loss of contact with reality.

Applying these overall parameters to Peter Sutcliffe in 1970 would clearly have placed him in the organised killer category. They would also – had the science been invented by then – have unquestionably warned that his killing spree would continue.

But useful though it was (and remains), Ressler's typology does not address the key question of motivation, and – in particular – what can be learned about the offender from studying the patterns of his behaviour. To do that – and therefore to be able to predict his likely future murders – requires a careful analysis not only of a killer's modus operandi but also of his (or, very rarely, her) 'signature'.

The difference between an MO and a signature is at the heart of an offender's motivation. MO will reveal the type of victim a serial killer typically selects, how he habitually approaches or overpowers them, the tools used, and any common pattern of time and place that the murders take place. But a killer's 'signature' identifies him far more precisely.

First coined by Ressler's colleague at Quantico, John Douglas, the term is defined as 'a personal detail that is unique to the individual, *why* he does it: the thing that fulfils him emotionally'. And while a serial murderer's MO may change as the killer comes up with a better technique or adapts to new circumstances, the emotional reason he commits the crime will never change.

What, then, was the 'emotional reason' behind Peter Sutcliffe's early offending? What drove him to smash in the back of his victims' heads with a hammer before inflicting savage wounds on their dying bodies? It was a question British police in the 1960s were simply not equipped to ask, let alone answer: in those days, murder was simply murder, and those who committed the most obscene killings were written off as 'beasts' or 'monsters' with little serious thought as to what their motivation might have been.

It would be easy to dismiss this as the wisdom of hindsight: had modern scientific understanding been applied to the succession of murders and attempts – all bearing very similar MOs – between 1966 and 1969, a revealing picture of Peter Sutcliffe would have emerged. A picture that could have predicted the trail of slaughter he would leave throughout the next decade.

But while twentieth- and twenty-first-century criminology and psychology have advanced the study of serial killers and their motivation for murder, the fundamentals were established in 1886 by the father of modern psychology, Richard von Krafft-Ebing. That year, he published the foundation text for all subsequent understanding of sex-based killing, *Psychopathia Sexualis*.

The perverse urge in murders for pleasure does not solely aim at causing the victim pain and – most acute injury of all – death, but that the real meaning of the action consists in, to a certain extent, imitating, though perverted into a monstrous and ghastly form, the act of defloration.

It is for this reason that an essential component ... is the employment of a sharp cutting weapon; the victim has to be pierced, slit, even chopped up ... The chief wounds are inflicted in the stomach region and, in many cases, the fatal cuts run from the vagina into the abdomen.

Krafft-Ebing's analysis described almost exactly Peter Sutcliffe's methodology. But even more crucially, it also identified the likely motivation – what the FBI analysts would later term the 'emotional reason' – for this type of murder: necrophilia.

For a phenomenon that – albeit rare – was first formally recorded by the ancient Egyptians (who took precautions against the known incidence of embalmers sexually violating corpses delivered to them), remarkably little scientific attention has been paid to understanding necrophilia. Krafft-Ebing himself, while coining the term, presumed that it was no more than 'a horrible manifestation of sadism'.

His successor, American psychiatrist and pioneering psychoanalyst Abraham Brill, published the first comprehensive examination of the subject in 1941. But working on a limited database, he concluded that necrophiles were either mentally deficient, psychotic or incapable of obtaining a consenting live partner.

That this was not necessarily true emerged during one of Britain's most celebrated post-war serial murder cases. Between 1943 and 1953, John Reginald Christie murdered at least eight women, including his wife, Ethel, by strangling them in his flat at 10 Rillington Place in London's Notting Hill. His first victim was a part-time prostitute who, according to his own subsequent admission, he killed during sex, but by his later murders Christie had progressed to having intercourse with the bodies of his dead or dying victims.

It would take another twenty-five years for a scientifically reliable study of necrophilia to be published. Forensic psychiatrists Phillip Resnick and Jonathan Rosman, from Case Western Reserve University, Chicago, analysed 122 proven homicides involving necrophilic acts or fantasies. Their research, bluntly entitled 'Sexual Attraction to Corpses', revealed two distinct variants of the condition – 'genuine necrophilia' versus 'pseudo-necrophilia' – and argued that conventional assumptions about necrophiles suffering from underlying mental illness or having a hyper-extended sexual deviance were misplaced.

> Neither psychosis, mental retardation nor sadism appears to be inherent in necrophilia. The most common motive for necrophilia is possession of an unresisting and unrejecting partner.

A genuine necrophile, according to Resnick and Rosman was someone with 'a persistent sexual attraction to corpses'. The pseudo-necrophile, by contrast, had a transient attraction to dead bodies, but these were not the prime object of his sexual fantasies: in fact this type of offender – often sadistic or opportunist – had a preference for living sexual partners.

From this empirical start, the psychiatrists were able to sift through their data – the largest-ever collection of validated information on necrophile crimes – to identify three clear types of 'genuine necrophile'.

> We classified the genuine necrophiles into three groups, based on the nature of their acts with corpses:
> A. Necrophilic homicide: murder to obtain a corpse for sexual purposes (14 cases)

B. Regular necrophilia: the use of already dead bodies for sexual pleasure (21 cases)

C. Necrophilic fantasy: fantasising about sexual activity with a corpse, without carrying out any necrophilic acts (15 cases)

The researchers then dug deeper into the background of the offenders. That, too, produced some unexpected results.

Marital Status: In our sample 60 percent were single, 26 percent were married, and 14 percent were divorced or widowed. The marital status of the true necrophiles and pseudonecrophiles was similar.

This implied that men (and almost every one of the offenders studied was male) were frequently able to maintain what appeared to be normal adult relationships while simultaneously indulging their taste for dead bodies. It was a conclusion borne out by a revelation about their sex lives away from corpses.

Nonnecrophilic Intercourse: Most of the true necrophiles (86 percent) had had nonnecrophilic intercourse prior to their necrophilic acts or fantasies ... Some of the subjects were involved in successful relationships when they committed their necrophilic acts.

Next, Resnick and Rosman examined how the offenders obtained access to dead bodies. They found that genuine necrophiles often chose occupations that put them in contact with corpses. Typically, they worked in cemeteries, morgues or hospitals. But even where these men could find corpses in their work, they quite frequently carried out murders to increase the number of bodies they sexually molested.

> The rate of homicide committed by true necrophiles was 28 percent. Most of these homicides were for the purpose of necrophilic acts.

But what did a necrophile killer actually do – sexually – with his victims? Some, according to the data, did have full sexual intercourse with the corpses. Others, though, either did not, or – more tellingly – were not able to do so.

> The fact that several of the regular necrophiles did not engage in vaginal intercourse supports ... [the] contention that coitus is not an essential component of necrophilia. Rigor mortis or the failure to obtain a full erection often makes it difficult to actually have intercourse. As in all perversions, the act is not as rewarding as the fantasy would suggest.

If that was the 'what' – the mechanics or MO – of a necrophile murderer's activity, the forensic psychiatrists were also able to establish the 'why': the emotional reason for a man to kill and then sexually abuse his victim's body. In the context of Peter Sutcliffe, and the development of his pattern of offending, it produced a revealing profile.

> Our data confirm ... [the] observation that necrophilia may appear as the culmination of a pattern of multiple and

increasingly perverse practices rather than as an isolated, abrupt detail …

We postulate that the following psychodynamic events could lead to necrophilia:

1. The necrophile develops poor self-esteem, perhaps due in part to a significant loss

(a) He (usually male) is very fearful of rejection by women, and he desires a sexual object who is incapable of rejecting him; and/or

(b) He is fearful of the dead, and transforms his fear of the dead – by means of reaction formation – into a desire for the dead.

2. He develops an exciting fantasy of sex with a corpse, sometimes after exposure to a corpse.

By the end of the 1960s, Peter Sutcliffe matched the criminological definition of an organised serial murderer; he also fitted remarkably precisely the clinical classification of a necrophile killer. If this is only visible with the benefit of some hindsight, after the publication of the various pieces of empirical research – and thus not to West Yorkshire detectives investigating the unsolved murders and attempted murders between 1966 and 1969 – it should certainly have been considered by police and prosecution at his trial. All the studies detailed in this chapter were published before then.

Above all, what they provide is a psychological photofit of the Yorkshire Ripper: both the 'what' and the 'why' – the MO and the emotional reason – of his offences.

And through that lens, it is possible both to understand what drove him to commit the crimes for which he would eventually be convicted, but also to place him in the frame as a suspect for a succession of unsolved murders that took place throughout the 1970s.

SEVEN

A STRAND OF ROPE

On Saturday, 14 March 1970, a Cheshire farmer stumbled across the body of a young woman on the edge of Square Wood, near the Cheshire village of Mere. She was lying face down in the mulch of the woodland floor and some of her clothes, including her fashionable miniskirt, had been removed and had been placed – seemingly neatly – next to her. Her purple maxi-length coat had evidently been removed with some force – some of its buttons had been torn off and were scattered nearby – but her killer had then carefully positioned it in such a way as to cover her body from view.

A subsequent post-mortem established that the woman was a teenager, and that she had been killed a week earlier. Her body bore evidence of both sexual assault and battering to the back of the head. Around her neck were the telltale marks of a ligature: the clear cause of death was strangulation with a strand of knotted rope or cable.

Within days, Cheshire Police matched her description to a missing person's report: the murdered girl was Jacqueline 'Jackie' Ansell-Lamb, an eighteen-year-old legal secretary who shared a flat with her best friend in Whalley Range, Manchester, but who had been in London for a party the previous weekend. Detectives began the familiar routines of homicide investigations by piecing together information about her last-known whereabouts and movements.

Jackie Ansell-Lamb had been born on 21 September 1951 and spent all her childhood in London's St Pancras district. But in September 1969 her parents decided to leave London and move to St Ives, in what was then still rural Cambridgeshire. Jackie, already established in a secretarial job, didn't want to leave London: she moved into a flat with her best friend, Judi Langrish.

Her decision was probably influenced as much by a reluctance to trade city life for her parents' new and distinctly quieter location as by a career decision. Friends and colleagues told the police that Jackie was 'typically modern': she liked dancing, discotheques and was known to have had a number of boyfriends. She kept a record of them in a diary in which she graded them on a careful scale – 'A-plus' being the best, gradually descending through the alphabet to a less-than-favourable 'C-minus'. One former boyfriend, Barry Klarnett, informed detectives that she had started the diary after seeing the Hollywood movie *Three into Two Won't Go*: in the film, actor Rod Steiger played a middle-aged man who began an affair with a young woman after picking her up while she was hitch-hiking. The detectives would soon discover that Jackie Ansell-Lamb's life imitated art in more ways than keeping a register of her boyfriends' qualities.

During February 1970, Jackie and Judi moved from London to Manchester: they rented a flat in Whalley Range and Jackie quickly got a new job as a legal secretary.

On Friday, 6 March 1970, both girls returned to London to collect the last of their clothes from the old flat: they were invited to a party in Earls Court and decided to make a weekend of it. At the party, Jackie met David Sykes, an attractive twenty-three-year-old man; she went back to his flat on the other side of London at Blackheath Park, and they spent the Friday night, all day Saturday and Sunday morning together.

Jackie had told Judi that she would catch a train to Manchester on the Sunday, but that afternoon she changed her plan. David Sykes drove her the fifteen miles across town to Hendon, where the M1 began: she had decided to hitch-hike. According to Mr Sykes, Jackie didn't relish the idea of hitch-hiking more than 300 miles to her home in Manchester, but neither she nor he had enough money for the train fare. He dropped her off at 2.30 p.m.: it was the last time anyone other than her killer saw her alive. In those pre-mobile phone days, she had no easy means to contact anyone who knew her; when she hadn't arrived back at the flat by the following morning, Judi Langrish reported Jackie missing.

The detectives' enquiries showed that neither Mr Sykes nor any other of her boyfriends could have had anything to do with her death. With few leads to pursue, the murder of Jackie Ansell-Lamb slowly languished in Cheshire Police's records of unsolved crimes.

Though they could not have been expected to know it – the science of criminology being almost unknown in Britain in 1970 – the investigators had missed the most telling evidence about Jackie's killer. While standard operating procedure at the time mandated a thorough enquiry into her known associates, and her 'little black book' was undoubtedly a tempting line to pursue, the most vital clues were to be found on and around her body in Square Wood.

The method of her murder – strangulation – was notable. The most popular means of homicide involves stabbing the victim, either with a knife or a broken bottle. Kicking or punching follows on in second place, narrowly ahead of use of a blunt object or shooting. On average, strangulation or asphyxiation is the cause of death in around 15 per cent of murders – a figure that has remained largely stable for decades.

Even when a man does murder a woman by strangling her, he most usually does so with his bare hands. The use of a ligature is a remarkably rare occurrence and today would raise a red flag in central police databases of offenders' known MOs. But in 1970 – and for many years thereafter – there was no national database and the sharing of intelligence between police forces was rare to the point of non-existence: the potential link between the murders of Lucy Tinslop in Nottingham and Jackie Ansell-Lamb in Cheshire was never made.

But unusual though it was, the ligature was not the most revealing evidence in Jackie's death. It was what the killer had done *after* strangling her that offered the most important insight into his mind: he had posed her body.

Crime-scene or sexual staging had first been recognised (in America, at least) as an important clue more than twenty years earlier in the infamous 'Black Dahlia' murder in Los Angeles. On 15 January 1947, the body of Elizabeth Short, a twenty-two-year-old waitress, was found on waste ground in the Leimert Park district of the city. She had been severely mutilated – cut and stabbed repeatedly around her breasts and thighs – and her corpse had been posed, with her hands over her head, her elbows deliberately bent at right angles and her legs spread wide.

Although the Los Angeles Police Department has never been able to solve the case, the highly unusual circumstances of the positioning of Short's body has led to a series of detailed scientific studies of crime-scene staging. Without exception, these have found that this is an extremely rare phenomenon – present in less than 1 per cent of all known homicides – and always offers vital evidence of both the murderer's MO and his emotional reason for killing. As one study[3] reported:

> The act of leaving a victim's body in an unusual position
> is a conscious criminal action by an offender [either] to
> thwart an investigation, shock the finder and investigators,
> or give perverted pleasure to the killer.

A subsequent research paper by former New York Police Department homicide detective Vernon Geberth[4] refined this analysis and found that there are three typical types of body posing in murders.

> Fantasy: Offenders pose a body to satisfy a perverse
> sexual fantasy through the manipulation of the victim's
> body, including posing and propping. Sadists rely heavily
> on fantasy and ritual to obtain satisfaction. At 71%,

---

[3] Keppel and Weiss, 'The Rarity of "Unusual" Dispositions of Victim Bodies: Staging and Posing', *Journal of Forensic Sciences*, November 2004

[4] Former Lt. Commander Vernon Geberth, 'Sex-Related Homicide and Death Investigation: Practical and Clinical Perspectives', *Law and Order Magazine*, February 2010

sexual mutilation of the body or body parts was the most common motivation.

Retaliation: Offenders pose a body out of anger or as retaliation. The offender uses staging or posing as a weapon to punish and degrade the woman. Typically the posing consisted of spreading open the victim's legs, inserting objects, or exposing the breasts to further degrade the victim. At 22 per cent, this is the second most common motivation.

Staging: Offenders pose a body to 'stage the scene' and make it appear to be a sex-related murder. The offender is consciously attempting to mislead and thwart the police investigation by making the murder appear to be sexual, when in reality the murder was based on interpersonal violence.

At 7 per cent, these are cases in which the offender actually committed the homicide while engaged in violent, but nonsexual, activity. The posing was essentially an after-thought or a countermeasure intended to mislead the investigative effort.

While the careful scientific analyses of Keppel and Weiss and then of Vernon Geberth were, at the time of Jackie Ansell-Lamb's murder, a long way in the future, had British police possessed any sort of effective national intelligence database, the clear sexual staging of her body should have been logged and flagged up when her killer struck again in similar circumstances. Peter Sutcliffe's proven MO and signature in several attacks for which he was eventually convicted matched almost exactly the circumstances of Jackie's death.

But could the Yorkshire Ripper have struck in Cheshire that spring of 1970? Where was Peter Sutcliffe at the time – and what was happening in his life?

By March 1970, Sutcliffe's relationship with Sonia Szurma was plainly both deep and permanent. She was belatedly about to take a series of O levels – the key to moving on to teacher training college – but she found time to visit her older sister, Marianne, who was a graduate member at the Royal Academy of Music in London. Although police have never released formal confirmation, anecdotal reports suggest that Sutcliffe often accompanied Sonia to Marianne's piano recitals and, tellingly, sometimes drove back to Yorkshire alone.

That summer, Sonia passed her exams: with seven O levels under her belt she won a place at the Rachel McMillan teacher training college in Greenwich, in South London; her first term began in September 1970. It would be her first extended time away from home, and her father insisted that she lodge with her sister.

Sutcliffe himself was still drifting from job to job. Although he was evidently not thrilled about his girlfriend moving south, the couple agreed that he would drive down to visit her most weekends. It may not have been an entirely altruistic move: according to one of his close friends, Sutcliffe fancied Marianne, carrying a photograph of her – clad only in bra and panties – in his wallet for several years. Either way, for a man who had already attacked women in the north of England, being the most probable attacker of Mary Judge, Lucy Tinslop and Jackie Ansell-Lamb, the trips to London opened up the entire country and offered fresh opportunities to kill.

Barbara Mayo was twenty-four, a trainee teacher living with her boyfriend in Shepherd's Bush, West London. In the first week of October 1970, the couple drove up to County Durham to buy four new wheels for their car. On the return journey, the car broke down at Catterick in North Yorkshire; with little other option, they abandoned it temporarily at a garage and both hitched back to London.

On Monday, 12 October 1970, Barbara got up at about 7.30 a.m. and half an hour later left home to hitch-hike back up to Catterick to collect the car. She took an Underground train to Hendon and held out her thumb at the beginning of the M1. It was the last anyone would see or hear of her.

When Barbara failed to arrive at the garage or make contact with anyone, her boyfriend reported her missing. Police began an extensive search of the motorway networks. They found no trace.

Six days later, on Sunday, 18 October 1970, a honeymooning couple stumbled across Barbara's body in bushes on the edge of a lonely wood off Hodmire Lane, Glapwell, near Ault Hucknall in Derbyshire. She was face down, with her clothing in disarray and her jacket spread over her; she had been beaten about the head and strangled with a ligature. Although Derbyshire detectives refused to say whether she had been subjected to a sexual assault, subsequent information suggested that they found a DNA sample – presumably from her killer's semen – on her clothing. Unless the sample derived from a previous intimate encounter, its presence indicated that there was a sexual element to her murder.

The location of Barbara's body was less than a mile from the M1, but exactly where she was killed was never established. Had her attacker strangled her somewhere else and transported the body? Or had he pulled off the motorway – with her still alive in the passenger seat – on a pretext and persuaded her to get out of the car in Hodmire Lane, before smashing in the back of her head and dragging her through a gateway into the wood where she was subsequently found? That second option certainly seemed the more plausible: it's very rare indeed for a murderer to kill in one location and transport the victim's body for several hours before dumping it.

Either way, the similarities between the deaths of Jackie Ansell-Lamb and Barbara Mayo led detectives from New Scotland Yard – quickly called in by Derbyshire Police – to suspect the same man had murdered both women. But despite intensive efforts involving 120 officers and an eventual tally of more than 47,000 statements from members of the public, Barbara's killer was never caught. For a while, police worked on an assumption – never explained – that she might have died in a drug-dealing dispute. There was no evidence to support this theory and eventually it was dropped. Barbara Mayo's case was consigned to the growing files of unsolved attacks on women – another ghost in the broken machinery of justice.

For the first few weeks of the autumn of 1970, Peter Sutcliffe drove up and down the M1 for weekends with Sonia in London. He then moved to London, taking on occasional jobs as a mechanic in a garage in the south-east London suburb of Deptford and living in bed and breakfast accommodation.

By his own account, he lived in London for a full year – though he was always vague about the precise dates. But he was certainly either in the capital or regularly making the lengthy journeys to it from Yorkshire when Gloria Booth was murdered.

At 8 o'clock on the morning of Sunday, 13 June 1971, a fifteen-year-old schoolboy doing his paper round in South

Ruislip took a shortcut from Nairn Road through Stonefield Park and came across the near-naked body of a young woman: she had apparently been dumped in brambles, the corpse elegantly posed and with no attempt at concealment.

Even to such an untutored eye, it was clear that the victim had been very viciously attacked: the only clothes on the body were a bra and blouse – both of which had been pushed up to reveal her breasts, and there was dried blood congealing in several nasty-looking wounds. The rest of her clothes and her shoes were strewn in the brush around the corpse.

The Metropolitan Police quickly established that the dead woman was Gloria Marlene Booth. She had been a wartime baby, born illegitimately on 8 November 1941 in Blaydon-upon-Tyne, Northumberland. Her mother, Mary Jane Banks, gave the baby to be brought up by her maternal grandmother until she married: at the age of ten, Gloria moved back into the family home, which now included several younger sisters.

In 1957, at the age of sixteen, Gloria left the north-east and moved to London to work in service – then still an available occupation for young working-class girls. Six years later, in June 1963, she married Peter Douglas Booth, a carpenter, and before long the couple moved into a new home in Ealing, West London.

By 1971, Gloria was twenty-nine; she was no longer in service, instead earning a steady wage as an office typist. She supplemented this income by working part-time as a barmaid at several pubs throughout the South Ruislip and Northolt area, five miles away from Ealing. Two of these – the White Hart on Yeading Lane and the Viking on West End Lane – were opposite South Ruislip Park.

On Saturday night, 12 June 1971, Gloria left work at the

White Hart around 11.30 p.m. Eyewitnesses told police that she was seen walking north along Yeading Lane and Ruislip Road towards the A40 roundabout. At 11.50 p.m., she stepped into a telephone box near the Polish War Memorial on Western Avenue. She phoned the barman at the Viking, with whom she had agreed to go to a party later that night. But before they could finalise the arrangements the line cut out.

Gloria then walked from the War Memorial on towards the Viking public house: at 12.30 a.m. on the Sunday morning, she was seen standing outside – apparently waiting for the barman to finish work from a 'lock-in'.

Eyewitnesses were also able to tell police that they had noticed her talking to a man of shortish height who was wearing dark clothing. From the accounts they managed to piece together, detectives concluded that Gloria had waited so long for the barman to finish work that she had missed her last bus back home. They began working on the assumption that she either accepted a lift from a stranger – perhaps the man with whom she had had a conversation outside the pub – or had decided to walk back to Ealing.

Around 1 a.m., Gloria was seen on Nairn Road, beside Stonefield Park. A footpath ran parallel with the road, along the hedge outside the recreation ground where, within two hours, she would be attacked and killed.

When police arrived at the scene that Sunday morning, they immediately cordoned off the entire area and sent for the pathologist. Dr David Pocock arrived at 11.30 a.m. and began an initial in situ examination of the body and its surroundings. He recorded what he found in an official report for West London Coroner's Court.

Injuries were noted to the breasts, throat and pubic region and there was mud staining the legs, iliac crest [a section of bone at the top of the pelvis] on the right side and left arm. Petechial haemorrhages were seen in the eyes. There was also some white material on the inner aspect of the right leg with a corresponding white substance on the ground beneath ...

Two hours later, Dr Pocock prepared himself – and Gloria's body – for a full autopsy examination at Uxbridge Mortuary. His report was written in the dry medico-legal language of a professional pathologist: despite that, it was a remarkably shocking document.

The deceased was a young adult woman, 5 feet 2½ inches in height ... the following injuries were identified.

Two small bruises, less than ¼ inch in diameter were seen in the centre of the upper forehead ... multiple small bruises were seen on both sides of the front of the throat.

Around both nipples for an area of some 4 inches in diameter over the breasts there were numerous bruised areas with a pattern strongly indicative of bite marks on both sides ... the nipples were not found having been apparently bitten off. There was no bleeding from the wounds on the breasts.

Dr Pocock also noted that there was oil and brick dust on Gloria's body and highly unusual injuries to her genital region: these suggested that her killer had most probably thrust 'a blunt instrument' into her vagina several times. But even more unusually, this mutilation appeared to have been carried out after she was dead – and strangely for what was apparently a sexually motivated attack, there was no evidence of conventional rape.

At the end of the autopsy, Dr Pocock summarised his conclusions on the form, which would be presented at Gloria Booth's inquest.

> Death has been caused by asphyxia following compression of the neck ... The majority of the injuries below the level of the throat have been caused after death ... The injury to the vulva is compatible with being caused by a blunt instrument, or could have been caused by the [killer's] shod foot.
>
> The post-mortem abrasions on the left side of the neck, breasts, pubic region and right arm would suggest that the deceased was laid in a prone position after death on an irregular surface, probably for a period of about half an hour or more with the right arm folded across the abdomen. This would have been before the deceased was placed in the position as found at Nairn Road.

In summary, the pathologist's report indicated that the man who murdered Gloria Booth had hit her about the head and strangled her – probably with a piece of rope containing two knots, which left the distinctive bruises on either side of her Adam's apple and one on the right side of her neck. After she was dead, he bit her breasts and repeatedly shoved something into her vagina. There were also, it appeared, small additional clues that Dr Pocock did not record on the official form. Police conducting house-to-house enquiries were instructed to discover if any of the men they interviewed had a gap in their front teeth.

Moreover, the 'white substance' on the ground – initially dismissed as bird droppings – was thereafter assumed to be dried semen. If so, it appeared that the killer had strangled the life out of Gloria, probably with a rope ligature, and then dragged her to the bramble patch where he undressed and posed her before mutilating the body and masturbating over it.

This highly unusual and distinctive 'signature' had strong similarities to the attacks Peter Sutcliffe had already carried out. But it is their resemblance to his future (and proven) killings that – with the benefit of hindsight – suggests that Gloria Booth was one of his unknown victims.

For a start there was the use of a knotted ligature: Sutcliffe used this technique on his last two victims – the murder of Marguerite Walls in August 1980 and in the foiled attempted murder of Dr Upadhya Bandara in September that year. When he was finally caught in Sheffield in January 1981, police discovered that he was carrying a three-foot-long piece of nylon rope knotted at each end for gripping and with two centre knots: exactly the sort of garrotting implement used to kill Gloria Booth.

Then there was the staging of the body and the partial removal of clothing to expose Gloria's breasts. This would be noted in all of the murders for which he was eventually convicted.

The mutilation of her pubic region had a strong parallel with his murders of Emily Jackson in January 1976 and Josephine Whitaker in April 1979. On Whitaker's body, as on Gloria's, police discovered distinctive bite marks around the breasts – bites made by a man with a gap in his front teeth. Peter Sutcliffe had exactly this dental distinction.

There were other smaller similarities, too – individually not conclusive, but when added to the tally, collectively persuasive. The oil and brick dust on Gloria's dead body, for example: Josephine Whitaker's corpse revealed the presence of milling-oil traces, transferred from Sutcliffe's working clothes. At the time Gloria was killed, he was working in a local garage: oil and brick dust would undoubtedly have been present on his garments.

The sheer number of parallels between the deaths of Gloria Booth – as well as those of Jackie Ansell-Lamb and Barbara Mayo – and the known victims of the Yorkshire Ripper make it statistically almost impossible for their attacker to have been anyone other than Peter Sutcliffe. What's more, the pattern of his offending – his MO and his emotional signature – quite clearly identifies him as an experienced serial murderer and necrophilic killer.

As the summer of 1971 ended, with no breakthrough in any of the three women's murders, Sutcliffe's obsession with sex and death was growing stronger.

When Sonia went back to the London Teacher Training College for her second year in September 1971, Sutcliffe told her that he would travel down to see her as often as possible. He continued this pattern through the winter and into spring 1972.

In 1972, Easter Monday fell on 3 April. Sonia had a fortnight's break from college and returned to Yorkshire. Two weeks later, Sutcliffe drove her back down to London. The following day, a twenty-two-year-old woman was found barely alive in undergrowth beside a lay-by near Hemel Hempstead.

Marie Burke was a drifter and 'truck hopper'. At 6.30 p.m. on 18 April, she was spotted thumbing a lift at the start of the

M1 in the North London suburb of Brent Cross. Two hours later, an off-duty policeman saw a pair of bright-pink trousers poking out of bushes beside the A414. He found Marie, unconscious but still breathing: she had been carefully covered with an imitation fur coat.

She was rushed to Mount Vernon Hospital, St Albans, where doctors discovered she had severe wounds to the back of her head: they had been caused by repeated blows from a blunt instrument. For three weeks, she was in a coma, hovering between life and death. When she did awake, she had no memory of the attack or events leading up to it.

For the next five years, Marie Burke received outpatient psychiatric care to help her cope with the effects of the attack. She received less help from the police: despite her best efforts – she regularly rang the incident room asking for updates for several years – the case was eventually written off as an unsolved traffic accident. In the 1980s, her file was destroyed in a force reorganisation.

Was Peter Sutcliffe the man who left Marie Burke for dead? There can be no certainty – not least because Marie has long since disappeared. But the attack has all the hallmarks of his signature. And there would, unquestionably, be many more victims in the years to come.

EIGHT

MIDLANDS, MURDERS AND MISCARRIAGES OF JUSTICE

Comberford Lane runs westwards for two miles from the pretty village of Wigginton through open fields to the main A513 road out of the Staffordshire market town of Tamworth. Exposed and rural, in 1972, it was popular with what newspapers euphemistically term 'courting couples'.

Around 6 p.m. on Wednesday, 7 June 1972, Judith Roberts left her home in Gillway Lane, Wigginton, and set off on a cycle ride along Comberford Lane. It was a pleasant summer's evening and numerous cars parked along the little road testified to its reputation as a place where couples could enjoy intimate encounters. Some would later report seeing Judith pedalling past them. Those would be the last sightings of her alive.

Judith Roberts was fourteen: a bright and popular girl, she lived with her parents and twin sister and attended Queen Elizabeth Grammar School in Tamworth. That evening, there had been a minor tiff in the Roberts' home. Judith had become self-conscious about her appearance and wanted to diet, her parents told her she was being silly – and she stomped out of the house in a bad temper. Wearing her school uniform – a blue-and-white-checked dress – tights, sensible lace-up shoes and a blue anorak, she borrowed her sister's green bike to ride the row out of her system.

When she had not returned by 10.30 p.m., her parents, Vincent and Judith, called the police. It would be the start of an intensive three-day search involving more than 200 officers, sniffer dogs, a mountain rescue team, troops from the army's Whittington Barracks, near Lichfield, and airmen from the RAF base at Stafford. Vincent Roberts was games master at Queen Elizabeth Grammar School and his fellow teachers joined the hunt for Judith.

By the morning of Saturday, 10 June, there was still no sign of her; police patrol cars drove through the villages and countryside broadcasting appeals for information.

At 4.30 p.m., two trainee soldiers were searching the fields surrounding Comberford Lane. Behind a twelve-foot hedge covered with leaves, plastic fertiliser sacks and sheet of corrugated asbestos, they stumbled across Judith's body. It was less than a mile from her home.

The murder bore all the hallmarks of Peter Sutcliffe's MO. Judith had been attacked from behind with a heavy blunt instrument and her skull was fractured into eighteen pieces. While lying face down and dying or dead, she had been stripped of her shoes and her clothing so that she was naked from the waist down; her blue anorak had been pulled up over her head.

There was also evidence that the attack had happened a little way from where the body was found: marks on the corpse, and on the ground, indicated that the killer had dragged Judith by her legs, face down, before positioning her clothes underneath the body and her shoes neatly next to her. While there was no sign of rape, it was plain from the circumstances and staging of the body that the murder had some sort of sexual motive.

There were other clues, too. One eyewitness told police he had seen a man wearing working clothes and wellington boots walking and talking with Judith at the High Street end of Comberford Lane. Another described seeing a Morris Minor car on the lane. Sutcliffe had already established a habit of approaching and talking with his victims before smashing them over the back of the head; he also owned a Morris Minor.

Staffordshire Police called in both regional crime squad detectives and senior investigators from New Scotland Yard. Over the next few weeks, they jointly interviewed more than 11,000 people and took 15,400 sets of fingerprints: none matched the single print discovered on Judith's bicycle.

They also began trawling through old case files: detectives pored over known sexually motivated murders in the country over the previous fifteen years and extended their research into neighbouring Warwickshire, where police had recorded a series of attacks on women in the Chelmsley Wood area. None of the details fitted with what had been done to Judith Roberts.

It was a sign of the stubborn parochialism of police forces in the 1970s that none of these efforts either sought out details of similar murders or attempted murders elsewhere across the country. Similarly, the fractured and hopelessly inefficient systems of national crime reporting ensured that none of the crimes Sutcliffe was on record as having committed was ever drawn to the attention of Staffordshire Police. Had the

Scotland Yard card index files containing his proven MO (and his conviction three years earlier for going out equipped with a hammer) made their way to Tamworth, not only would he have become an immediate and prime suspect but – at the very least – the specific details of the Judith Roberts crime scene would have alerted West Yorkshire Police seven years later when they discovered Helen Rytka's body similarly hidden underneath a sheet of corrugated asbestos.

Equally, had Staffordshire Police embarked on a thorough murder case collaboration with either force or regional intelligence offices in Cheshire or Derbyshire – both of which had common boundaries with Staffordshire – they surely would have noticed similarities with the killings of Jackie Ansell-Lamb and Barbara Mayo.

But there would, above all, have been another incalculable benefit: an innocent and vulnerable young man would not have been locked up for twenty-five years for a crime he did not commit.

Andrew Evans was seventeen in June 1972. His life up to that point had been difficult and unsuccessful: he was almost illiterate, suffered from chronically low self-esteem and was both physically and mentally ill. He had joined the army a year earlier, hoping that military service might address the problems of his childhood; they had not. His health deteriorated so badly that he was on heavy doses of Valium and the army decided to discharge him on medical grounds: on the evening of 7 June, he was one day away from handing in his uniform and leaving Whittington Barracks for good.

Four months after Judith's battered body was discovered – sixteen weeks in which the local and some national press had published extensive coverage of the murder – Andrew Evans walked into Longton police station in Stoke on Trent. Shaking and stuttering, he told detectives that he had had a disturbing dream in which he believed he saw the face of a murdered girl. According to evidence presented at his trial, he said, 'I keep seeing a face. I want to see a picture of her. I wonder if I've done it.'

Investigating officers from the regional crime squad initially believed the plainly disturbed teenager was either deranged or a fantasist. Nonetheless, they took him into custody and began three days of relentless interviews. Despite his evidently vulnerable state – and his age – these were conducted without his parents, a solicitor or a doctor present. After seventy-two hours, Andrew Evans had confessed to the murder of Judith Roberts.

Even the detectives sitting across the table from him doubted the credibility of the admission. For a start, his confessions were riddled with claims about the attack and the body that simply did not fit the evidence (and which the real murderer would have known to be untrue). Evans himself was also remarkably equivocal: when his interviewers asked if he had ever been to Tamworth, he replied: 'I don't know. I don't know. I could have been. I forget where I have been.' When they questioned, point-blank, if he had murdered the girl, he told them: 'This is it. I don't know. Show me a picture and I'll tell you if I've seen it.'

Nor was there a shred of physical evidence to place him at the scene of the crime: not a spot of blood on any of his clothing, and not a clothing fibre or a witness ever connected him with Comberford Lane, much less the brutal attack on Judith Roberts. The sole fingerprint on her bike was not his. The only evidence was his inability to provide an alibi for the evening of 7 June – and his painfully unreliable admissions. Despite this, he was charged with murder and sent for trial.

By the time that trial took place, at Birmingham Crown Court in June 1973, Evans had retracted his confessions. Both prosecution and defence lawyers agreed that the young man in the dock was mentally ill. The court was also presented with evidence that at some point in the police station he had been injected with Brietal – a 'truth drug' that would later be shown to have the opposite effect by creating false memories.

Nonetheless, the jury convicted Evans of the murder and the judge imposed the mandatory sentence of life imprisonment. He would languish behind bars for the next twenty-five years until, in 1997, his conviction was quashed and the Home Office paid out a record £1 million in compensation.

Andrew Evans was – unquestionably – the victim of a terrible miscarriage of justice: he was not the killer who smashed in the back of Judith Roberts' skull, pulled up her clothing and carefully staged the body. If the real murderer was Peter Sutcliffe, he was never interviewed for the crime and would be free to attack and kill for ten more years.

At the end of 1971, Peter Sutcliffe had started a new job. Abandoning his patchwork of casual work – sometimes in Yorkshire, often in London – he had joined his friend Trevor Birdsall on the production packing line at Baird's television factory in Bradford. He gave notice on his Deptford bedsit and moved back into the Sutcliffe family home in Cornwall Road, Bingley.

He continued, however, to make his weekend trips to London, where Sonia was now in her second year at teacher training college. With no other accommodation available – she had moved into a dormitory with a strict 'no male visitors' policy – he either slept in his car or erected a small tent on waste ground and camped.

But Sonia Szurma was struggling: away from her family in the anonymity of London, she was becoming both physically and emotionally isolated. Before long, her behaviour became erratic and alarming. In class she was noticeably detached and uncommunicative, but outside the confines of college she started displaying signs of what would – before long – be diagnosed as schizophrenia: soon her outbursts of rage and delusions began to cause serious concern.

By the middle of 1972, she had lost a full stone in weight: she was also becoming a danger to herself. In the short period between two of his regular weekends with her, Sutcliffe received a telegram from Sonia. In the terse lexicography of telegrams (paid for by the word) it told him bluntly: 'Meet me at King's Cross station'. There was, however, no indication of what day, let alone what time the rendezvous was meant to take place.

For all his apparent devotion to Sonia – and her evident mental instability –Sutcliffe did not drop everything and rush down to his girlfriend's side. Instead, he took the telegram round to her father: it was Bohdan Szurma who dashed from the house to catch the first train to London.

It was as well that he did: Sonia's illness had reached a dangerous phase. She had become convinced that all the machinery on the planet was stopping and that the world itself was about to come to an end. In the grip of this delusion, she had wandered out into the streets around her dormitory – late at night and wearing only her pyjamas. Fortunately, she had been found and shortly afterwards admitted to hospital.

By the time she was transferred to Linfield Mount psychiatric hospital in Bradford, Sonia's mental condition had deteriorated even further. Doctors reported that her delusions now included a belief that she was an aeroplane or that she was 'the second Christ' – she told them that she could see stigmata on her hands. There was plainly no chance of her returning to London and resuming her studies.

Accounts of the ensuing few months differ, depending on who is giving them. One version paints Peter Sutcliffe as a constant and attentive presence in Sonia's slow road to recovery; an alternate history suggests that Bohdan Szurma asked him to stay away from his daughter for a little while after she was discharged back to the family's care.

Whatever the truth, one thing was not in doubt: Sutcliffe displayed such determination to 'pull Sonia through' (as he put it to Bohdan and Maria) that any separation was short-lived. Despite his misgivings at Sonia's appearance – she was now both overweight and lethargic from the medication prescribed for her illness – his patience and gentleness with her impressed the Szurmas.

It also appears to have helped Sonia: before too many months had passed, she was well enough to attend Trevor Birdsall's wedding and occasionally to go out drinking with Sutcliffe in the pubs around Bradford and Halifax. She also managed a brief stint as a student teacher.

But it was not to last. Late in 1972, Sonia suffered a relapse and her previous highly agitated behaviour returned: this time, though, she was prone to tearing her clothes off in public. Once again she was treated for schizophrenia and once again Peter Sutcliffe was at least partially excluded from her company.

As 1972 slipped into 1973, Sutcliffe was largely left to his own devices outside of working hours. His previous lackadaisical approach to timekeeping appears to have improved, as he was offered a salesman's job by Baird's – but he turned it down because, in his own words, he didn't want to spend time away on the road.

It was an odd decision and an even stranger excuse: by this time in his life, Sutcliffe had spent several years driving up and down the country. His obsession with cars – buying, renovating and selling on 'old bangers' – continued and he was evidently more than happy to spend large swathes of his free time at the wheel.

No night out with Trevor Birdsall would be deemed a success without their habitual trawling of West Yorkshire's red-light districts. Together they would quarter the sad and shabby streets of Manningham or Chapeltown, tailing prostitute after prostitute. Frequently, the hunt would end with Sutcliffe opening negotiations with his quarry over the price of sex. When she quoted £3, he would offer £2: if she accepted, he would taunt her, saying, 'Is that all you're worth?', before driving away, laughing.

In April 1973, he quit his job at Baird's and started work at Anderton International's Britannia Works factory in Bingley. His new job differed in one crucial regard from his previous employment: it was a permanent night shift. While this curtailed his visits to the red-light districts, it left him free during the days to explore new haunts. And since he rarely saw Sonia other than at weekends, he now had a great deal of free time on his hands.

Bakewell is a traditional English market town, nestled in the picturesque hillside of the Derbyshire Dales. It was founded in Anglo-Saxon times, its name probably deriving from a spring or stream belonging to a man named Badeca. By the time the Normans took control of the country, the settlement had gained local prominence: it is mentioned in the Domesday Book, which records that its church boasted two priests.

Bakewell has two chief claims to fame: its position in the Derbyshire National Park has made it a mecca for walkers, ramblers and hill climbers, and the local confectionery invention of a pastry case filled with jam, egg and almond paste – the Bakewell Pudding – has put the town on the culinary map, too. That sweet dessert is, however, routinely misnamed as 'Bakewell Tart', and in 1973 the term was equally inappropriately applied to the victim of a brutal murder.

A little after 12 noon on Wednesday, 12 September, Wendy Sewell stepped briskly out of her office at the Forestry Commission in Bakewell. She was heading for the local cemetery in Yeld Road. It was a short journey – but one that would cost Mrs Sewell her life (and, posthumously, her reputation) and lead to an innocent man being locked away behind bars for twenty-seven years.

Wendy Sewell was thirty-two. She had been born Wendy Crawshaw in 1944 and grew up as the only child of loving parents living in Bakewell. In the early 1960s, she went to art school in Sheffield: here she met her future husband, David, a physicist three years her senior. In March 1964, the couple married and moved into their first home in Bakewell.

The marriage was not a success: David Sewell's job kept him away from home for considerable periods and his spare time was often consumed by his passion for restoring vintage cars. Wendy began seeing other men and, by 1967, had moved out of the marital home. At some point, she gave birth to an illegitimate child and gave the baby up for adoption.

In July 1971, the Sewells found a way to patch up their marriage: the couple reconciled and moved to a period farmhouse in the historic village of Middleton by Youlgreave, five miles outside Bakewell. After a short stint as a legal secretary, Wendy got a job at the Forestry Commission. As far as her husband was aware, their relationship had survived its early difficulties and was a happy one. His beliefs were shortly to be brutally undermined.

Exactly why Wendy Sewell left her office that September lunchtime has been the subject of argument and dispute for more than forty years. Her family insist that she was going to the cemetery to do historical research connected with a plan to put up a memorial to a relative. But others in the town – usually anonymous – would tell grateful reporters that she was known to meet male friends there for lunchtime trysts: she would go down in newspaper history as 'The Bakewell Tart'.

What is definitely known about the sequence of events that morning is that Wendy Sewell was overheard talking in her office to an unknown man who had a distinctive high-pitched voice. Shortly afterwards, she told her boss that she was stepping out for some air and began to make her way to the cemetery. At about 12.50 p.m., she was seen by several people entering the graveyard through its main entrance off Yeld Road. At the same time, a seventeen-year-old local cemetery worker called Stephen Downing was about to leave the burial ground to walk home for a short lunch break.

Just after 1 o'clock, Wendy Sewell was subjected to a

sustained frenzied attack close to the consecrated chapel in the cemetery grounds. She was garrotted with a ligature, smashed on the back of her head from behind at least eight times with a pickaxe handle and stripped of most of her clothing. A few minutes later, Stephen Downing walked back up Yeld Road and found Wendy, face down and heavily bloodstained but still alive, lying on the footpath in the cemetery. He immediately went to her aid and knelt beside her.

Downing was a quiet and unassuming teenager, suffering from severe learning difficulties. Faced with a near-naked and evidently very badly injured woman, he was unsure what to do: he decided the best course of action was to get help from his workmates who had also just returned from lunch.

On their return, Stephen discovered that Wendy had moved: she was now lying twenty-five yards away in among old gravestones. She had staggered briefly to her feet before falling backwards, further injuring the back of her head on a large gravestone. She then lapsed in and out of consciousness.

The police were called but, for reasons never explained, the officer who arrived on the scene did not administer first aid or immediately call for an ambulance. By the time Wendy finally arrived at Chesterfield Royal Hospital it was 2.40 p.m., and she had lapsed into a coma. She died two days later without ever recovering consciousness.

From the outset, Derbyshire Police viewed Downing as the prime suspect. He was taken to the local police station and, despite never being told that he was under arrest, was subjected to nine solid hours of intensive questioning before being remanded in custody. His parents were not allowed to see him even though he was legally a minor; nor, despite the fact that he twice asked for one, was a solicitor present during the interrogation.

Stephen Downing had the reading age of an eleven-year-old child and was, in the parlance of the time, known to be 'slow'. The police interviews with him were unquestionably rough and oppressive: he was shaken to keep him awake and told he would be questioned all night if he did not admit to the attack on Wendy Sewell. At some point, a confession statement was written in pencil by police officers, which he painstakingly inked over and signed. It stated that he had hit Wendy Sewell twice over the head with a pickaxe handle taken from a pile in the cemetery works building, pulled up her clothing and then pushed his fingers inside her vagina.

There were numerous problems and inconsistencies in Stephen Downing's confession – not least the fact that he could give no motive for the attack. The language itself was beyond anything Downing himself could have come up with, and above all what the police claimed he said simply did not fit the facts. Wendy Sewell had not been hit twice but at least eight times; the pickaxe handle had not come from the cemetery store – all of those shafts bore a plate with the council's name on them and, in any event, were accounted for. And there was absolutely no mention in the statement of a ligature.

Nonetheless, immediately after Wendy Sewell died, Derbyshire Police charged Downing with her murder. By the time he came to trial in February 1974 – and having finally had the benefit of legal advice – Stephen had retracted his confession: he told Nottingham Crown Court that the police had suggested what it should say, then written it themselves and pressured him to sign.

But the key evidence against him was a small area of blood spatter on his overalls. A forensic scientist, Norman Lee, testified – without seeing the clothing – that this was 'a textbook example … which might be expected on the clothing of the assailant'. Stephen Downing's explanation that the blood had got on his clothes when he knelt down to help Wendy Sewell was dismissed: the young man was convicted and sentenced to life imprisonment.

Stephen Downing would serve twenty-seven years in prison for the murder of Wendy Sewell before, in January 2002, the Court of Appeal ruled that the coercive nature of his alleged confession – as well as new forensic evidence that undermined Norman Lee's 'textbook' certainty – meant that his conviction was unsafe. It was quashed and Stephen Downing – now forty-four years old – emerged from the penal system to which he had lost most of his adult life.

It was a humiliating moment for Derbyshire Police: following the Court of Appeal's ruling, it launched a new investigation into Wendy Sewell's murder. At a cost of £500,000 they interviewed 1,600 witnesses and were forced to admit that in 1973, far from Stephen Downing being the only man in the frame, there had been twenty-two solid suspects.

Nonetheless, a year later, in February 2003, the police issued a press release that announced that all except Stephen Downing had been 'eliminated' from their enquiries: as a result, there were no plans to reopen the case. It was a shabby and dishonourable way to imply – without ever actually stating – that Stephen Downing had been guilty all along. And it relied on the withholding of one crucial piece of evidence.

Alan Usher was a Home Office pathologist. At 2.45 p.m. on

Saturday, 15 September 1973, he carried out a post-mortem on Wendy Sewell's corpse. His findings, clearly set out in a typed report, were never provided to any of the courts that considered Stephen Downing's case. The report was – whether accidentally or otherwise – buried in Derbyshire Police HQ around the same time as Wendy Sewell's body was interred in Bakewell Cemetery. For more than forty years – and despite requests under the Freedom of Information Act – it stayed that way: a formal statement by the police made clear that it would not be considered for public release until 2032.

But when, in 2013, a copy was leaked, Professor Alan Usher's findings were startling. As well as concluding that Wendy had been subjected to a frenzied attack to the back of her head, which shattered her skull, he noted the presence of other wounds.

> She had been most violently assaulted almost certainly by someone using the pick axe handle though some of her injuries might have resulted from kicking with heavy boots.

He also drew conclusions from the positioning of the body and clothing:

> Though the removal of this woman's clothing below the waist seems to indicate a sexual motive for the attack, there is no real evidence to show that intercourse took place.

But it was his observations about Wendy Sewell's neck and throat that were most revealing. The pathology report stated that there were 'massive ecchymoses [the escape of blood into the tissues from ruptured blood vessels causing a bruise] in the mucus membrane below the level of the false vocal cords … [and] some bruising of the deep cervical muscle'. In plain English, this indicated that Wendy had been strangled with a knotted garrotte before being struck on the back of the head. There had been no mention of this at Stephen Downing's trial (nor, indeed, at his subsequent appeals) – presumably because it didn't fit with his confession.

It – and the rest of the forensic evidence – did, however, fit with Peter Sutcliffe's known MO. The smashing in of the back of the skull, the pulling up and rearranging of the victim's underwear, the sexual motive without clear evidence of intercourse: all of these are hallmarks of his method. The garrotte, too, is another piece of confirmatory evidence: it would feature in his proven 1980 attacks on Marguerite Walls and Upadhya Bandara.

The original detectives could have been forgiven for not linking the attack on Wendy Sewell in Derbyshire with the criminal record of Peter Sutcliffe in Yorkshire (though a more efficient intelligence system would have thrown up his name as a possibility); but in 2003, when their successors closed the case with a cynical nod and wink at Stephen Downing as the killer, there was no such justification. Sutcliffe's MO was known and proven – and two separate police investigations had concluded that he had certainly been responsible for many more murders.

Stephen Downing was simply in the wrong place at the right time. His return to Bakewell Cemetery that lunchtime almost certainly interrupted Wendy Sewell's killer. As in other proven Sutcliffe attacks, an innocent member of the public had interrupted the Ripper before he could slash and mutilate the body and masturbate over it. The vulnerable teenager paid the terrible price both of Peter Sutcliffe's crime and of shoddy police investigation.

It was not the first case, nor would it be the last, of an innocent man spending nearly half a lifetime in prison for a murder very probably committed by Sutcliffe. Nor would it be the last time inconvenient truths about the Yorkshire Ripper's bloody trail of unavenged victims were covered up.

NINE
OF MAPS
AND MURDER

It was a French lawyer who first showed the connection between maps and crime.

In 1829, André-Michel Guerry was employed by the Ministry of Justice in Paris; fascinated by statistics, Guerry began analysing data on crime collected by the General Office for the Administration of Criminal Justice – the world's first centralised national system of crime reporting. He quickly saw that the raw information pointed at patterns of offending and that, properly studied, these could help predict how individual types of criminal chose the location for their activities.

That year, together with an Italian geographer called Adriano Balbi, Guerry published the first scientific attempt at what we now call crime mapping. It was no more than one very large sheet of paper, but it displayed three maps of the various *départements* of France, shaded to demonstrate the location and incidence of violent crimes against persons and those against property.

Within a few decades, this innovative approach – visually displaying patterns in crime across geographic regions – had spread to England. In 1849, the early Victorian statistician Joseph Fletcher created maps that showed the rate of male imprisonment for serious property and violent crimes across counties in England and Wales. Twelve years later, the journalist and social reformer Henry Mayhew built on this and published a series of maps highlighting the frequency of rape, assault, bigamy and abduction in counties throughout England and Wales.

The belief that analysing the geographical spread of offending – particularly the relationship between the scene of the crime and the perpetrator's home – could predict the most likely places for, say, murderers or rapists to operate grew deeper in the 1930s.

Two Chicago sociologists, Clifford Shaw and Henry McKay, constructed a detailed map showing the precise locations of almost 3,000 male delinquents in Chicago during the period from 1927 to 1933. The map featured shading to indicate rates of delinquency. Subsequently, Shaw and McKay also constructed maps identifying the homes of 10,000 male delinquents who had come before the juvenile court of Cook County in the years 1934 to 1940. From these, they showed that there was a highly defined link between the scenes of crimes and the geographical circumstances in which the offender lived and worked.

Put simply – or, rather, translated from the lexicography of academic criminologists to the more direct language of police detectives – one of the most important clues an offender leaves behind him is the crime scene itself: not just in whatever forensic evidence can be gathered from it, but also the geographical location itself. By mapping the physical sites of crimes – especially in cases of an unknown suspect committing serial offences such as rape or murder – it is possible to predict not only where he may strike next but also where he is most likely to live.

The basics of what has become known as either geographical profiling or murder mapping have been well established for more than seventy years. By 1973, when Peter Sutcliffe was almost a decade into his bloody career, it was being refined by academics to highlight how far offenders travel to commit their chosen crimes. While some of this would not be formally published until the early 1980s, the essential truths were well known and would have been available to any police force that chose to consult a university criminologist.

What the science shows is that – like anyone else – criminals are restricted by both time and space. Again, like the rest of the population, offenders will usually operate on the 'least effort' principle: they will take the opportunity to commit crimes within the parameters of their daily lives. And so, for example, there will be a direct relationship between the areas in which they offend and the journeys they routinely make for work, shopping and leisure. In many ways this is no more than common sense: a rational decision (however irrational the act) to choose a location that is easy to get to and from, as well as one in which their targets are easy to find.

Different types of crime display different – and very distinct – patterns. Crimes against property – typically burglary and car theft – generally happen very close to the offender's home: he (or she) rarely travels more than fifteen minutes to commit the offence.

By contrast, murderers – and especially serial murderers – roam much more widely. They are statistically very likely to kill more than fifteen minutes' travel time away from their home base. In part this is no more than another rational choice: it is easier to remain anonymous in towns or streets where no one knows you. But the science also shows that serial murderers *expand* their area of activity: while they may start relatively close to home, as they gain confidence and expertise, their 'killing zones' are spread more widely. But even with this pattern, the iron rule of expending the least possible effort by attacking while on a familiar or routine journey applies.

It is for this reason, above all, that national crime databases and the sharing of information between regional and local police forces, so catastrophically absent in British policing in 1973, are so vital. If ever a dysfunctional system was tailor-made to assist an offender, the fractured and parochial state of British policing was a gift for Peter Sutcliffe.

And then, on New Year's Eve, a new factor entered the equation: one that would give Sutcliffe even more freedom to roam, hunt and kill.

Throughout the early 1970s, the British economy was plagued by high rates of inflation. To tackle it, Edward Heath's Conservative government capped pay rises in the public sector (and encouraged private industry to follow suit). Since wages began to fall well behind consistent hikes in the price of even basic foodstuffs, the policy caused deep unrest among trade unions. And the most powerful union in the country was the National Union of Mineworkers.

Coal was then king: it powered industry and private homes and was the mainstay of the country's heat and light. Mining was then still a nationalised industry, and, in protest at the suppression of wages, the NUM instructed its members to work to rule. This involved stopping overtime and greatly reducing output. In those pre-Thatcher days, it placed a chokehold on the nation: importing coal was politically unthinkable and economically unattractive. As coal stocks slowly dwindled, an international oil crisis made the situation ever more parlous.

Heath's government began lengthy and ultimately fruitless negotiations with the NUM. By the end of 1973, Britain's coal stocks were at an all-time (and very dangerous) low. To reduce electricity consumption and preserve precious supplies, Heath ordered an unprecedented move: a three-day working week.

From midnight on 31 December 1973, British industry could only have electricity on three consecutive days: for the rest of the week, factories would completely shut down.

Peter Sutcliffe was then working as a furnace operator on the night shift at Anderton International. With the company's very heartbeat stopped for lack of power, he suddenly found he had extra free time on his hands: he used it to roam far and wide in search of new victims.

Rosina 'Rosie' Hilliard was twenty-four and a working prostitute. She had been born, illegitimate, in Loughborough on 17 June 1949 and had been in and out of care for much of her short life. After leaving home, she had graduated to a shabby flat in Leicester and begun working the streets of the city's red-light district. Small and slightly built, she patrolled her beat in the Charnwood district wearing a shoulder-length blonde wig over her natural brown hair. By February 1974, she had become a familiar figure to vice squad police on their regular patrols of the area.

At 7 o'clock on the morning of Friday, 22 February, Rosie Hilliard's lifeless body was found by a lorry driver on a building site in Spinney Hill Road. It was splayed across an unmade road in a pathetic tableau that should – had police possessed an intelligence system fit for purpose – have been grimly familiar. An attempt had plainly been made to strangle her – possibly with a ligature – before her skull was shattered from behind with one massive blow, probably with a hammer.

Murders were not terribly common in 1974 Leicester: the city was then yet to experience the massive expansion that followed wave upon wave of immigration. It was, therefore, unsurprising that the police immediately assigned 120 uniformed officers and detectives to finding Rosie's killer. But other than establishing that the young woman had been spotted by vice patrols at 1.30 a.m. on the morning of her death, touting for trade at the corner of Berners Street and Melbourne Road – half a mile from the building site – the only potentially useful evidence related to two cars.

Witnesses told police they had noticed a Morris Minor and Ford Escort. Since some of these witnesses came from the loose community of Rosie's fellow prostitutes, it's reasonable to assume they did not recognise the vehicles as belonging to regular kerb-crawlers: certainly, as the weeks dragged by, Leicestershire Police issued ever more desperate appeals for information about the cars and their drivers. The urgency was reinforced by the discovery of tyre prints – almost certainly from the Ford – on the rough dirt of the building site, and the belief that this vehicle might have driven over her body.

This, as it turned out, was unlikely to have been a deliberate act. A young man, walking his girlfriend along Humberstone

Road at 2 a.m., disturbed Rosie's killer in the moments after she was attacked. Although the couple didn't witness the murder, they heard the sound of a high-revving engine – evidently trying to free itself from muddy ground – coming from the building site.

These circumstances would be repeated three years later when Peter Sutcliffe was forced to abandon his attack on Marilyn Moore in Leeds. Sutcliffe, in his subsequent confession statement, would describe being disturbed and revving his engine fiercely in a desperate bid to get away from the crime scene.

> I saw some people walking along about 40 yards away on the narrow road at the top. I jumped in my car and started it up. I put my foot down but the back wheels started spinning and I couldn't drive off at first. When the car got a grip I slewed round to the right and I drove away with a lot of wheel spin.

This matches to the letter what appears to have happened in the murder of Rosie Hilliard. It could explain why Rosie was not undressed or her body posed in Sutcliffe's now familiar MO. In his haste to get away he simply abandoned Rosie's body, running over her as he struggled to power his vehicle out of the rough and muddy ground and fracturing her spine and collarbone in the process.

Tracing vehicles with no more than the manufacturer's name – especially such common makes as a Morris Minor or a Ford Escort – makes searching for a needle in a haystack look simple by comparison. As West Yorkshire Police would discover to their cost within a few short years, trying to identify one car in tens of thousands inevitably overwhelms even the biggest of manhunts. Almost inevitably, Leicestershire Police were doomed to failure.

What its detectives needed was a second – and preferably a third – piece of information with which to narrow down their trawl. Once again, the lack of a functioning national intelligence system proved fatal. Had Leicestershire Police been made aware of Sutcliffe's known MO, he would undoubtedly have been investigated as a serious suspect: Rosie Hilliard's sad corpse displayed three of the key (and significantly rare) portions of his criminal 'signature' – the targeting of a sex worker who was then strangled and felled with a lethal blow to the back of the head. But it would also have flagged up Peter Sutcliffe as the owner – in succession – of a Morris Minor and a Ford Capri (which could easily have been mistaken for an Escort of the period in the murk and gloom of a February night).

Could Sutcliffe have travelled to Leicester to attack Rosie Hilliard? The twin sciences of murder mapping and offender profiling strongly indicate that his hunting zone would have substantially expanded by 1974. The three-day week would also have given him the opportunity to roam further afield throughout his cancelled night shifts. And the location of Rosie Hilliard's body was also telling: Spinney Hill Road is just off the A47 – the main trunk road leading to the M1 motorway and which connects the East Midlands with West Yorkshire. The pattern of Sutcliffe's known offending in the north shows that he typically favoured sites offering a clear and quick escape route to the motorways.

Like the deaths of Fred Craven, Mary Judge, Lucy Tinslop, Jackie Ansell-Lamb, Barbara Mayo, Gloria Booth, Judith

Roberts and Wendy Sewell, the murder of Rosina Hilliard would never be solved. She, like the others, was killed by a man whose method, technique and emotional signature very closely matched that of Peter Sutcliffe. But she, like the others, was destined to fade from police memory; another unexplained death, another ghost in the machinery of justice. And she would not be the last.

Kay O'Connor might well have been alive today had the three-day week ended seven days earlier. On Thursday, 28 February 1974, Britain went to the polls in a general election designed – in the words of Edward Heath – to decide who ruled the country: was it to be the elected government or (as Heath saw it) the unelected barons of the trade union movement? After months of power cuts and economic chaos, the stage was set for a showdown, with the electorate as the judges.

In the event, the voters could not decide – or at least not decisively. Although the Conservative Party polled the most votes by a small margin, Labour won more seats in the House of Commons. The outcome was a hung Parliament in which no single party seemed to have a mandate to govern.

Heath decided not to resign but instead to attempt a cobbled-together coalition with the Liberal Party. In this, he was to be disappointed: humiliated, he stomped out of 10 Downing Street to be replaced by Harold Wilson and the Labour Party.

Wilson set about attacking the most immediate problem facing Britain – an ongoing full-scale strike by the National Union of Mineworkers. By 6 March – and following intervention from the new government – the NUM and the National Coal Board agreed to settle their differences with a substantial pay rise for miners. Two days later, the three-day week was abandoned –

although restrictions on the use of domestic electricity continued to cause power cuts in homes across the land.

But the outbreak of industrial peace and the resumption of normal working hours came too late for Kay O'Connor. On Friday, 1 March, the clothing factory where she worked as a shorthand typist was still shut down: as a result, the thirty-seven-year-old was at home in Wickham Road, Colchester, Essex. This, coupled with the fact that she lived in an area of the town where crime was almost unknown and where everyone left their front doors unlocked or open, set the stage for her murder.

On that Friday afternoon, Mrs O'Connor – married but childless – walked from Wickham Road down Butt Street to the shops in Alexandra Road; she called in at the post office to collect her mother's pension before heading back home between 2.30 p.m. and 3.30 p.m.

Just after 4 p.m., a next-door neighbour in Wickham Road heard strange noises coming from Kay O'Connor's kitchen: she peered in through the back window of Number 8 and saw Kay lying in a pool of blood on the kitchen floor.

When police arrived shortly afterwards, they found that some of her clothing and one of her suede boots had been ripped off. They also discovered that Kay had been strangled – probably garrotted – and then stabbed, kicked and punched in a frenzied attack: there was also evidence of what detectives would vaguely characterise as 'a sexual motive'.

The murder had been carried out brutally and quickly, giving her no chance to even scream, much less to call for help. Colchester Police assigned more than a hundred officers to the investigation. Over the coming days and weeks, they took statements from 2,000 people. Reporters visiting the incident room for interviews and updates were impressed to see the walls covered with blackboards on which the hunt for the killer was 'mapped out like a military campaign'. They also noted that the man in charge, Detective Inspector Cliff Stolley, 'could not conceal his pride in the formidable crime-busting team'.

Sadly, despite public appeals, poster campaigns and the genuinely determined efforts of DI Stolley and his men, the closest they would ever get to the murderer was an artist's impression of a man seen in the area shortly after Kay O'Connor was killed. He was, according to eyewitnesses, 'tough-looking', around five feet six inches tall, of medium build and wearing heavy work clothes. His most noticeable feature was a pair of large and bushy sideburns that almost met the corners of his mouth.

Had Colchester detectives had access to a functioning national database, they would have seen that the brutal nature of Kay O'Connor's murder matched that of other attacks – solved and unsolved – up and down the country. Even in 1974 – a year before the first official Yorkshire Ripper attack – some of these showed Peter Sutcliffe's name as the perpetrator. What's more, the handful of police mugshots attached to them showed Sutcliffe to favour either a full beard or exactly the sort of distinctive sideburns depicted on the artist's impression on their incident room wall.

Had they had access to any of this vital intelligence, Peter Sutcliffe's name should unquestionably have been highlighted as a possible suspect. DI Stolley's team would then have had to ask whether there was any reason for a Bingley-based furnace-man to be more than 200 miles from home in Essex. At which point, they would – or should – have discovered that his sister, Maureen, lived less than fifty miles away in neighbouring Cambridgeshire, and was in the last month of her second pregnancy. They would also have found that Sutcliffe was in the habit of driving to his sister's home to visit her and his four-year-old niece. His most likely and logical route took him very close indeed to Colchester.

Motive, means and opportunity: the holy (or unholy) trinity of any crime. Coupled with the science of geographical profiling, or mapping, and Sutcliffe's history of almost identical attacks on women, his name should unquestionably have been in the frame. But with no working access to national intelligence it was never considered – and Kay O'Connor became another sad entry in Britain's list of unsolved murders.

The Easter holiday period of 1974 was blessed with unusually fine weather. Wednesday, 10 April dawned bright and sunny with temperatures reaching an unseasonal high of 16 degrees Celsius (or, in the measurements of the time, 60 degrees Fahrenheit); it would end with another murdered and mutilated young woman.

Caroline Doreen Allen was seventeen: she worked as a part-time nanny during her holidays from boarding school. That evening, she left her employers' house in Walnut Avenue, in the Nottingham suburb of Bramcote. She planned to catch a bus to her home fifteen miles away in the little village of Kinoulton. By 8 p.m., the weather had turned: the night was cloudy and overcast, with visibility rapidly fading.

When she didn't arrive at home, Nottinghamshire Constabulary began a missing persons inquiry. Because Caroline was known to have frequently hitch-hiked locally, they worked on the assumption that she had done so that evening. More than a hundred officers combed the area with tracker dogs, and public appeals were made for any sightings.

One of these turned up an eyewitness report of a girl matching Caroline's description – long brown hair, blue jeans, a fawn smock top over brown knee-length boots and a tapestry bag over her shoulder. She was seen talking to the driver of a lime-green-coloured Lotus Europa car in Edwalton – roughly halfway between Bramcote and Kinoulton. What made the sighting more memorable was that the driver had been travelling in the opposite direction and had apparently turned around when he saw the young girl hitch-hiking. After a brief conversation, she was seen to get into the vehicle, which then drove off southwards along the arterial A46 connecting Nottingham with Leicester.

It would be the last sighting of Caroline Allen alive. The next time she would be identified was twenty months later, in isolated woodland near Melton Mowbray. On Thursday, 3 December 1975, a walker out for an afternoon's shooting found a skeletal and fully decomposed body in Old Dalby Wood at Little Belvoir, Leicestershire. The lonely spinney was just six miles from Caroline's home; although the corpse was too badly decayed for any visual identification, police found a watch with Caroline's name engraved on it still clinging to the remains. The long-standing missing persons inquiry became a murder hunt.

Later that day, Home Office pathologist Dr Victor Pugh began the grisly task of the post-mortem. It was not an easy autopsy: more than a year and a half's exposure to the elements (and local wildlife) had stripped the body of any flesh. Without any tissue or organs to examine for stab wounds, bruises or evidence of strangling, it was impossible to pinpoint the cause of death. But from the remains of her skull Dr Pugh was definitely able to establish that Caroline Allen had been beaten around the back of the head.

The other telling piece of evidence was found – or rather, was not found – at the scene. While much of the victim's clothing had rotted on her corpse, her jeans were missing from her body: this strongly suggested that they had been removed by her killer, implying – at the very least – a sexual motive.

Police redoubled their efforts to pursue their only solid lead – the lime-green Lotus Europa. It should have been a profitable line of enquiry. Lotus – one of the small handful of British sports car companies – produced fewer than 10,000 Europas in the nine years between 1966 and 1975. Unlike subsequent fruitless searches by West Yorkshire Police's Ripper Squad for mass-circulation cars seen in the vicinity of murders, tracking down a lime-green version of such a limited-issue vehicle was a distinctly more manageable operation. And yet it produced only one possible suspect – who was then eliminated for the very good reason that he had a cast-iron alibi.

It is a truism of any police inquiry – and in particular of murder investigations – that the least reliable evidence of all is that of an eyewitness. Scientific studies have consistently shown that, in case after case, what appears to be solid and dependable identification by someone present at the scene often turns out to be dramatically wrong. Not only does the contemporaneous mood and stress level of the eyewitness have a bearing on the accuracy of their observation, but the more fundamental factors of weather and darkness can lead them quite honestly to misidentify what they have fleetingly seen. Which could well explain why Nottinghamshire Police was searching for entirely the wrong vehicle – and provide one reason for questioning whether Peter Sutcliffe could have been Caroline's killer.

In 1974, Sutcliffe owned a lime-green car. He used it – by his own subsequent admission – to trawl for victims. But the vehicle wasn't the exclusive Lotus Europa: it was, instead, a somewhat more prosaic Ford Capri. At first glance, these would appear to be very different vehicles. But, as with eyewitnesses, there is a subtle psychological process at work here. Because the Lotus is a status car, while the Ford is very much more mundane, we *assume* that there is little similarity. And yet placing drawings and photographs of the two side by side reveals that their shapes have much in common.

Added to this are two factors: at the time the witnesses reported seeing Caroline Allen get into the lime-green car it was dark, cloudy and – in poor visibility – they were a significant distance away. What's more, Sutcliffe's Capri had a black vinyl roof that, in poor lighting, would make the rear slope of the vehicle appear very similar to the raked and cut-away shape of the back of the Europa.

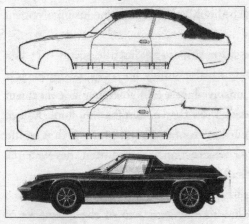

(top to bottom): Side view of Ford Capri/ Showing profile in poor light /Side view of Lotus Europa

On its own – and despite the limited evidence that Caroline had suffered a crushing blow to the back of the skull – this would not be enough to make Sutcliffe a suspect. If he had the means and – unquestionably – the motive, there would need to be some indication of opportunity: something that could, conceivably, place him in the area at the time. There was.

On 1 April 1974 – just nine days before Caroline Allen disappeared and was murdered – Maureen Sutcliffe gave birth to her second child. Peter Sutcliffe's nephew was delivered in Ely Hospital, and within a week was back home with his parents in Duxford, Cambridgeshire.

The most logical route for Peter Sutcliffe to have taken to visit his sister and her family – visits he was known to make regularly – would take him past Melton Mowbray, on through Leicestershire and past the southern edge of Nottinghamshire where Caroline Allen disappeared.

Did he do so? Only West Yorkshire Police (and Sutcliffe himself) ever knew or discovered the answer to that. And – as we shall see – West Yorkshire Police still refuses to release much of the crucial evidence about Peter Sutcliffe and his involvement in other murders.

If the factual basis for suspecting Sutcliffe seems – at first glance – coincidental, it is not simply born of a desire to clear up troubling and unsolved cases by blaming a convenient scapegoat. The investigation that underpins this book looked at other unsolved murders from this period for which it would have been possible to construct an argument that they were the work of the Yorkshire Ripper.

For example, what became (briefly) infamous as the Headless Body of Cockley Cley bore at least two of the hallmarks of

Sutcliffe's killings. On Tuesday, 27 August 1974, a farm labourer heading to work on Sir Peter Roberts' estate near Swaffham in Norfolk found the badly decomposed and decapitated body of a young woman lying in undergrowth beside a popular lovers' lane at Cockley Cley.

The manner of the mutilation matches what Sutcliffe would inflict on his known victim Jean Jordan in October 1977: he would ultimately tell the Ripper Squad that he had sawn off Jean Jordan's head with a hacksaw 'to create a mystery about the body'. Additionally, although she was never fully identified, the Norfolk victim was, like many of Sutcliffe's targets, believed to have been a working prostitute.

But these two facts alone are not enough to make him a convincing suspect. While he could, in theory, have been responsible, there are simply not enough points of similarity – much less any evidence placing Sutcliffe in the vicinity – to make this any more than an outside possibility. The sad story of this unnamed woman serves instead as a control – a way of constraining the over-eager assignation of blame.

There is, by contrast, something that makes him an unlikely suspect. Because in August 1974 an event occurred that would change – at least temporarily – the pattern of Peter Sutcliffe's life.

TEN

MARRIAGE, MISTAKES – AND MORE MURDERS

On Saturday, 10 August 1974, Peter William Sutcliffe married Sonia Szurma. It was the bride's twenty-fourth birthday.

The couple had been courting for eight years and their friends had long been asking whether they were ever going to tie the knot. Sutcliffe's answer was always the same: they were saving up for the deposit to buy their own home.

If so, there was precious little evidence of a substantial income between them. Sutcliffe was still working the night shift at Anderton's and, although she had recovered from the worst of her illness, Sonia was not holding down a regular job. She was intermittently well enough to take on short stints as a student teacher, but she still lived at home with her parents in Tanton Crescent, while Peter based himself at Cornwall Road. He was, though, almost a ghost in the family home: working nights meant that he was going to bed at the time they got up in the morning and left around the time they walked back through the door. Coupled with his ritual of spending every weekend with Sonia, it ensured that his parents and siblings saw little of him.

But the atmosphere in the Sutcliffe family house was increasingly tense. John and Kathleen Sutcliffe rowed almost constantly about his alleged womanising. It added impetus to Peter's thinking about marriage.

It was Sonia who chose the wedding venue. Clayton Baptist Church was a pretty chapel, solidly built of Yorkshire stone and situated in the heart of the picturesque Clayton village, less than a quarter of a mile from the area in which she had grown up. It was an odd choice, in some ways – Sonia had been brought up a Catholic and Peter had a generalised loathing of all religion; nonetheless, it offered the perfect backdrop for what Sonia pictured as a traditional romantic white wedding.

Peter Sutcliffe went to see the vicar alone. He explained that Sonia was too shy to come with him or to discuss the impending marriage. The Reverend William Nelson firmly explained that, since he had never seen either of them in his church, the would-be bride needed to come along for a serious discussion about the Christian sacrament of matrimony. If he thought, by this, that he would learn much more about the young couple, he was to be disappointed; at the next meeting, Sonia said very little, only able to explain that she had chosen Reverend Nelson's church because she had once been to someone else's wedding there and had liked both the building and the service. But since she lived locally and there seemed to be no reason not to marry them, he agreed to perform the ceremony. It would be the last time he saw either bride or groom.

The wedding provided the spur to sort out the Sutcliffes'

living arrangements. Until they could afford a place of their own, Bohdan and Maria Szurma offered the newly-weds the permanent use of the backroom at Tanton Crescent.

After a wedding reception in the Quarry Arms – a small neighbourhood pub just a few streets away from both the Szurma family home and the church – the new married couple set off for a honeymoon in Paris. They stopped en route with Peter's sister Maureen in Duxford, Cambridgeshire. By coincidence – and, without other evidence, it can be no more than that – they arrived on the very day that the nameless victim was murdered and decapitated fifteen miles away in Cockley Cley.

When they returned from Paris, the Sutcliffes started their new life in the Szurma family home. Neither of Sonia's parents ever publicly commented on their impressions of their new son-in-law, but the relationship between them seems to have been friendly. It was in marked contrast to the succession of bitter rows that broke out between the Szurmas and Sonia. She was still erratic in behaviour and could be temperamental: neighbours reported loud and frequent arguments between her and Bohdan in particular. In the ensuing months, the relationship deteriorated to the point where father and daughter communicated largely by leaving each other notes.

Throughout those early months of marriage, Peter Sutcliffe continued working the night shift at Anderton International. His lime-green Ford Capri would arrive back in Tanton Crescent at breakfast time and depart again in the early evening. It was hardly the best start for a young couple, but it did have one noticeable benefit: tied to the twin demands of job and marriage, he had little or no opportunity to trawl the streets hunting for new victims.

At some point in the autumn of 1974, Sonia Sutcliffe suffered the first of a succession of miscarriages. Around the same time – whether by coincidence or not – more victims were found with a similar modus operandi.

Gloria Wood was twenty-eight. Like Sonia, she was a student teacher and lived less than five miles from the Szurmas' house in Clayton – and less than fifteen minutes' drive from Anderton's. Unlike Sonia, however, Gloria had successfully given birth to two children. But her relationship with her husband had broken down and she had placed the children in temporary care while she redecorated a new home for them.

That home was a flat on the Holmewood Estate on Bradford's south-east fringes. At around 7.30 p.m. on Monday, 11 November 1974, Gloria was crossing the playing fields close to the flats.

As I was coming through the school grounds this man approached me. He came up to me and said, 'Can I carry your bag, love?' I said, 'No thanks – I haven't got far to go.' He seemed a right big man with staring eyes; dark-brown eyes. And he was olive skin-coloured – not black, not white, but Mediterranean-looking: Greek or Italian. He had a beard – a black beard, and black hair.

That impression would be the last thing Gloria Wood knew until she woke up in a Leeds hospital the following day. She had been smashed on the back of her head with a ball-peen hammer and had slumped, unconscious, to the ground.

I remember waking up in the hospital with my mother and my father near the bed. I wondered why the police were there: it just didn't register on me that I'd been attacked. I didn't feel a hammer blow. I didn't even feel it hit me.

But the medical notes were quite clear. Gloria had suffered a brutal attack in which the hammer had struck four blows, caving in her skull and leaving tiny splinters in her brain. Only two things had saved her life: the skill and speed with which she had been operated on, and the fact that, according to police, her assailant had been disturbed.

There were some youths at the end of the snicket: it must have interrupted him. And a little girl found me. She went into her mother and said, 'There's a lady on the grass who's had paint all over her.' That must have saved my life, really.

Gloria Wood would remain in hospital for some time – losing, for several years, custody of her children to her estranged husband. She would also need decades of psychological support to come to terms with what had happened to her. But despite the terrible trauma and its lingering aftermath, she was able to give police a very clear description of the man who had attacked her: no more than five feet eight inches tall, medium build, with a short dark beard and moustache.

Gloria Wood was attacked no more than three miles away from the street in Manningham where, five years earlier, Peter Sutcliffe had been arrested late at night in possession of a ball-peen hammer. His subsequent conviction was a matter of record

– albeit for the relatively minor offence of going equipped for housebreaking. Similarly, his caution in September 1969 for attacking a Bradford prostitute with a stone in a sock was also on file.

Quite how Bradford Police failed to notice the similarity between these two incidents and the hammer attack on Gloria Wood defies understanding. That they failed to cross-check with earlier hammer attacks on Fred Craven, John Tomey and Mary Judge in other parts of West Yorkshire – let alone the sad litany of near-identical murders across the rest of England – is, perhaps, more understandable: the continuing absence of any national criminal database made the trading of intelligence between forces a matter of pure luck. But to miss such clear and previous evidence from within their own patch was inexplicable.

Instead of this basic checking of criminal records, the police in Bradford seemed convinced that Gloria's attacker must have been someone known to her: they pressed her repeatedly to give them a name.

The police thought that I knew who had attacked me. But I couldn't tell them – I didn't know. I couldn't think of anyone who'd want to attack me. I just told them what I did know – that my attacker was a man with olive skin, quite tall, a beard, black hair. They wrote it all down and went away. Didn't hear from them for ages after that.

Gloria Wood would never hear the news she longed for: that the man who so nearly ended her life had been caught. Her ordeal remains, gathering dust, in the unsolved case files of West Yorkshire Police. She is convinced that her attacker was Peter

Sutcliffe – and is angry that he has never been charged, despite evidence gathered by detectives that placed him very close to the scene of the attack. At 8.30 p.m. on Monday, 11 November 1974 – less than an hour after Gloria's skull was smashed with a ball-peen hammer – Peter Sutcliffe clocked in at work at Anderton International: the distance between the crime scene and the factory was no more than six miles.

As 1974 ended, the British economy was sliding even deeper into crisis. Inflation was rising, the balance of payments was dangerously in deficit and industrial unrest was leading unions to call an increasing number of strikes. That December, Prime Minister Harold Wilson received a sobering report from one of his most senior advisers.

Lord Balogh was an economist by training and occupied the key governmental post of Energy Minister. He warned that the balance of payments deficit could provoke a 'violent withdrawal' of short-term money and that there was a very great risk of 'possible wholesale domestic liquidation starting with a notable bankruptcy ... The magnitude of this threat is quite incalculable.' To complete the gloomy picture he added: 'Should inflation accelerate further, a deep constitutional crisis can no longer be treated as fanciful speculation.'

Britain was on the verge of a major economic meltdown – a crisis that would, within a year, lead the government to go cap in hand to the International Monetary Fund begging for a bailout. The effect on businesses – particularly those in the engineering sector – was dramatic: the chill language of layoffs and redundancies began to be heard on the nightly news.

Anderton International was one of those companies affected.

In February 1975, it asked its workforce for volunteers to take redundancy: Peter Sutcliffe was one of those who applied. The severance package he was granted handed him a lump sum of £400 – no small amount in the mid-1970s, and enough to pay for a series of HGV driving lessons.

The course was run by the APEX School of Driving at Cullingworth, a small village sitting in the folds of hills between Bingley and Keighley. It would require Sutcliffe to spend many hours learning to control a heavy goods vehicle through the narrow and steep streets of West Yorkshire villages and towns.

Keighley – with its solid concentration of light industrial mills and factories – would be a prime training ground. A disused army base – 'the Dump' – between the nearby villages of Steeton and Silsden would be the location for the test he was to sit four months later.

But before then the Sutcliffes had an appointment to keep in London. And it would coincide with another murder matching at least one element of Sutcliffe's known MO.

Saturday, 22 March 1975 was the date set for Sonia's sister, Marianne, to marry her long-term boyfriend. He was a North London solicitor and the couple's wedding was to be held at Wembley Methodist Church. In preparation for the big day, Sonia and Peter journeyed south at the start of the week, staying in the bride-to-be's future home in Alperton, in the north-central London borough of Brent.

Four days before the wedding – at 5.25 p.m. on Tuesday, 18 March – Eve Stratford was discovered face down on the floor of her East London bedroom: her hands were tied behind her back with a stocking and a belt and her blue negligee had been ripped open. Her throat had been cut so violently – at least eight to twelve times – with a large knife that her head was almost severed.

On the face of it, there is little to connect this killing with Peter Sutcliffe. Although Eve Stratford had been almost decapitated – a highly unusual murder signature but one that was very similar to the unidentified victim of Cockley Cley, and to what Sutcliffe would do to Jean Jordan just over two years later – there was no evidence of a hammer attack, no serious sexual posing and the circumstances of Eve Stratford's young life would readily suggest a less specifically motivated killer than the Yorkshire Ripper.

Certainly – and with reason – the Metropolitan Police focused its investigations on more local and seemingly relevant offenders. But six months later another young woman was murdered on the other side of London. It would take another thirty-two years, but eventually forensic tests would link the two killings. And since the second bore the familiar Sutcliffe trademarks, a process of reverse engineering requires that the Stratford case be re-examined.

Number 45 Park Lane was, in 1975, one of the most fashionable venues in London. Behind its prestigious doors it boasted a casino, two restaurants and a stylish bar officially called 'The Playroom'. The formal title of the high-rent premises was the Playboy Club – though it was known more usually as the Bunny Club. It was the British outpost of Hugh Hefner's ever-expanding adult empire and its staff were – as his company's policy required – young, pretty women dressed in the absurd (if revealing) Bunny Girl uniforms of tight-fitting bodice, matching 'ears' and a white fluffy tail.

Perhaps few other buildings embody so precisely the different age that was the early 1970s: feminism might have announced itself at the start of the decade with Germaine Greer's seminal book *The Female Eunuch*, but Britain was then still a country of everyday sexism. This – together with the then substantial annual salary of £2,000 – goes a long way to explaining why hordes of young women eagerly competed for jobs at the Playboy Club.

Eve Stratford became a Bunny Girl in 1973. She was nineteen, the daughter of a medic with the Royal Army Corps and a woman he had met while stationed on post-war duties in Germany. She had spent much of her childhood moving around the world according to her father's military postings.

When she was seventeen, her parents, Albert and Liza, had settled in Warrington near Manchester. Eve had met and begun dating a young aspiring musician during her father's last posting in Aldershot: she decided to stay in the south when her parents moved north. The young couple moved into a run-down four-bedroomed flat in Lyndhurst Drive, Leyton, East London – sharing it, at various times, with other members of the boyfriend's band. There was evidently little spare money since there was no proper bed in the flat, but simply a double mattress laid on the floor.

But Eve Stratford had ambitions: she was young, glamorous and had a friend who had started working at the Playboy Club. With her help, Eve successfully applied to become a Bunny Girl.

Within a year, she was mixing with the rich and famous celebrities of the day – Sid James and Eric Morecambe, to name but two – who spent their evenings (and their money) at Number 45 Park Lane. She was a popular figure at the club, but she wanted to taste fame and fortune for herself, not just bask

Top left: Fred Craven, murdered in April 1966 in Bingley, West Yorkshire.

Top right: John Tomey in 2003. He survived an attempt on his life in March, 1967 in Oxenhope, West Yorkshire.

Middle right: Jacqueline Ansell-Lamb, murdered in March 1970 in Mere, Cheshire.

Below left: Coverage of the murder of Mary Judge in February 1968 in Leeds.

Mossdale rescue

Front Page Yorkshire Evening Post Friday 27 February 1968

Honeymooners find M1 girl strangled

At 11.30 a.m., on 13th June I attended at Nairn Road, Ruislip where in an adjacent field I was shown the body of the deceased, subsequently identified to me by Detective Chief Superintendent Frew as the above named woman. The body was that of an apparently young adult woman lying on her back on brambles and bracken. The deceased was completely unclothed apart from a blouse and brassiere which were pushed up to the top of the chest. Rigor mortis was fully established and the body temperature taken in the rectum was 71°F. The ambient temperature at the time was 72°. Injuries were noted to the breasts, throat and pubic region and there was mud staining the legs, iliac crest on the right side and left arm. Petechial haemorrhages were seen in the eyes.

Injuries to the genitalia.

In the region of the right vulva a split in the epithelium was found extending into the soft tissues but not into any cavity or organ. This injury showed strands of soft connective tissue running from side to side at its deeper aspect suggestive that the injury was caused by a blunt instrument although the edges of the wound were clean and no evidence of vital reaction was seen at this site. On either side of the vulva small irregular abrasions were noted that also showed no vital reaction. The laceration of the vulva measured 2" in length.

Internal Examination.

Skeletal System: No bony injury was identified. On the under aspect of the scalp there were diffuse petechial haemorrhages. A single bruise on the right side in the soft tissues of the throat below the angle of the jaw was found and also two small bruises were found in the soft tissues of the throat, one on each side of the tyroid cartilage.

Above left: Barbaro Mayo, murdered in October 1970 in Ault Hucknall, Derbyshire.

Above right: Newspaper report on the couple who found Barbara's body 'in the bushes'.

Inset: Gloria Booth, murdered in June 1971 in South Ruislip, West London.

Below: Extracts from the Gloria Booth pathology report.

Top left: Marie Burke, who survived a murder attempt in April 1972 in St Albans, Hertfordshire.

Top right: Judith Roberts, murdered in June 1972 in Wigginton, Staffordshire. Her body displayed head injuries identical to those of murdered Carol Wilkinson (1977) and Yvonne Pearson (1978), on whom a walling hammer was used.

Middle left: Andrew Evans, imprisoned for 24 years having been wrongly accused of Judith Roberts' murder.

Middle right: Judith Roberts murder scene off Comberford Lane in Wigginton.

Below: The incident room in St Editha's Church hall, Wigginton.

Above left: Wendy Sewell, murdered in September 1973 in Bakewell, Derbyshire.

Above right: Wendy Sewell was dragged on her back by her legs some 25 yards to the headstone pictured. The washing label from her bra was found torn off en route.

Below: An extract from Wendy Sewell's 'buried' pathology report that reveals injuries to the thyroid, cervical muscles, trachea and air passages – classic evidence of ligature (garrote) usage, which was not in possession of the accused nor found at the scene of the crime.

Top: The bloodstained trousers and heels of Wendy Sewell's pumps suggest she was garrotted and beaten on the footpath before being stripped of her lower clothing and bra and then dragged 25 yards across the grass area.

Middle: Number 3 indicates a bow torn from clothing; Number 4 is the clasp from her bra.

Left: Stephen Downing served 27 years, having been wrongly convicted of the murder.

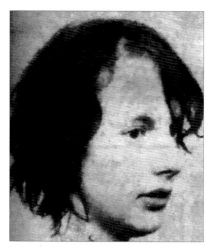

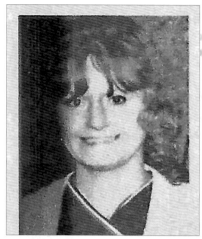

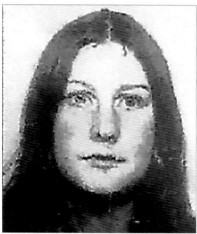

Top left: Rosina Hilliard, murdered in February 1974 in Leicester.

Top right: Kay O'Connor, murdered in March 1974 in Colchester, Essex.

Middle left: Caroline Doreen Allen, murdered in April 1974 in Old Dalby Wood, Leicestershire.

Middle right: The 'Headless Body of Cockley Clay' found in August 1974 in Norfolk.

Below right: Gloria Wood, who survived a murder attempt in December 1974 in Bradford, West Yorkshire.

Above left: Eve Stratford, murdered in March 1975 in Leyton, East London. DNA fingerprinting techniques connected her murder to that of Lynne Weedon.

Above right: Lynne Weedon, murdered in September 1975 in Hounslow, West London.

Below: Extracts from the Bradford *Telegraph & Argus*, detailing the attempted murder of Rosemary Stead in January 1976.

Bradford Telegraph & Argus 7 January 1976 article:

ce seek weapon after vicious attack in snicket

Thug leaves gir unconscious in pool of blood

A vicious attacker battered a teenage girl unconscious and left her in a pool of blood as she walked home down a dark, muddy snicket.

Today 18-year-old Rosemary Stead, who got engaged only two months ago, was "fairly comfortable" in Halifax Royal Infirmary.

VICTIM: Rosemary Stead

Bloodsoaked, Rosemary staggered the few yards to her Queensbury home after she came round and fell into the arms of her brother, Peter. Another brother, Allan, 15, described what had happened last night.

"As we lay in the chair and got her arms round it, there was no colour out at all, and we didn't see how heavy she was.

"She was all set in the light we could see that her nose and face were all swollen and bleeding and covered in the dirt, in the back of her head – her collar was coated in blood."

Rosemary had left out of the Summerville supermarket in Wakefield Road, Bradford, slightly late, and had walked her usual way home to 9 Thornacre Close, near Queensbury's new supermarket.

BEATEN

She sought the 6 am

"It was a while before she could tell us what happened," said Allan. "Her glasses had been smashed and she had lost the bag she was carrying.

"She told us that after getting off the bus she heard someone behind her, she started to walk faster, but the footsteps were still there so she turned round.

"After that she can't remember anything."

APPEAL

On November 4, her eighteenth birthday, Rosemary became engaged to the boyfriend she had been going out with for over a year, Allan Elsey of Checkheaton.

Det. Supt. Len Shakeshaft describes the attack as "vicious and apparently motiveless." He said there was no apparent connection with the two recent murders in the Aire Valley.

He appealed for passengers on the bus to come forward.

"We particularly want to contact anyone who got off at the same stop," said Rosemary. Rosemary was wearing a checked overcoat, red polo-necked jumper, a white skirt and navy-blue platform shoes.

"We are still searching for the weapon."

Rosemary, who has two brothers and a sister went to Buttershaw Middle School. Neighbours described her as a quiet, steady person.

Police name stabbed woma

Detectives are still trying to find the motive behind the stabbing of a 39-year-old mother of four found lying in a shop doorway in Listerhills, Bradford, early on Saturday.

Although seriously injured with several wounds her condition is improving in Bradford Royal Infirmary.

She has been named as Mrs. Maureen Hogan, of Edward Street, Bradford.

Det. Supt. Dick Holland is trying to trace Mrs. Hogan's movements in the four hours between he leaving a Bradford club and being found by a milkman at 5.40 a.m.

Mrs. Hogan spent some time in the Europa Club in Bradford and then went on to the Pentagon night club.

"She left the club at about 1.30 a.m.," said Supt. Holland.

The police have appealed to anyone who may have seen Mrs. Hogan en route from the Pentagon in Westgate to St. Andrew's Villas to come forward. They also want to hear from anyone who heard screams in the Great Russel Street area early on Saturday.

Mrs. Hogan

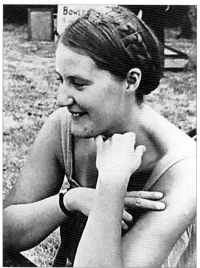

Top: Extract from the Bradford *Telegraph & Argus* revealing the name of victim Maureen Hogan, who was found seriously injured in August 1976 in Bradford.

Middle left: Elizabeth Parravicini, murdered in September 1977 in Isleworth, West London.

Middle centre: The body of Carol Wilkinson, murdered in October 1977 in Bradford, displayed injuries identical to Yvonne Pearson, murdered by Sutcliffe in January 1978 using a heavier walling hammer.

Middle right: Anthony Steel, wrongly convicted of the murder of Carol Wilkinson, served 20 years and died aged 52.

Below left: Alison Morris, murdered in September 1979 in Ramsey, Essex.

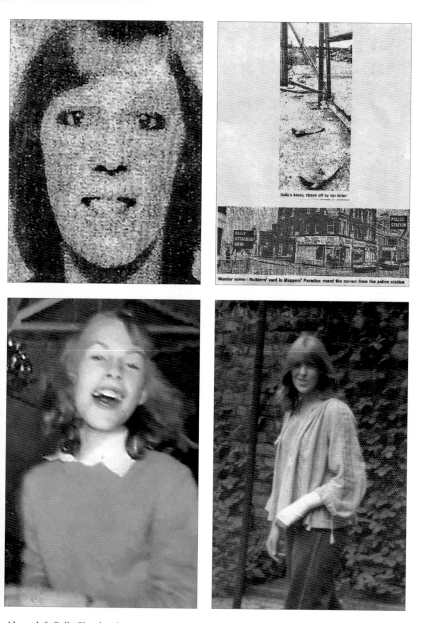

Above left: Sally Shepherd, murdered in December 1979 in Peckham, South East London.

Above right: Details of the Sally Shepherd murder scene, suggesting she was killed in 'Ripper fashion'.

Below left: Patsy Morris, found murdered in June 1980 on Hounslow Heath, West London.

Below right: Maureen Lea survived an attempted murder in October 1980 in Leeds.

Above left: Author Chris Clark as an Intelligence Officer in the 1980s.

Above right: Author Tim Tate circa 1978.

Below: Part of the statement Sutcliffe made to police on 10 February 1981 after six pieces of rope and cord were recovered from his garage, lorry and home, including his bedroom.

Peter William Sutcliffe

7. During 1969 an otherwise unremarkable young man named Peter William Sutcliffe came to the notice of the police on two occasions in connection with incidents involving prostitutes. Sutcliffe, who at that time was 23 years of age, was a native of Shipley, West Yorkshire and lived there with his parents. He was not notably abnormal, although he had gained a reputation for a rather macabre sense of humour whilst employed as a grave digger at Bingley. During his late teens he developed an unhealthy interest in prostitutes and spent a great deal of time, often in the company of his friend Trevor Birdsall, watching them soliciting on the streets of Leeds and Bradford. There is no evidence that he used the services of prostitutes at that stage although it is clear that he was fascinated by them and spent a considerable amount of time acting as a kind of voyeur. It is apparent that at some point during 1969, Sutcliffe's interest in prostitutes attained a new dimension with a desire on his part to inflict physical injury upon them. Although the police files on two incidents involving Sutcliffe during that year were destroyed some time ago as part of a perfectly legitimate "weeding" process there is no doubt that on one occasion Sutcliffe attacked a prostitute in Bradford with a cosh consisting of a large stone inside a man's sock. He had left Birdsall in his car before the incident and told him about what had happened when he returned. Surprisingly he was not charged with any offence. During the same year Sutcliffe was arrested in a prostitute area in Bradford whilst in possession of a hammer. He was not suspected of having the hammer for the purpose of inflicting violence to the person and the meagre police records remaining show that he was subsequently charged with "going equipped for stealing". At the time of these attacks Sutcliffe was courting Sonia Szurma whom he was to marry in 1974.

8. Between 1969 and the start of the known Ripper crimes in 1975, there is a curious and unexplained lull in Sutcliffe's criminal activities and there is the possibility that he carried out other attacks on prostitutes and unaccompanied women during that period. I should perhaps say here that I have given considerable thought to the extent of my responsibility in this review of the Ripper Case having regard to the opportunity it has given to interview Sutcliffe and his associates and in particular, Birdsall. I came to the conclusion that consideration of any other crimes which might have been committed by Sutcliffe and any of his associates was a matter for the West Yorkshire Metropolitan Police and the other police forces where such crimes might have been committed. I believe that it is sufficient for me to add that, in the light of the evidence adduced during the review, we feel it is highly improbable that the crimes in respect of which Sutcliffe has been charged and convicted are the only ones attributable to him. This feeling is reinforced by examining the details of a number of assaults on women since 1969 which, in some ways, clearly fall into the established pattern of Sutcliffe's overall modus-operandi. I hasten to add that I feel sure that the senior police officers in the areas concerned are also mindful of this possibility but, in order to ensure full account is taken of all the information available, I have arranged for an effective liaison to take place.

9. Whatever activity Sutcliffe did or did not engage in between 1969 and 1975, in the latter year he is known to have embarked on a campaign of murderous attacks on prostitutes and unaccompanied women in the West Yorkshire and Greater Manchester Police areas which was to

Extracts from the Byford Report, 1982. The withheld parts 10 and 11 underlined below.

Police files show a shocking catalogue of earlier crimes linked to Sutcliffe

EXCLUSIVE

BY DAVID BRUCE

CHIEF CRIME REPORTER

DETAILS have emerged of a chilling document suggesting that 13-times killer Ripper Peter Sutcliffe committed FORTY SEVEN other crimes across the country.

The list will add weight to calls for Sutcliffe never to be released.

The YEP can reveal that Ripper Squad detectives listed the 47 crimes – including murders and sex attacks – on an official TIC (taken into consideration) form still held in West Yorkshire Police archives.

Detectives strongly suspected that lorry driver Sutcliffe, now 58, was responsible for the crimes which dated back to when the serial killer was in his late teens.

Details of the 47 other offences which Sutcliffe was linked to were drawn up after investigations into crimes across Britain as police hunted a killer who brought fear to the North.

One of the officers involved in compiling the list, retired detective constable Alan Foster, said today that he believed all the crimes should be re-investigated bearing in mind advances in DNA technology. He said crimes were included only if there was strong suspicion that Sutcliffe could have committed them – and matched his lorry journeys around the country.

Mr Foster said he believed the families of all victims had an absolute right to know who had killed their loved ones.

He claimed that Sutcliffe may have eventually admitted to many more offences – had it not be for a senior officers cutting short an interview with the serial killer at Dewsbury Police station shortly after his arrest.

He said the purpose of compiling the TIC list was to eventually challenge Sutcliffe with the crimes, and to take statements from him admitting his guilt. He believed that the Ripper was never confronted with the additional crimes.

The first offence on the TIC list, he said, was the murder of a bookie at Bingley, in about 1965, when Sutcliffe was just 18. Among witnesses interviewed by detectives was Peter Sutcliffe's father, who recently died. He recalled that the Sutcliffe family lived close to the bookies.

Another attack happened about 12 months later when a taxi driver picked up a fare near Leeds University. They ended up on moors above Oxenhope, near Keighley. The taxi driver was repeatedly hit over the head with a hammer – Sutcliffe's favoured killing weapon – but amazingly survived. The victim told police his attacker looked like an Arab with black crinkly hair and a high pitched voice who was not particularly tall, a description closely resembling Sutcliffe.

Another murder on the list involved the killing of a young woman in Hemel Hempstead. The victim, who was never identified, was believed to have been a prostitute, like several of Sutcliffe's other victims in later years

Above: An extract from the *Yorkshire Evening Post* on 3 February 2005.

in its limelight. She decided that she would become a model and was convinced that she could make it to the top.

In 1974, she certainly seemed on course to realise her ambition. She was chosen for the (then) ultimate Bunny accolade of being test-photographed as a candidate for *Playboy* magazine's 'Playmate of the Month'. But despite her evident beauty she was rejected for the heinous sin of being 'too plump'.

Undeterred – and in breach of *Playboy* rules – she posed for a photo shoot for one of Hefner's arch-rivals, *Mayfair* magazine. In the March 1975 edition, she appeared naked in a series of explicit photographs as 'Miss March', under the professional *nom-de-sexe* Eva von Bork. The magazine proclaimed her to be 'the most classic blonde we've ever uncovered'. More disturbingly, in the accompanying text – purportedly an interview with Eva, though in reality no more than a copywriter's fantasy – *Mayfair*'s 400,000 monthly subscribers were informed of her sexual preferences: 'I like to be dominated, not whipped or tied up or things like that, just kept in my place.' It was, at best, an unfortunate statement – and potentially far worse.

The magazine hit the newsstands in February 1975; when it reached the attention of the Playboy Club management, Eve was ordered to clear out her locker and was suspended.

At the beginning of March, Eve posed for a further nude photo shoot as well as a session for a South African crime-fiction book cover in which she had to show off her cleavage and look terrified as a knife was held to her throat.

On Tuesday, 18 March, Eve went to Camden in North London at lunchtime to see her photographic agent before heading west to Bayswater for a meeting with a publisher.

Afterwards, she bought some dried flowers and carried them with her on the Tube journey back to Leyton. She arrived at Leytonstone Underground station around 3.45 p.m. and set off to walk the three-quarters of a mile to her home along Fairlop Road. As she left the station it started to rain.

By 4.10 p.m., she was home and she took off her wet clothes in her bedroom. But she was not alone for long: a neighbour heard Eve and a man talking in the flat around 4.30 p.m. Around 5.15 p.m., the same neighbour heard a loud thud like a chair falling over and footsteps going down the stairs onto the street; the phone began ringing and was left unanswered.

Ten minutes later, Eve's boyfriend arrived home from work to find her lying face down on her bedroom floor. She was wearing a pink bra and panties under a blue transparent negligee, open at the front, and her hands were tied behind her back with a stocking and dressing-gown belt. Her throat had been cut violently around eight to twelve times with a large knife, the cuts so deep that her head was almost severed.

Although there were no other obvious signs of a struggle, a post-mortem later determined that Eve's killer had silenced her by clamping his hand over her mouth as he cut her throat. There was evidence that she'd had sex that afternoon but it was not clear whether this had been consensual or rape. More puzzlingly, whoever killed her had also tied a second nylon stocking around one of her ankles.

Enquiries by the Metropolitan Police quickly established that Eve Stratford was definitely not killed by her boyfriend. Perhaps understandably – given her chosen line of work – detectives focused on the possibility that she had met her murderer either at the Playboy Club (though its rules strictly forbade Bunnies from dating customers) or through the glamour-modelling photo shoots. Certainly, in the days before her death, she had told friends that she had received mysterious telephone calls in which the caller hung up without speaking; she had also complained of a man hanging about and following her. Eventually, though, the leads ran out and the case languished in Scotland Yard's unsolved files.

What, then, links the brutal killing of Eve Stratford with the Yorkshire Ripper? On the surface there would appear to be little or no connection. While it is true that he was known to buy what friends described as 'nuddy books' – more particularly the over-the-counter variety of pin-up magazines such as *Mayfair* – in this, he was hardly uncommon: volume 10, number 3, which introduced 'Eva von Bork' as 'the most classic blonde', was purchased by 462,841 people, with a likely ultimate readership of at least double that figure.

Certainly, Peter Sutcliffe was in London in the week of Eve's murder, and if he was her attacker he had an escape route along the North Circular Road to his sister-in-law's home. But even with the single similarity of signature – the near-removal of his victim's head – to other murders, these factors hardly amount to conclusive evidence.

It would take another killing six months later – and eventually the application of modern forensic science in 2006 – to pinpoint the key that could unlock the mystery.

DNA – deoxyribonucleic acid – was first isolated in 1869 by the Swiss physician Friedrich Miescher after he discovered a microscopic substance in the pus of discarded surgical bandages. But it was not until 1953 that the British scientists James Watson and Francis Crick revealed the double-helix structure of what has come to be known as the most fundamental building block of human genetics.

For the generations raised on episodes of *CSI* and its British television equivalents, DNA testing is now taken for granted as the most important forensic science tool in crime investigations. Yet it was only in 1986 that the technique was first used, in the hunt for a man who had raped and killed a sixteen-year-old schoolgirl.

At 9.05 a.m. on Monday, 10 September 1984, the pioneering geneticist Sir Alec Jeffreys made a revolutionary discovery: every person on the planet had a unique chemical code, imprinted on the cells that made up their bodies. He had uncovered what we now call the 'genetic fingerprint'. When, two years later, Leicestershire detectives sought his help to identify the killer of Dawn Ashworth, he was able to test semen left on the body and isolate the genetic profile of the man who had left it. It was a breakthrough that had two important immediate consequences: it proved that the original suspect was innocent – and it helped convict the real murderer.

When Eve Stratford was killed and dismembered in her London flat in March 1975, DNA fingerprints were still the stuff of science fiction. But the Metropolitan Police retained all the forensic material taken from the murder scene in its evidence archives; it was to prove a remarkably far-sighted decision.

Late on the evening of Wednesday, 3 September that year, Lynne Weedon was walking home from an evening in the pub with friends. Lynne was sixteen and lived with her parents in Lampton Avenue, Hounslow.

At 10.30 p.m., she left her local – the Elm Tree in New Heston Road – in the company of her school friends. At 11.10

p.m., the group split up at the junction where Upper Sutton Lane meets the A4 Great West Road. From there Lynne took her usual shortcut home: an alleyway known locally as 'The Short Hedges'. At 11.15 p.m., she was halfway down the path when she was attacked – her skull smashed from behind with one massive blow from a blunt instrument.

As she lay in the dirt, her killer removed her blue jeans and panties, leaving her naked from the waist down; he then began sexually molesting her dying body. But he was disturbed by someone walking down the alleyway. He either threw the slight schoolgirl over a five-foot-high wire-mesh fence or dragged her through a hole in it and into the grounds of an electricity substation. Here he left her for dead.

Lynne was found at about 7.30 a.m. the next morning, unconscious and slumped at the bottom of the garden of Lampton School caretaker's house, which adjoined the substation. She never regained consciousness and died at West Middlesex Hospital a week later from a haemorrhage of the brain.

Police painstakingly searched the alleyway and surrounding area, but they could not find the weapon that had been used to cave in Lynne's skull. However, post-mortem examination later established that it was most likely to have been a heavy walling or lump hammer.

There were clear similarities between the murder of Lynne Weedon and that of Gloria Booth two years earlier. Both had been attacked late at night on their way back from pubs, in or near alleyways very close to the main westbound arterial roads out of London. Hounslow, where Lynne was attacked, is also less than ten miles from Ruislip, where Gloria had been killed.

But the most telling aspect was the removal of the lower parts of both girls' clothing.

Despite this, the Metropolitan Police did not connect the two murders – much less link up with other forces across England where disturbingly similar attacks and killings remained unsolved. Nor did they associate the Lynne Weedon case with the brutal slaughter of Eve Stratford on the other side of London six months earlier. For this, they could have been forgiven: the evidence of MO was so completely different that conventional investigative wisdom would suggest that two different killers were at work.

But, as it would turn out, both young women were murdered by the same man. In 2006, a new Metropolitan Police squad – the Murder Review Group – was undertaking cold-case examinations of long-unsolved killings in the capital. They were helped by the fact that in both the Eve Stratford and Lynne Weedon cases samples of forensic evidence taken from the bodies or the scene had been retained. Using Sir Alec Jeffreys' DNA fingerprinting techniques, they were able to show that the same unique genetic fingerprint was present in both cases.

Detection – particularly cold-case murder investigation – is often a process of reverse engineering: following the evidence back through the overgrown thickets of time and place. What the Met's 2006 breakthrough revealed was not simply that the same man killed both Lynne Weedon and Eve Stratford, but also that he had varied his MO radically between the two attacks. In turn, that brought into the frame all those whose known criminal signatures matched either set of circumstances. And that means Peter Sutcliffe, the Yorkshire Ripper.

But what about opportunity? Where was Sutcliffe in the

early summer of 1975, and what is known about his life and the pattern of his offending? Three very significant events had taken place in Yorkshire that summer: each strongly increases his candidacy for Lynne Weedon's murder – and others that would follow.

The first occurred on 4 June: two days after his twenty-ninth birthday, Peter Sutcliffe gained his heavy goods vehicle licence. He celebrated by buying himself a second car, a white Ford Corsair to join his lime-green Ford Capri, and began looking for a lorry driver's job – a search that would prove successful by the end of September. The second and third events were related – at least geographically – to the first. In the course of his HGV training, Sutcliffe had become very familiar with the narrow streets of Keighley and the nearby moorland village of Silsden. That summer of 1975, the Yorkshire Ripper would strike in both. It would mark the start of his most concentrated campaign of killing.

ELEVEN

'A CHARMING MAN'

Officially – in the files of the Central Criminal Record Office and the accounts of West Yorkshire Police – Peter Sutcliffe's career of murder and attempted murder began on 5 July 1975 with the attack on Anna Rogulskyj in Keighley. Those same official accounts record two further offences that year: the non-fatal hammer assault on Olive Smelt in August and the killing of Wilma McCann – his first killing – in October.

There is no mention in that authorised version of the 1969 stone-in-the-sock attack on a Bradford prostitute; nor does it mention the names Fred Craven, John Tomey, Mary Judge, Lucy Tinslop, Jacqueline Ansell-Lamb, Barbara Mayo, Gloria Booth, Judith Roberts, Wendy Sewell, Rosina Hilliard, Kay O'Connor, Caroline Allen, Gloria Wood, Eve Stratford or Lynne Weedon – despite there being very strong evidence pointing to Sutcliffe.

But there is another name to add to that list: the name of a young girl who in the summer of 1975 was – unquestionably – attacked and left for dead by the Yorkshire Ripper. Her name is Tracy Browne, and her story reveals much about Sutcliffe's methods – and the remarkable catalogue of police errors and dubious decisions that explain how the official account of his murderous reign has been censored.

The village of Silsden sits at the point where the rough moors of Brontë country meet the softer hills and valleys of the Yorkshire Dales. It was recorded in the Domesday Book as 'Siglesdene', but to many of its older inhabitants it is, and always was, 'Cobbydale': a reflection, perhaps, of the local determination to establish an identity more rural than its proximity to the industrial West Riding might suggest.

That historic county appellation had itself been abolished in 1974, when a major administrative reorganisation created the new county of West Yorkshire. It was a change that accompanied another major restructure: the neighbouring (and often intensely rivalrous) city police forces of Leeds, Bradford and other urban centres had been folded, along with their more rural counterparts, into a new service – West Yorkshire Metropolitan Police.

This change was intended both to improve financial efficiency and to recognise the importance of intelligence sharing on criminals who paid no heed to the arbitrary boundaries of the old police districts. It may have succeeded in the former – the traditional local bobbies' substations would soon disappear from villages such as Silsden – but by the summer of 1975 the latter was still little more than an optimistic ambition.

Upper Hayhills Farm is a little way outside Silsden, up the long steep road that leads out of the village and on towards the moors and dales. In August 1975, it was home to Anthony and Nora Browne and their four daughters.

Theirs was a close and warm family, maintained by love and sensible parental discipline. One of the rules was that, when the Brownes' twin teenage daughters, Mandy and Tracy, went out of an evening, they had to be home by 10.15 p.m.

That summer had been a good one – long and warm days, with pleasant balmy evenings. The night of Wednesday, 27 August was clear and bright, the village and farmland lit up by the moon. It was the last week of the summer holidays and the twins had gone into Silsden for a night out: since there was no school to worry about the next day, they had been given permission to be home half an hour later than usual.

Around 10.30 p.m., they set off together up the long road home. On the outskirts of the village Mandy quickened her pace while Tracy hung back to chat a few minutes longer to her friends. Some minutes later, she began to climb the hill alone; she was a mile away from the farm.

As I was walking up my feet were hurting: I was wearing those platform shoes that were in fashion. So I decided to sit down on these bricks and take my shoes off.

By the time Tracy had eased the shoes off her aching feet, she found she was no longer alone.

I just happened to look up and was aware of this man walking towards me. And he stood there for a couple of seconds and then started walking up the road.

I remember how dark he looked. He had this beard,

Afro-style hair and very dark eyes: I remember his eyes being almost black. He was only short – about 5 foot 8.

As I set off home again I was walking quick and he was walking quite slow, so I fell into step with him. We were chatting, just passing the time of day and it was quite calming: even the way he spoke was quiet and unassuming, and that's probably why he didn't make me feel nervous.

He asked me my name and I told him. He said, 'There's nothing much doing in Silsden, is there?' And I said: 'No, not really.' And then he said: 'Have you a boyfriend?' He seemed a really charming, nice man. I'd no reason to think that I was in a dangerous situation.

Every so often he'd hang back, to tie his shoelaces or blow his nose: this happened about three times. It didn't feel that I was in a dangerous situation: he didn't make me feel uncomfortable, even though I knew he was a stranger.

It was just about 50 yards from the gateway – I could actually see our farm – when he hung back again. I was just about to turn round to thank him for his company. But before I turned he hit me. And he hit me again. And again. And again.

I was shouting, 'Please don't, please don't.' And at the same time I could hear his grunts with the sheer impact of the blows. Sort of, *urgh*, *urgh*.

Tracy was hit five times on the back of the head with a ball-peen hammer. It smashed her skull, leaving her stunned and covered with blood – but still conscious. Only the lights of a car coming up the hill towards her stopped the attack – and saved her life.

As soon as that car got near to us I think he just wanted to get me out of the way as quickly as possible. He lifted me up like a baby, threw me over a barbed wire fence and ran off. I can still hear him running off now.

I remember scrambling along the fields. And I remember feeling really weak, although I wasn't aware that I was nearly bleeding to death. I was covered from the head to the waist in blood.

Somehow Tracy staggered over the fields until she came to a farm worker's caravan. She banged on its side, begging for help.

The man who lived there eventually opened the door and just said, 'Oh, my God'. By that time I couldn't speak: my mouth was opening but the words wouldn't come out and I started shaking because my body had gone into shock.

The farmhand took Tracy home and her parents called an ambulance. She was rushed to Chapel Allerton Hospital in Leeds – the nearest specialist head unit – where, after five hours' emergency neurosurgery, doctors finally removed splinters of bone from her brain. The surgeons saved her life that night, but for the next two years she would need constant medication to prevent seizures.

Despite her appalling injuries, Tracy Browne was able – and very willing – to talk to the police. The man who took charge of the investigation into what was plainly an attempted murder was Detective Superintendent Jim Hobson – then head of CID in Leeds – who would, in the years to come, lead the hunt for the Yorkshire Ripper. He asked Tracy if she could provide a description of her attacker.

He asked me if I could do an identikit picture, which I did. He was very dark with these really mysterious, dark eyes, a full black beard and almost Afro-style hair. For me you couldn't have got a picture more perfect than the one which was done. It was pinned up on shop windows and shop doors for a few weeks after that – with police asking, 'If people recognise the man, please come forward.'

But no: a week, two weeks went by and no sign of any man being pulled in with Afro hair and dark beard.

Photofit of Tracy Browne attacker

Nor was Tracy's the only description. Her photofit of the attacker was confirmed by a witness who told detectives that he had seen a dark-haired, bearded man in Silsden that night. He also said the man had been seen standing near a Ford car. Its description joined those in the local shops and in the weekly newspaper, the *Keighley News*.

Jim Hobson was a good and highly experienced copper. He had learned his trade as a detective in the old Leeds City Police and had an outstanding reputation as a murder investigator. It was a track record that would, in time, lead to his being promoted to head the hunt for the Yorkshire Ripper. And yet not only did Hobson never connect the attack on Tracy Browne with Peter Sutcliffe, he also failed to link it to the attempted murder of Anna Rogulskyj in Keighley – no more than four miles from Silsden – just five weeks earlier on Saturday, 5 July.

Like Tracy, Ms Rogulskyj had been hit on the back of the head with a hammer by someone who was disturbed mid-attack and ran off; as with Tracy, the man who attacked her had engaged her in conversation before attempting to kill her; and like Tracy, Anna had described her assailant as around five feet eight inches tall, with dark hair and a beard.

Two identical attacks carried out in such a short space of time and geographically very close to one another: two attacks where

Photofit of Anna Rogulskyj attacker

the description of the would-be killer matched in crucial regards – how could police not have joined the dots?

More disturbingly still, there had been a third remarkably similar attempted murder in the few short weeks between the attacks on Anna Rogulskyj and Tracy Browne. On Friday, 15 August – less than two weeks before Tracy's ordeal in Silsden – Olive Smelt had been struck twice on the back of the head with a hammer in Halifax. She, too, had survived and been able to describe her assailant: a youngish man – no more than thirty years old – who was slightly built with dark hair and a beard. And as in the Anna Rogulskyj and Tracy Browne cases, the suspect had started up a conversation with his victim before smashing in the back of her skull.

How were these three cases not immediately linked? And why was Sutcliffe's known MO – attacking women alone at night and being caught with a hammer in suspicious circumstances – never pulled up from the card-index files of previous convictions at West Yorkshire Police headquarters?

It is a question the force has never wanted to answer. The only attempt to do so would be made – in the bitter aftermath of the Ripper's trial – by its Chief Constable, Ronald Gregory. In his (handsomely remunerated) memoirs, published in the *Mail on Sunday*, he claimed that the attempted murder of Tracy Browne had not been connected with Peter Sutcliffe because 'Tracy was not a prostitute ... and all the other attacks were in city areas'.

This is arrant – and self-serving – nonsense. Neither Olive Smelt nor Anna Rogulskyj – both established as Ripper victims – was a prostitute, and Keighley, where Anna was attacked, was a small town. The truth is that the new Metropolitan force was no better at accessing and sharing information between its divisions than the old city and rural police had been before reorganisation.

It was a fatal blindness and one that – despite the repeated and valiant efforts of Tracy and her family to persuade Hobson's men that she had been a victim of the Yorkshire Ripper – would leave Peter Sutcliffe free to continue his murderous career for years to come. It would also form an integral component of the eventual cover-up of the true extent of Sutcliffe's crimes.

TWELVE

A YORKSHIRE RIPPER

By the beginning of September 1975, there were two separate police investigations into the near-identical attacks on Anna Rogulskyj and Tracy Browne. Despite the fact that both were attempted murders within a few miles of each other – and both by a man wielding a hammer – there appears to have been little if any coordination between the inquiries.

Meanwhile, had the police but realised it, the most likely suspect was living in Tanton Crescent, in Bradford – less than a dozen miles away.

An examination of Peter Sutcliffe's movements that August reveals that he had the opportunity to attack Tracy Browne – and that a week later in early September he was in London at the exact time when Lynne Weedon was killed. In the week of her death, he and Sonia joined the Szurma parents on a holiday visit to some of their relatives in Czechoslovakia. En route, they stopped off at Marianne Szurma's home in North London before flying out of Heathrow Airport, less than four miles from where the teenager's skull was smashed with a hammer. At best it was a remarkable coincidence.

The lives of Peter and Sonia Sutcliffe were once again about to change. During September, Peter – armed now with his HGV licence – looked for employment as a driver, while Sonia decided to complete her teacher training and enrolled at the Margaret McMillan College in Bradford.

Then, on Monday, 29 September, Sutcliffe found work: he was taken on as a driver by the Common Road Tyre Company, in the Bradford suburb of Oakenshaw. The job was to have a profound effect on his ability to seek out victims – and would quickly highlight yet more flaws in the police intelligence system.

Oakenshaw is situated at the junction of the M62 motorway – the arterial route linking Yorkshire and Lancashire – and the M606 spur into Bradford. Its position provided Sutcliffe with a perfect base from which to expand his attacks, and since his job involved short- and medium-distance hauls all over the north and the Midlands, he was given ample opportunity to familiarise himself with the network of motorways and trunk roads linking its towns and cities – the quickest and best means of making an escape from the scenes of his forthcoming crimes.

But just over a fortnight after he began work, he once again ran into trouble. On 15 October, he was caught stealing second-hand tyres and the police were called: Sutcliffe was arrested and, after a brief appearance at the local magistrate's court, bailed to appear for trial in the spring of the following year.

His arrest should have revived police interest in him: it was certainly entered into his intelligence file, and, since this contained details of the stone-in-the-sock attack and the offence of going equipped with a hammer, he should have been flagged up as a suspect for the attempted murders of Anna Rogulskyj and Tracy Browne. That he wasn't is a symptom of the very limited understanding of the importance of criminal intelligence in the 1970s.

True, an intelligence system had been put in place as far back as 1968: in all large town and city divisions, a full-time collator maintained criminal records and disseminated all crime information into workable intelligence for the uniform and CID operational officers of that area. This was also backed up by further intelligence officers working at each force headquarters, and on a less parochial level each region (a collection of police forces) had a regional crime intelligence office with a further officer stationed permanently with the Metropolitan Police's C11 intelligence squad at New Scotland Yard.

But any system is only as good as the officers who operate it. If they don't grasp the vital need to spread information out (as well as gather it in), there will – inevitably – be failures.

This problem had been recognised the previous year by the Association of Chief Police Officers. Starting in August 1974, an ACPO committee chaired by the Assistant Chief Constable of West Midlands Police, G. H. Baumber, began examining how information about criminals and their activities was disseminated by collators across the country. What Baumber found was an unqualified mess – 'haphazard and controversial', to use his own words – in which intelligence was at best treated as something with only short-term and limited relevance, and at worst was jealously kept within divisional areas by detectives who viewed themselves as possessing a monopoly of expertise over their neighbouring rivals.

When it finally reported in May 1975, the Baumber Committee made wide-ranging calls to sweep away the inefficient patchwork of regionally based approaches to intelligence and to replace them with a standardised national way of ensuring that officers investigating crimes anywhere in the UK should have access to a functioning intelligence system. It would, in time, lead to the first attempts at a national database – but the key phrase is 'in time'. Institutions are rarely revolutionised quickly and police forces – with all their historic rivalries – are among the slowest organisations to embrace change.

All of which meant that, in September 1975, the index card on one Peter William Sutcliffe of Tanton Crescent, Bradford – a young man who had acquired a succession of convictions for larceny and road traffic offences from 1963 through to 1966 – remained, together with his series of police mugshots, stuck, variously, in filing cabinets at the Bradford collator's office, the overall force intelligence office in Leeds and the regional crime intelligence office situated at Wakefield.

Had any one of those collators noticed Sutcliffe's arrest for the stone-in-the-sock and hammer incidents and mentioned them to detectives investigating the hammer attacks in Keighley and Silsden, Detective Chief Superintendent Dennis Hoban might not have been called to Prince Philip Playing Fields off Scott Hall Road on the morning of 30 October 1975. And the hunt for Peter Sutcliffe might not have been diverted down a fatal blind alley.

Dennis Hoban had given all his adult life – and with it his health – to catching criminals. He had worked the streets of Leeds for many years, developing a network of informants who provided both tips and unique knowledge of the different strata of criminals operating within the city. As a result, Hoban was a walking encyclopaedia of criminal knowledge – a detective who knew the names and likely locations of almost every class of villain: it enabled him to arrest everyone from petty thieves and fences to organised and violent robbers.

But the body he stared down at, that foggy morning, worried him. Wilma McCann was a known prostitute – and that made it quite possible that she hadn't known her killer.

There are, at the most basic level, only two motives for murder – sex or money. However complicated or confusing the circumstances of a homicide might look, experienced detectives like Hoban knew that they all ultimately came down to one or other of those two fundamental drivers. He also knew that – contrary to the pervasive narratives of crime novels and films – women are very rarely killed by a stranger: nine times out of ten the murderer either knows or is related to his victim.

The problem was that the other 1 per cent of cases often involved women who hawked their tired bodies for sex on the streets; the essential nature of the transaction – illegal and stigmatised – meant that there was frequently no more than a brief and largely anonymous 'relationship' between the buyer and the seller. And when one of these strangers killed, the investigation was destined to be long and difficult.

On Thursday, 29 October – exactly a fortnight after his arrest for theft – Peter Sutcliffe made deliveries to the Skipton and Barnoldswick areas. His work over, he drove to Leeds' red-light district of Chapeltown. He arrived during the early hours of 30 October.

At the same time as Sutcliffe was finishing work, Wilma McCann left her flat to go drinking in the pubs of Chapeltown.

She had four children, all under the age of nine: it was not the first time she had left them alone at night and her eldest child had become used to acting as babysitter.

Around 1.30 the following morning – and having enjoyed a heavy drinking session – Wilma started to make an erratic and unsteady journey back to her council house on Scott Hall Avenue. She never arrived.

At 5 a.m., a neighbour found Wilma's eldest two children huddled together at a bus stop, cold, confused and frightened: they cried and told him that their mummy hadn't come home.

Six hours later, a milkman stumbled across Wilma McCann's body, sprawled face upwards on the sloping grass embankment of Prince Philip Playing Fields off Scott Hall Road. She was just a hundred yards from home.

Sutcliffe had struck her twice on the back of the head with a hammer before stabbing her fifteen times. Her hair was matted with blood and her body obscenely exposed: her trousers were pulled down below her knees and her jacket and blouse were torn open. The post-mortem revealed that the stab wounds to her neck, chest and abdomen were made after she had been killed by the blows to her head. It also discovered semen on the back of her trousers and panties, where Sutcliffe had masturbated over her. Microscopic examination of the sample revealed the presence of the rare type B blood group – but if that was a potentially useful lead for Dennis Hoban and his team, it was quickly undermined by the unwelcome news that whoever had left the semen was what forensic scientists called 'a non-secretor'.

The human body stores a variety of differing types of fluid, but they break down into just two categories: excreted and secreted. The former includes sweat, earwax, bile, vomit and – naturally – faeces; the latter includes blood, urine, saliva and semen.

But not all bodily fluids contain sufficient genetic material to provide useful forensic information. Where they do not, this is primarily because the individual does not have sufficient levels of protein in their bodily fluids to enable a match to be made with blood or semen found at a crime scene: such individuals are termed 'non-secretors'. The percentage of non-secretors versus secretors in the population is remarkably low, but that is small comfort to detectives presented with a forensic sample from a crime scene that then turns out to contain no useful information.

And so, despite an extensive inquiry involving 150 police officers taking 11,000 interviews and working 53,000 hours, Hoban and his team were unable to identify Wilma McCann's killer.

With little else to go on – and without the crucial intelligence sharing that would have flagged up both the unsolved hammer attacks over the previous nine years and Peter Sutcliffe's criminal record – the detectives began pursuing a line of enquiry that would ultimately dominate and derail the hunt for the Yorkshire Ripper: they focused on the fact that Wilma McCann was a prostitute.

In fairness, Hoban had little other obvious option, and, however disastrous the decision would eventually turn out to be, he and his team worked extraordinarily hard. Most weeks were seven working days, and each working day began before dawn and often ended after midnight.

The problem was that, by its very nature, the fixation on sex workers excluded the possibility that Wilma McCann's killer might also have attacked non-prostitute women. It was then – and remains to this day – a serious danger in a major incident investigation: assuming – from limited facts – a particular pattern of the offender's criminal behaviour can screen out an acknowledgement that the pattern may have changed or may even be more inclusive than first thought. It's a tempting trap for even the most senior of investigating officers because it allows them to eliminate from consideration cases that don't fit the pattern they have decided is the hallmark of the offender. Unfortunately, some of those cases could actually provide the most telling clues.

And it is also a self-perpetuating problem. Once a particular focus is fixed in the investigators' minds, there is a perfectly natural tendency to make that pattern work no matter what other evidence might suggest. In the weeks following the discovery of Wilma McCann's sad, brutalised body, valuable leads and clues were lost by neglecting the attacks on Tracy Browne and Anna Rogulskyj and the other victims scattered throughout Yorkshire and indeed the rest of England.

At the start of 1976, Peter Sutcliffe would commit two attacks that precisely encapsulated the problem. One fell within the detectives' criteria and would be used to bolster the growing suspicion that a killer was stalking prostitutes; the other fell outside that narrow perception and would be disregarded.

On the evening of Wednesday, 6 January, eighteen-year-old Rosemary Stead left work at Sandmartin Supermarket in Wakefield Road, Bradford. She was slightly late in finishing and as a result missed her usual bus home. By the time she got to Queensbury – a bleak and lonely village on the moors outside the city – it was close on 6.30 p.m. and darkness had long since fallen.

As Rosemary walked along a road next to open fields, she was suddenly and viciously attacked from behind. A blunt object was smashed into the back of her skull, knocking her unconscious: only the evident traffic – both cars and pedestrians – disturbed her attacker and caused him to run off. Those witnesses were able to give police a clear description of him: twenty-five to thirty years old, five feet nine inches tall, slim build, with dark hair, a moustache and beard.

On its own this should have rung alarm bells: the description matched closely those given by Anna Rogulskyj and Tracy Browne. Despite this, the man leading what would turn out to be a fruitless search for Rosemary's attacker felt able to inform the local evening paper, the *Bradford Telegraph & Argus*, that there was no connection with their cases.

The attack on Rosemary Stead also had significant similarities to the murder of Wilma McCann: blunt instrument or hammer attacks to the head from behind were – and thankfully remain – extremely uncommon. Yet the fact that Rosemary was a shop assistant, not a sex worker, prevented her case from being linked with the hunt for Wilma's killer.

By contrast, the murder of Emily Jackson two weeks later was almost instantly matched with the Wilma McCann case, and Dennis Hoban was assigned to lead the search for what was assumed to be the same man.

Mrs Jackson was forty-two, married with three children (a fourth had died in an accident five years earlier), and living on the outskirts of Morley, one of Leeds' sprawling western suburbs. The family was struggling financially: as a result, just before Christmas 1975, Emily had agreed with her husband, Sydney, that with his help she would temporarily 'go on the game'.

The couple owned an old Commer van: they installed a mattress in the back and drove to the car park of the Gaiety pub, at the heart of Chapeltown and the red-light district. Sydney would sit inside drinking while Emily conducted business in the vehicle; then, when work was done, he would drive them both home.

On the evening of Tuesday, 20 January 1976, the Commer van arrived in its now familiar corner of the pub car park. After a quick drink with her husband, Emily set out to trawl for business. When she didn't return at closing time, Sydney was not unduly worried: he assumed she was having a busy night and, since she would need the vehicle, took a taxi home.

Just after 8 a.m. the next day, Emily's mutilated body was found in a derelict cul de sac off Roundhay Road by a worker on early shift. It was less than half a mile from the Gaiety, where Sydney had waited in vain for his wife to finish work.

A few minutes later, the teleprinter in Millgarth police station – the headquarters of Leeds CID – spat out news that a prostitute had once again been murdered.

FROM THE ACC NUMBER 2 AREA WEST YORKS METRO POLICE
TO ALL DIVS [DIVISIONS] WEST YORKS, ALL SURROUNDING FORCES, POLICE GAZETTE AND POLICE REPORTS.
THE BODY OF EMILY MONICA JACKSON, 42 YEARS, HOME ADDRESS 18 BACK GREEN,

CHURWELL, WAS FOUND IN A DERELICT BUILDING IN MANOR STREET, LEEDS 7, AT 8.05 AM TODAY 21ST JANUARY 1976.

IT IS KNOWN THAT THE WOMAN HAS RECENTLY BEEN AN ACTIVE PROSTITUTE IN THE CHAPELTOWN AREA OF LEEDS ... THE DECEASED SUFFERED SEVERE INJURIES TO THE CHEST, ABDOMEN, AND THROAT, POSSIBLY CAUSED BY AN INSTRUMENT SIMILAR TO A PHILIPS SCREWDRIVER (CROSS PATTERN TYPE).

ASSAILANT MAY BE HEAVILY BLOODSTAINED AND IS BELIEVED TO HAVE BEEN WEARING HEAVY RIBBED RUBBER BOOTS OR HEAVY WELLINGTON BOOTS.

THOUGH THERE HAS BEEN NO SEXUAL INTERFERENCE TO THE VAGINA THE BRA WAS MOVED TO POSITION ABOVE THE DRESS AND THERE ARE SEVERAL INDICATIONS THAT THE PERSON RESPONSIBLE FOR THIS CRIME MAY ALSO HAVE BEEN RESPONSIBLE FOR THE DEATH OF THE PROSTITUTE WILMA MCCANN AT LEEDS ON 29/30TH OCTOBER 1975.

MOTIVE APPEARS TO BE HATRED OF PROSTITUTES ... A SEARCH OF RECORDS FOR PERSONS CONVICTED OF SERIOUS ATTACKS UPON PROSTITUTES WOULD BE APPRECIATED ...

And there it was: the assumption that the murderer was driven by a 'hatred of prostitutes' specifically, rather than by the sexual pleasure of killing – necrophilia.

By January 1976, West Yorkshire Metropolitan Police's force records had documented eight serious attacks on unaccompanied women, all of which had occurred within a twenty-mile radius over the preceding three years. These details had been fed into the West Yorkshire criminal records force intelligence office in Wakefield, as well as various divisional collators' offices at Keighley, Bradford, Halifax, Leeds and Wakefield: they had also been sent to the regional crime intelligence officer based at New Scotland Yard. Five of these attacks had occurred during the previous six months and involved the use of a hammer: two had been fatal while in the remaining three the offender had been disturbed before he was able to murder.

All of the survivors described the offender as a shortish man of medium build with dark curly hair, dark eyebrows, and a short beard and moustache. Because he had engaged them in conversation, they were also able to identify his accent as local to Yorkshire and, most probably, the Bradford area. Three of them had even provided remarkably similar photofits.

Unquestionably, all of these attacks should have been logged as a recurring series by the same offender. That they weren't was due to the fatal assumption that directed police enquiries to a search for men with a known loathing of sex workers.

In fairness, Dennis Hoban's public statements in the immediate aftermath of Emily Jackson's case did recognise a likely sexual motive: at his first press conference he told reporters that Emily had been stabbed with a ferocity 'that bordered on the maniacal'. He also issued what would, before long, become an all-too-familiar warning.

I believe the man we are looking for is the type who could kill again. He is a sadistic killer and may well be a sexual pervert.

But despite this, the criteria set out for the trawling of intelligence files were narrowly focused on the way Emily Jackson and Wilma McCann had earned their sad and tawdry livings. The instructions were:

That the victim should be a prostitute.
That she should have been hit over the head with a hammer.
That her clothing should have been disarranged to expose her body.
That stab and slash wounds should have been inflicted to the body.

As a result, the investigators threw out intelligence files on non-prostitute victims – even where these involved the offender smashing in the back of his target's head – and on 23 January the first and formative reference to the Victorian streetwalker killings was made in a national newspaper headline that warned of a 'Jack the Ripper Killer' on the loose.

At the time, the real murderer was living quietly with the Szurma family in Tanton Crescent: to them, and to those who knew him, Peter Sutcliffe seemed to be an unassuming and normal family man. But as winter turned to spring his criminal record was augmented.

On 5 March 1976, he appeared before magistrates at Dewsbury and pleaded guilty to stealing five second-hand tyres from his employers. He was fined £25 and, one month later, was sacked – ostensibly for poor timekeeping. He would be unemployed for the next six months.

The loss of his job meant a reduction in income for Peter and Sonia. She, however, managed to make up some of the shortfall by taking casual work at a local private nursing home. Her mother already worked there on Saturday and Wednesday nights, and Sonia's shifts were arranged so that the two women worked together. This, coupled with his own unemployment, left Sutcliffe free to pursue his passion for trawling the streets in search of new victims: it is no coincidence that most of his crimes during this period were committed at weekends. When Sonia and her mother arrived home in time for an early Sunday morning breakfast, they were accustomed to finding Peter exhausted and soundly asleep upstairs: they could not have known that the reason he slept so soundly was because he had spent half the night quartering the red-light districts of Bradford and Leeds.

Sunday, 9 May was typical – both for the pattern of family life in Tanton Crescent and of Sutcliffe's increasingly urgent desire to kill. It would also lead to another blunder by West Yorkshire Police.

After Sonia and her mother left for work on the Saturday night, Sutcliffe climbed into his white Ford Corsair and headed for Leeds. He slowly drove through the streets of Chapeltown searching for a victim, but it was not until just before 4 o'clock the next morning that he spotted Marcella Claxton.

Marcella was twenty years old. Born on the Caribbean island of Saint Kitts, she had come to England with her parents ten years earlier. Her childhood had been hard and unhappy: her father was not averse to harsh discipline and his daughter bore the physical and mental scars of it. At school she was officially listed as educationally subnormal, with an IQ of just 50.

By 1976, she was unemployed and living in one of the run-down terraces of back-to-back houses off Roundhay Road, a few hundred yards from the Gaiety pub in Chapeltown. She was single, with two young children – both in temporary foster care – and was three months into her third pregnancy.

In the months to come, West Yorkshire Police would describe Marcella as a prostitute: it was a charge she denied, and certainly on the morning of 9 May there was nothing to suggest that she was working the streets – nothing but the fact that she was alone and staggering homewards through the red-light district. She had spent the evening at a West Indian drinking club and was very definitely not sober.

So, when a white car pulled up beside her in Spencer Place and its driver asked if she was 'doing business', she denied she was a prostitute, but nonetheless asked him for a lift. Instead of driving her home, he drove her to Soldiers' Field in Roundhay Park and offered her £5 to get out of the car and undress for sex on the grass. Rapidly sobering up, she told him she needed to urinate and went to hide behind a clump of nearby bushes.

Minutes later, she felt a vicious blow to the back of her head, swiftly followed by a second. Dazed, she lay back on the grass looking at the blood on her hand where she had touched her head. Her attacker stood nearby – enabling her to register his black hair, beard and moustache. She also saw he was masturbating as he watched her bleeding on the ground. Afterwards, he went back to the white car to get tissues to clean himself up; he then threw them on the ground and pushed a £5 note into Marcella's hand, warning her not to call the police.

Marcella was covered in blood, but somehow she managed to half-walk, half-crawl to a nearby telephone kiosk to call an ambulance. As she sat on the floor and waited for help, she saw the white car drive past the phone box several times. Finally, it stopped: the driver got out and walked back to the bushes where he had attacked her. Finding his victim gone, he drove off.

At Leeds General Infirmary, surgeons discovered eight severe and gaping wounds in the back of Marcella's head: each was about an inch long and it took a total of fifty-two stitches to patch up her bloodied scalp. But other wounds took much longer to heal: not only was Marcella plagued by nightmares in which her attacker came back and found her, but she also lost the baby she had been carrying.

After six days in hospital, Marcella Claxton was finally allowed to return home. She provided police with a very detailed description of the man who had tried to kill her: it enabled detectives to put together a photofit showing a smartly dressed white man with dark hair, a beard and moustache. It was remarkably similar to the one Tracy Browne had provided nine months earlier.

For reasons never explained by West Yorkshire Police, the investigating officers chose not to believe her description – insisting instead that the attacker was most likely to have been black. Whether this was due to the overwhelmingly Afro-Caribbean demographic of the local population or the result of the endemic racism of the 1970s, Marcella's photofit picture was disregarded and her file removed from the growing investigation into attacks on Leeds prostitutes. It would not be until after the Yorkshire Ripper was finally caught that the police added her name to his tally of victims.

Photofit of Marcella Claxton attacker

But Marcella Claxton would encounter Peter Sutcliffe again. Not long after she came out of hospital she went with friends for a drink at the Gaiety. While she was there, the man who had assaulted her walked in and took a long look round the pub before stepping out again. Shocked and distressed, she told her friends that she had just seen the person police were looking for – but by the time they rushed outside he had gone.

The encounter was an unhappy coincidence: Sutcliffe was not looking for Marcella that night and there is no certainty that he even noticed her. But his presence in the Gaiety was very far from accidental: he was scouting the location for potential victims – and nine months later he would find one.

The dismissal of Marcella Claxton's evidence was yet another major blunder by the police. The search for Yorkshire's own Jack the Ripper was by then headed by a man whose name would become increasingly familiar: West Yorkshire Assistant Chief Constable George Oldfield. As the long, hot summer of 1976 progressed with no sign of his quarry, he restructured the team and made several changes of command: none made any real difference.

But, in any event, the attacks on prostitutes seemed to have stopped. By August there were no further reports – and therefore no new leads. It would be another seven months before the next grim discovery of a sex worker's body in the Leeds red-light district – a pause that would always puzzle the experienced investigators working diligently on the inquiry. They knew – as Dennis Hoban had warned – that serial killers rarely stop their grim trail of murders unless and until they are arrested. What then could explain the apparent lull?

The answer is that there was no such lull, only a tragic misreading of the nature of their quarry. Focused so narrowly on prostitutes, the detectives missed another attack on what Oldfield would have described as 'an innocent woman' and which bore at least some of the hallmarks of Sutcliffe's MO.

It happened in the early hours of Sunday, 29 August. Maureen Hogan, a thirty-nine-year-old housewife, had been on a night out in Bradford. She had visited the Europa Club before moving on to the Pentagon nightclub in the city centre: she left there at 1.30 a.m. to walk home. Shortly afterwards, she was attacked from behind and collapsed in a shop doorway; five hours later, a milkman out on his rounds stumbled across her unconscious body.

Surgeons at Bradford Royal Infirmary discovered that Mrs Hogan had suffered severe head injuries and had been repeatedly stabbed in the abdomen. Although she was not able to provide any details of her attacker, these wounds were – at the very least – remarkably similar to those inflicted on Wilma McCann and Emily Jackson: they also bore a strong resemblance to the attacks on Anna Rogulskyj, Tracy Browne and Olive Smelt (as well as the other still open case files from police forces across the rest of England). The man leading the inquiry, Detective Superintendent Dick Holland, would shortly be appointed to the growing team working on the Ripper attacks – but because

Maureen Hogan was not a prostitute, no connection was made with the murder investigations.

Two months later, Peter Sutcliffe's life changed once again: after many months of unemployment, he finally found a new job. T. & W. H. Clark (Holdings Ltd) was a small engineering transport firm with contracts to deliver all over the UK. Its yard and offices were situated on the Canal Road Industrial Estate between Shipley and Bradford – a convenient location for the arterial M62 and M1 motorways – and very close to the Szurma home in Clayton. In October, Peter told Sonia the good news that Clark's had hired him as a lorry driver.

Aside from the much-needed extra cash that this brought in, the job brought Sutcliffe two very personal benefits. The firm owned four six-ton rigid lorries as well as a Ford Transcontinental – then the most advanced (and, at a price of £250,000, the most expensive) HGV of its time. Sutcliffe revelled in the power, mass and speed of the truck and devoted the hours between loading and unloading to cleaning and polishing both the inside and outside of his vehicle.

But above all else, his new position offered him the opportunity to roam far and wide in search of women to attack: his journeys in the lorry took him all over the country, frequently requiring overnight stops. He would bed down in the bunk at the rear of the cabin, free from family to account to and left for lengthy periods to his own devices. It was the key element in the resumption of his killing spree.

THIRTEEN

STATE
OF FEAR

1977. In the Queen's Silver Jubilee year, the Sex Pistols posed outside Buckingham Palace to promote a new and deliberately disrespectful punk take on the national anthem. The economy was sliding ever deeper into trouble, and with it the Labour government, which out of desperation formed a short-lived electoral pact with the Liberal Party. Shockwaves from across the Atlantic arrived with news that Elvis Presley had died, and that doctors had observed the first signs of a mysterious new disease that would, in time, come to be called AIDS. By any standards, 1977 was a busy and landmark year.

It was also a year in which fear – tangible, overwhelming fear – was felt in the towns and cities across Yorkshire. For 1977 was the year in which Peter Sutcliffe's sad roll call of victims began to increase rapidly. He would carry out six confirmed attacks on women – five of them fatal. But there would also be four other murders that should have been investigated by the ever-growing specialist squad tasked with catching this most brutal of killers.

The first official Ripper attack of the year occurred on the night of Saturday, 5 February. The victim was, once again, a Leeds prostitute: but there was much more to the killing of Irene Richardson than simply the gruesome dispatch of yet another desperate woman forced by poverty to roam the miserable alleys of the red-light district. In the manner of her death lay clues both to the future crimes of the Ripper and, crucially, to the trail of unsolved murders dating back almost a decade.

Irene was twenty-eight years old and for more than a decade her story had been one of misery and deprivation. She was born Irene Osborne into a large working-class Glaswegian family – she had six sisters and three brothers; when she was in her mid-teens, the Osbornes left Scotland and split up both emotionally and geographically: the various sons and daughters were scattered from coast to coast across England. In 1965, Irene was to be found in London, completely cut off from all her siblings, and very shortly to give birth to the first of two children. When she proved unable to cope, they were taken into care and eventually fostered. By 1970, she had moved to Blackpool and found work in the local Pontins holiday camp. She also met and married George Richardson, a plasterer: the couple would have two daughters and enjoy what was – by the standards of Irene's life up to then – a relatively settled existence.

But in the summer of 1975, she abruptly disappeared from home: her husband tracked her down to London, where they settled for a few more months before Irene once again vanished. This time George didn't look for her, and eventually their two daughters were taken into care.

By February 1977, Irene Richardson was sick, homeless and working the rough streets of Chapeltown for £5 a time. After several nights sleeping rough – including bedding down in a public toilet – she managed to find a room in a shabby bed and breakfast on Cowper Street in the heart of Leeds' red-light district.

On the night of Saturday, 5 February, she left the rooming house at 11.15 to search for business. Within an hour, she would be dead.

That night – with his wife and mother-in-law out at work – Peter Sutcliffe had gone out kerb-crawling in his white Ford Corsair. He spotted Irene not far from the Gaiety pub and stopped his car a few yards ahead of her. Evidently relieved to have found a customer, she jumped in quickly. He drove to Soldiers' Field in Roundhay Park – the scene of his attempted murder of Marcella Claxton.

When Irene got out of the car to urinate prior to having sex, Sutcliffe slipped a hammer and Stanley knife into his pocket. As she was crouching, he delivered three heavy blows to the back of her head with his hammer: one drove a piece of her skull almost two inches into her brain.

As she lay dying, he ripped open her jacket and blouse and began to stab at her body with the knife – first in her neck and then three more times in the abdomen. The blade opened up a gaping wound in her throat, exposing her larynx – identical to the savage cuts inflicted on Eve Stratford – and ripped her stomach apart so that her intestines spilled out onto the ground. He then pulled up her skirt and pulled down her tights, stuffing her panties inside them. Satisfied with this grisly tableau, he opened his flies and masturbated.

Shortly afterwards, he heard voices and a car nearby; after carefully positioning Irene's inert and bloodied body, he climbed back into the car and drove off.

At 7.30 on the morning of Sunday, 6 February, a man out jogging in Soldiers' Field spotted Irene Richardson's mutilated corpse. She was lying face down, her hands under her stomach and her head turned to the left. Her cheap, imitation-suede fur-trimmed coat had been draped over her buttocks and legs, with only her feet showing. Her calf-length brown boots had been carefully placed over her thighs.

There was a wealth of intelligence in that crime scene: the lifting and removal of a woman's lower garments, the highly unusual 'signature' of hammer blows to the head, followed by the slashing and stabbing of her body. These all pointed to a sexually driven killer and bore remarkable similarities to the succession of attacks across the country over the previous nine years – something that a brief consultation with their regional crime intelligence officer and a search of the method index located at New Scotland Yard would have identified.

But to West Yorkshire Police it was not these clues that dominated the inquiry: instead, they homed in on the fact that Irene Richardson was a prostitute – the third street girl to be killed in West Yorkshire in less than eighteen months. It reinforced the belief that sex workers were the killer's target – and that therefore, by definition, 'innocent women' were not at risk.

Nor was this to be their only significant mistake. Police searching Soldiers' Field that February morning discovered tyre marks near the body; they assumed – correctly – that these had been made when the killer drove onto the soft ground. Analysis showed that the tyres were made by three different companies –

Esso, Pneumant and India Autoways – and that they could only fit twenty-six types of car. But while this was a limited number of models, the actual number of potential vehicles exceeded 100,000. Not for the last time, valuable investigative hours would be wasted on what was – by any standards – a search for a needle in a field of haystacks, rather than on examining local and national criminal record offices for men with a history of unusual attacks on women.

Certainly, had a functioning cross-border police intelligence system been in existence, the increasingly harassed detectives of West Yorkshire Police would not have missed the next two murders.

The first occurred on Tuesday, 22 March, thirty-two miles south of Leeds in South Yorkshire. Barbara Ann Young was twenty-nine years old and lived on the Happy Days caravan site at Hatfield, near Doncaster. She had two small children and supported the family by working as a prostitute.

At 8.45 p.m., Barbara was found by a female friend crumpled on the ground in Broxholme Lane, on the town's north-eastern edges. It was close to the main arterial road leading to the M1 and was dotted with lorry parks and cheap transport hotels; it was also an area that Sutcliffe knew from his driving jobs and had discovered to be a good place to pick up sex workers.

Barbara was conscious, but clearly suffering from severe head injuries. She told her friend that she had gone with a punter to an alleyway between Broxholme Lane and Christchurch Road, where he had attacked her. Around midnight, another friend took Barbara home and put her to bed; she died from her injuries during the night.

A post-mortem revealed that her skull was fractured, causing a massive haemorrhage. South Yorkshire Police began a murder inquiry – but despite the very clear similarities to the deaths of Wilma McCann, Emily Jackson and Irene Richardson (let alone the catalogue of identical unsolved attacks that preceded them), there is no evidence that they passed the information on to their colleagues in Leeds. Had they done so, the detectives hunting the Ripper would have realised that he was far more mobile – that his killing grounds extended significantly beyond Leeds – than they assumed.

West Yorkshire detectives concentrated their efforts on the red-light district of Chapeltown, warning the area's sex workers that a prostitute killer was at large. Many women decided to relocate to safer vice districts in Manchester, London and Glasgow. Those who could not or would not be displaced so far from home shifted their operations to nearby Bradford, where customers knew to seek out women in the triangle of down-at-heel terraced streets between Manningham Lane and Lumb Lane.

Whether or not this accounts for Peter Sutcliffe's selection of his next victim is open to speculation. What is certain, however, is that Debbie Schlesinger would die at his hands as the long winter months gave way to spring.

Thursday, 21 April 1977 was the Queen's fifty-first birthday, and as ever the royal family's celebrations were private, though reported on the news. That evening, a group of young women went into Leeds for drinks in a city centre pub; among them were Pat Power and her best friend, Debbie Schlesinger. Debbie was eighteen; she lived with her parents on the Hawksworth Estate in Horsforth – a semi-rural suburb on the road leading from Leeds to Bingley – and worked in a supermarket. In common with many youngsters of her age, she loved dancing and was a familiar figure at local discos.

The girls got off the bus together and walked up to the rows of neat detached houses in Cragside Walk. They parted company at Pat's home and Debbie walked on towards her house, fifty yards down the street. Before she could get there, a man appeared – apparently from nowhere – and stabbed her through the heart. She screamed – once and loudly – before somehow summoning the strength to run towards the neighbourhood Conservative Club, her attacker following closely behind. Here she collapsed and died in the doorway, just as Pat, her father and other neighbours arrived. Pat would later recall how quickly it happened.

I came running and found her slumped in the club doorway. There was no movement – but I never thought she was dead at that time: I just thought she'd fainted or something.

Disturbed, the attacker ran off, disappearing into the night. The eyewitnesses were, however, able to get a good look at him. He was a white man with dark hair and a beard, about thirty years old and five feet six inches tall.

The man put in charge of the investigation was Detective Superintendent Jim Hobson – the head of Leeds CID and the man who, two years earlier, had led the unsuccessful hunt for Tracy Browne's attacker. Asked the next morning by a local television news crew if he had any idea what the motive might be for Debbie's murder, his answer was frank, if less than reassuring.

No, not at this stage. She hadn't been sexually assaulted and robbery doesn't seem to be the motive at this stage.

Hobson was rather more bullish when speaking to the Schlesinger family. Debbie's sister, Karen, recalled that the detective was certain the killer would be caught quickly.

The police said from the start it was somebody local and it would be sorted by the weekend – they would have this person, no problem.

He was not 'had' by the weekend. Nor would he ever be arrested.

Since by April 1977 the local press was feverishly following every attack on a woman in the city and its suburbs, West Yorkshire Police was inevitably asked whether Debbie could be the latest victim of the so-called Ripper. The answer was an unequivocal no. Nor was it only the press speculating: when, two days later, a known prostitute was killed five miles away in Bradford, Pat Power asked detectives about any link to her friend's death.

It was a Ripper case and I asked if he could be responsible for Debbie's murder, because there was no motive to kill her. But they said it wasn't the red-light area where he usually worked so there was no way that it could have been him. And so I just had to accept what they said – but I always had in the back of my mind that it could have been him. Always.

It would take another twenty years for Pat's suspicion to be confirmed – unofficially – by a brave policeman determined to bring justice to the families of the Ripper's unacknowledged victims. He would discover evidence that placed Peter Sutcliffe very close to Debbie Schlesinger's home on the day she died – evidence that had somehow not been found by the men hunting the Ripper that April of 1977. It was a single sheet of paper: a worksheet for Peter William Sutcliffe, provided by his employers, T. & W. H. Clark (Holdings Ltd), showing that late in the afternoon he delivered 104 empty axle squares and one front axle to a company called Kirkstall Forge. Its premises were less than a hundred yards from Cragside Walk.

But that determined detective and his rigorous reinvestigations were, that spring of 1977, two decades in the future. Before then, there would be many more bodies – and more terrible errors by West Yorkshire Police.

* * *

Patricia Atkinson, known as Tina, was thirty-two, divorced, and living with three children in a small flat on the edge of Bradford's red-light district. Within the safety of these four walls – she was mindful of the threat to women on the streets – she plied her trade as a prostitute.

Tina was slim, dark-haired and always smartly dressed. Outside her working environment she had no shortage of men friends and, on Saturday, 23 April 1977, she set off for a night out in the busy pubs around Manningham. In them, she had a well-earned reputation for heavy drinking.

At 11 p.m., she was seen walking towards Church Street;

shortly afterwards, she encountered Sutcliffe, who was hunting in the area's grim streets. Tina was thoroughly intoxicated and banging on the roof of a parked car. When Sutcliffe accosted her and suggested 'business', she readily got into his vehicle and he drove them back to her flat in Oak Avenue.

As they entered through her front door, Sutcliffe hung up his coat, pulled his hammer from its pocket and delivered four massive blows to the back of Tina's head. She collapsed to the floor. He hoisted her up again and, as the blood poured from her wounds, began to remove her overcoat. He then carried her to the bedroom, threw her down on the bed and ripped open her black leather jacket and blue blouse. Next, he pulled up her bra to reveal her breasts and pulled her pale-blue jeans and pants down to her ankles.

With a chisel he had removed from his pocket, he began to stab at Tina's exposed stomach; he then turned her over and stabbed her in the back before flipping her dying body over once again and stabbing at her stomach a further seven times. Before he left her, he partly pulled her jeans back up and threw the bed linen over the top of her body. When Sutcliffe left the flat, Tina was still making gurgling noises.

Sutcliffe drove home to Tanton Crescent. Methodically, he washed his victim's blood off his jeans in the kitchen sink and hung them up to dry, before cleaning other traces of blood off his boots. As he climbed into bed beside the sleeping Sonia, Tina Atkinson slowly died.

There were two vital elements to the murder of Tina Atkinson. The first was a clue that West Yorkshire Police were quick to spot: without realising it, Sutcliffe had left a size 7 boot print on the bottom bed sheet – an imprint that matched those left at the scene of Emily Jackson's death. The second was less obvious but, in terms of understanding the nature of the killer, even more important. Tina had been attacked in her own flat, not out in the rough streets of the red-light district: the Ripper was evidently both willing and able to vary his MO. It should have rung warning bells in the incident room at Millgarth: if the killer was not, as the police had assumed, wedded to his pattern of outdoor attacks, he might equally not fit the other assumption – that he was solely targeting prostitutes.

Neither hypothesis was seriously questioned. Detective Superintendent Jim Hobson directed the attentions of the 120 officers working on the Ripper cases firmly towards the streets. Since, by the time Tina Atkinson died, they had not received much in the way of useful help from prostitutes, pimps or punters, Hobson tried a new strategy: he put undercover female police officers on the streets of Chapeltown. It was a risky operation. The officers were disguised as prostitutes and equipped with short-wave radios: if a man approached them asking for sex, they alerted colleagues parked a few streets away.

As a tactic it could only ever be short term: since none of the undercover 'vice girls' could ever get into a customer's car, their presence was quickly clocked by both prostitutes and punters alike. But the main problem was that it relied on a misunderstanding of the killer's motivation: that assumption – that he was driven by a hatred of prostitutes – was shortly to be fatally exposed.

Meanwhile, the man they were seeking was – to all outward appearances – getting on with the business of married life. Sonia Sutcliffe was approaching the end of her teacher training and confident that she would pass her exams before the coming summer: this would mean a full-time job and a significant rise in the couple's income. Buoyed by this, she and Peter began to search for a home of their own.

Number 6 Garden Lane, Heaton, was a detached four-bedroomed house, covered with light-pink rendering, in a resolutely middle-class area of Bradford. The asking price was £15,000 – no small sum in 1977 – but potentially affordable: the Sutcliffes arranged to view it on Saturday, 25 June.

Later that night, Sutcliffe dropped his wife off for her night shift at Sherrington Nursing Home before setting off for a night out with two regular drinking companions. The trio visited three pubs in and around Bradford, and at closing time bought a late supper of fish and chips before heading home. It was well past midnight when Sutcliffe dropped off his friends but instead of going into his home he drove away from Bradford and headed for Chapeltown.

Jayne MacDonald was also out in Leeds that night. She was sixteen years old and had recently started her first job as a sales assistant in the shoe department of a local shop. She kissed her father goodbye and left their home in Chapeltown for an evening with friends at the Hofbräuhaus, a German-style 'Bierkeller' in the city centre. There she met and danced with an eighteen-year-old boy, and when the pub closed at 10.30 p.m., the two set off, as part of a crowd, in the direction of Briggate, Leeds' main shopping street. Jayne suggested finding somewhere to buy a snack; by the time they found a chip shop and had enjoyed a late supper, Jayne had missed her last bus.

She and her new friend sat on a bench until about midnight, before walking towards where he lived on an estate near St

James' Hospital. The young man said that if his sister was at home she would give Jayne a ride back to her house. But when they arrived it was obvious that there was no one at the young man's house. Instead, the couple walked on up Beckett Road in the direction of Chapeltown, and the MacDonalds' address in Scott Hall Avenue: by cruel coincidence this was just six doors away from the home of Wilma McCann.

The youngsters parted company outside the main gates of the hospital at around 1.30 a.m. Jayne planned to call for a cab from a taxi firm's kiosk at the corner of Harehills Road. But when she received no reply at the kiosk, she decided to continue on walking through the maze of tired and shabby streets. Her route took her up past the Gaiety, where Emily Jackson had last been seen, and she was walking along the Chapeltown Road pavement, close to an adventure playground, when Peter Sutcliffe pounced.

Two young children found Jayne MacDonald's body in a corner of the play area at 9.45 the next morning. She was lying face down, her skirt disarranged and her white halter-neck top pulled up to expose her breasts. Sutcliffe had struck her on the back of her head with his hammer, dragged her dying body twenty yards from the pavement, and then smashed two more blows into the back of her skull. He had then stabbed her more than twenty times in the chest and back. A post-mortem revealed that a knife had been used – and that it had been thrust repeatedly into one of the wounds.

Jayne MacDonald was not a prostitute. Other than living in Chapeltown, she had no connection to the vice trade. Nor was the spot where Sutcliffe attacked her known as a regular haunt of street women. Her murder should have given West Yorkshire

Police pause for thought: it was plainly the work of the man now universally dubbed 'the Ripper', but the sixteen-year-old did not fit the detectives' assumption that he was exclusively targeting those who sold their bodies for sex.

Instead of questioning their theory, the police made another misguided supposition. In the immediate aftermath of Jayne's death – and beset by howls of newspaper anguish that 'an innocent young woman has been slaughtered' – Chief Constable Ronald Gregory appointed his most senior detective to oversee all the Ripper investigations and to placate the public with a reassuring statement that the killer had simply made 'a mistake'. Assistant Chief Constable George Oldfield duly obliged.

> It looks very much to me as if he is selecting these women of the streets as his targets. I think it was a mistake that he attacked Jayne MacDonald: probably in her case he mistook her for being a lady of the streets because she was out in that area at the time she was.

Oldfield would go on to become the most visible – and most visibly haunted – police officer of the entire Ripper inquiry. He was an old-school copper and no stranger to controversy. Three years earlier, he had led a rushed, careless and corrupt investigation into the IRA's bombing of a coach on the M62 motorway: the subsequent conviction of a mentally ill woman called Judith Ward would ultimately be quashed when it was revealed that her highly improbable confession had been manipulated by detectives to ensure she was found guilty.

The hastily issued statement that Jayne MacDonald's death had been a slip-up by a killer obsessed with murdering prostitutes would not be the last – nor even the most serious – mistake Oldfield would make in the hunt for the Ripper.

But even if, in the fevered circumstances of that June of 1977, it was understandable, it defies belief that no one in West Yorkshire Police connected the MacDonald case with the previous attacks on Anna Rogulskyj, Tracy Browne, Olive Smelt and Marcella Claxton. Had they done so, they would have quickly discovered an identical description from each incident of a man with a local accent, dark crinkly hair, beard and moustache: in other words, a picture of Peter Sutcliffe.

And had they cross-referenced this with Sutcliffe's criminal record, at least twelve women would not have died at his hands over the coming four years, and four others would not have had to endure the life-shattering pain of surviving his attacks.

FOURTEEN
THE INNOCENT AND THE DEAD

On 31 August 1977, Peter Sutcliffe sold his white Ford Corsair. There was nothing wrong with the car: Sutcliffe was a good mechanic and devoted many hours to ensuring his vehicles were in excellent condition. The decision to get rid of it was driven by an urgent need to get it as far away as possible from the road outside his home in Tanton Crescent: he had discovered that his most recent victim had survived, was talking to detectives and that she – or an eyewitness – could potentially identify the Ford.

If anything gives the lie to his subsequent claims of mental illness and diminished responsibility, it was this seemingly banal action. Far from being in the grip of an intractable schizophrenia, getting shot of the key piece of evidence connecting him to an attempted murder shows his mind to have been clear, cunning and calculating.

The attack itself had followed a familiar pattern. On the night of Saturday, 9 July – two weeks after killing Jayne MacDonald

– he left Sonia at home in Tanton Crescent with her parents and climbed into the white Corsair with its distinctive black vinyl roof. He headed straight for Lumb Lane in the red-light district of Bradford.

In the aftermath of the MacDonald murder, the *Yorkshire Post* – the regional morning daily – and its sister paper, the *Evening Post*, published an open letter, addressed to 'The Ripper': it pleaded with him to surrender to police.

> You have killed five times now. In less than two years you have butchered five women in Leeds and Bradford. Your motive, it is believed, is a dreadful hatred of prostitutes, a hate that drives you to slash and bludgeon your victims.
>
> But, inevitably, that twisted passion went terribly wrong on Sunday night. An innocent sixteen-year-old lass, a happy, respectable, working-class girl from a decent Leeds family, crossed your path.
>
> How did you feel yesterday when you learned that your bloodstained crusade had gone so horribly wrong? That your vengeful knife had found so innocent a target? Sick in mind though you undoubtedly are, there must have been some spark of remorse as you rid yourself of Jayne's bloodstains.

It was a fine and emotional piece of journalism. Unfortunately, led by the conviction of West Yorkshire Police that the killer was obsessed with sex workers, it completely misread the motivation of the man it sought to address. Proof came ten nights later when he set out to kill again: like Jayne, his victim that evening would not be a prostitute, but a woman in the wrong place at the wrong time.

Maureen Long was forty-two, the mother of several (largely grown-up) children and separated from her husband. Her life had been typical of many working-class Yorkshire women: tough, unforgiving and punctuated by occasional – if minor – brushes with the law. But one thing was certain: she was not – and never had been – 'on the game'.

That Saturday night, Maureen left the home she shared with an occasional partner in the Leeds suburb of Farsley, for a night on the town in Bradford. She visited a number of pubs, and at one of them met her estranged husband – with whom she remained on good terms – and made arrangements to stay at his home in Laisterdyke, Bradford, later that night.

Maureen Long loved dancing and so it was no surprise that she ended up at the Mecca ballroom in Manningham. In her long black dress, and noticeably worse for drink, she was a memorable figure on the discotheque dancefloor that night. Witnesses observed that, by the time she left just after 2 a.m., she was distinctly drunk.

Sutcliffe spotted her coming out of the Mecca and, after cruising slowly behind her, pulled over as she unsteadily made her way past the long queue of people waiting for taxis. He asked her whether she was going far; she enquired whether he was offering her a lift. When he said that he was, if she wanted one, she climbed unsteadily into the passenger seat of the Ford Corsair.

Her defences undermined by drink, Maureen explained that she lived with an ex-boxer, whom she described as a 'spoilsport'. Close to home she asked the slim, rather handsome driver whether he fancied her. Sutcliffe said that he did, and she said that if no one was at home they could go inside to have sex. When she discovered that the home wasn't empty, she told him that she knew a place where they could park up in nearby Bowling Back Lane.

But first she needed to empty her bladder. Maureen got out of the car and crouched down to urinate. As she did, Sutcliffe smashed the back of her head with a hammer. When she slumped to the ground he pulled down her girdle, tights and panties and stabbed her in the chest, abdomen and back. One slashing wound opened her from her breasts to below the navel.

But before he could finish her off – or relieve himself by masturbating over her body – he was disturbed by a dog barking close by. Leaving Maureen for dead, he threw himself into his car and sped off into the night.

Two women living in a nearby gypsy caravan found Maureen at 8 o'clock the following morning. She was still alive, but seriously injured. Only emergency surgery at Bradford Royal Infirmary kept her alive long enough for a transfer to the specialist head injuries unit at Leeds General Hospital. She would undergo a succession of major neurological operations over the next nine weeks.

The blows to Maureen's head had wiped much of her memory: when George Oldfield and his team interviewed her, they found she could not accurately describe her attacker or the vehicle in which he had picked her up. Because of this – and despite the very clear similarities to the Ripper attacks – Oldfield was sceptical that she was the serial killer's latest victim. The detectives focused instead on the possibility that the man they were looking for was a taxi driver. It was a decision that would lead to vital time being lost.

In truth, the atmosphere inside the major incident room at

Millgarth police station that September was one of fear. Fear that, despite a truly herculean effort – 300 officers had worked 343,000 man-hours, taking 12,500 statements – they were no closer to their quarry. But fear, too, that the Ripper investigation could become contaminated by evidence stemming from attacks that might look like the Ripper's handiwork but which were actually no more than coincidental. It was this fear that led Oldfield and his men to exclude the Tracy Browne, Olive Smelt and Marcella Claxton cases from their enquiries – and, for a time, to discount Maureen Long as a likely Ripper victim. It was a perfectly understandable concern: but its effect was to leave Sutcliffe free to search for his next victim.

The press, though, was less constrained. Whatever Oldfield had decided, the attempted murder of Maureen Long was a major story. Soon newspapers reported that the nightwatchman whose barking dog had disturbed the attacker had given police a description of a car he saw driving away. It was enough to convince Sutcliffe that he had to sell the white Ford Corsair.

The following month saw two major changes in the lives of Peter and Sonia Sutcliffe. She was, at long last, ready to start full-time employment and was set to join Holmfield First School in Bradford at the start of the autumn term. The couple had also exchanged contracts on the house in Garden Lane: the date for moving into their first home together was set for the end of September.

Although full records of the Sutcliffes' movements are – more than thirty-five years later – still locked away from public scrutiny in West Yorkshire Police evidence archives, there is reason to believe that, before the pressure of their new life took hold, the couple paid a visit to Sonia's sister in Alperton, north-west London, when the Szurma family took their regular late summer holiday at the start of September. If so, it could link Sutcliffe to the murder of a young mother on holiday there at the same time.

Elizabeth Parravicini (*née* Graham) was a twenty-seven-year-old English mother of two pre-school-age children. She was married to an Italian accountant called Rick Parravicini and the family lived in Rome.

That September, Elizabeth came back to England for a short holiday: she and her children stayed at her parents' home in The Grove at Osterley. On the evening of Thursday, 8 September, she went out to a West End cinema with friends before catching the last Tube train home: it arrived at Osterley station at 12.45 a.m. on the Friday morning. She walked east along the main A4 Great West Road and then turned right, walking along Osterley Road past St Mary's Church and the playing fields of Isleworth Grammar School.

As she drew level with the driveway of the private Parkfield Housing Estate, 200 yards from the safety of her parents' home, Elizabeth was attacked from behind: someone repeatedly smashed a blunt instrument – almost certainly a ball-peen hammer – into the back of her head. Her skull fractured almost instantly. The killer then dragged Elizabeth's body across the road and dumped her, fully clothed, face down into a private front garden shrubbery, leaving her handbag and shoes on the footpath at the scene of the initial attack.

Her parents had decided not to wait up and had gone to bed, but sometime during the night her father woke and realised that Elizabeth hadn't come home. He contacted her friends, who confirmed that she had caught the last Tube: at 3.30 a.m.,

Mr Graham rang the police and reported his daughter missing. At first light, he set out with his other daughter to search the area: after a two-minute walk, he found Elizabeth's shoes and handbag. Then they discovered her body.

The Metropolitan Police used the press to issue a warning to women in West London to be on their guard.

> This was a most brutal attack on a perfectly respectable married woman. We are looking for an extremely savage individual; she was a very striking woman.

But it was the coda to the statement that was most revealing: 'There are similarities with the murder of Lynne Weedon which are being considered.'

London's detectives had made no progress in finding the man who had killed Lynne almost exactly three years earlier. That attack had taken place just one and a half miles from the place where Elizabeth Parravicini died: it too had involved an attack from behind with a blunt instrument, smashing the schoolgirl's skull into fragments. Nor did the similarities end there: in both cases, the killer had dragged his victim's dying body away from the street and into the cover of shrubbery. And while Lynne's assailant had removed her jeans and panties, leaving her naked from the waist down, the detectives worked on the theory that Elizabeth's attacker had been disturbed and had fled before interfering with her corpse.

On its own, the MO evident in the Elizabeth Parravicini murder bore a strong resemblance to the attacks by the man being sought by West Yorkshire Police. The linking of it to Lynne Weedon's killing strengthened that link considerably.

Yet once again the lack of a joined-up national intelligence system ensured that the investigation in London never considered the possibility that 'their' murderer could be operating nationally. Elizabeth Parravicini joined the growing list of remarkably similar unsolved murders across England.

On Monday, 26 September, the man who was the most likely suspect for all of these attacks completed two purchases. He and Sonia finally completed the legal paperwork and moved into their new home in Garden Lane, Heaton. On the same day, he bought a car to replace the white Ford Corsair: aside from its colour – red – his new vehicle was all but identical to its predecessor. Within days he would use it to stalk and kill his next victim.

On Saturday, 1 October, Peter Sutcliffe spent the day working on his new car in the drive of his new house. In the evening, he drove to Manchester, where at 9.30 p.m. Jean Jordan climbed into the red Ford Corsair as it kerb-crawled through the city's Moss Side red-light district. Jean Jordan, also known as Royle and more colloquially as Scotch Jean, was twenty and the mother of two small children. She lived with them and her common-law husband in a small flat in Lingbeck Crescent. Two years earlier, with little or no money coming in, Jean had turned reluctantly to prostitution: by October 1977, she had clocked up two police cautions for soliciting.

That evening, Sutcliffe spotted her slim figure amid a small group of women. He stopped and asked her if she was 'doing business'. She had been about to get in another car, but changed her mind and opted for Sutcliffe and his red Corsair. They haggled briefly about the price before Sutcliffe agreed on the standard charge of £5, to be paid in advance. She then directed him to a spot on Princess Road, Chorlton, near the Southern Cemetery. It was an old allotment area, now an overgrown wasteland and shielded from the traffic by high hawthorn hedges. It was a favourite haunt of the Moss Side prostitutes and their clients, as well as courting couples.

Sutcliffe handed over a brand-new £5 note, which he had received in his pay packet from T. & W. H. Clark two days earlier. Jean carefully stowed the note in a hidden compartment in her handbag and then made her way across the derelict ground. Sutcliffe followed her, before smashing his hammer into the back of her head thirteen times: the blows shattered her skull into fragments.

As Jean Jordan lay dying, Sutcliffe realised that he was in danger: other prostitutes were servicing punters amid the bushes and rubble. Crouching over the corpse, he saw a car's headlights come on and, hearing the car's engine being started, realised that it would soon be pulling away. He quickly dragged Jean's body nearer some bushes to hide it.

No sooner had the first car pulled away than another vehicle pulled in and parked in the same spot. Panicking, he scrambled back into the Corsair and started the lengthy drive out of Manchester to the M62 motorway, over the Pennines and back to Sonia and their new house.

As he drove home, Sutcliffe realised he had made a potentially fatal mistake: in the rush to get away from the scene of Jean Jordan's murder, he had remembered to pick up the hammer, but had left a piece of even more incriminating evidence that could lead the police directly to him. If detectives found the brand-new £5 note he had given her, he knew they could check its serial number with the bank: that, in turn, would lead them to discover that it had been part of a consecutive run of notes issued to his employers. He had two alternatives: either turn around and go back to find it, thereby running the substantial risk of being spotted, or continue on to Bradford and sit it out. He chose the second option, but with a determination to monitor the local papers for any news of the killing that might force his hand.

Four years later, the saga of Sutcliffe's £5 note – and the police hunt for its owner – would become one of the more memorable parts of his trial. But what was never considered was the importance of the story to understanding the Ripper's state of mind. And yet even a cursory account of his actions that night and in the following week clearly shows that they were not those of a deranged individual in the grip of paranoid schizophrenia: instead, they reveal the calculating brain of a clever and ruthless necrophilic killer.

On Monday, 3 October, Sutcliffe picked up the paper and was surprised to see nothing about the Ripper having struck for the first time in Manchester. The same absence of reports occurred for the rest of the week. He was forced to conclude that Jean Jordan's body had not been discovered.

On Sunday, 9 October, Peter and Sonia held a housewarming party. When the celebrations wound down a little after midnight, he drove his parents back to their house in Bingley, but instead of returning home he headed for Manchester. Since it was late on a Sunday night, traffic was light, and he arrived at the outskirts of the city within three-quarters of an hour of dropping off his parents. Fifteen minutes later, he was parked by the Princess Road allotments and was heading into the wasteland to find Jean Jordan's body.

When he found it, he began searching for her handbag. He checked the area around – and even under – her body: it was not there. He then began to work over a larger search pattern, but still he couldn't find it. He became frustrated, and with mounting rage, pulled Jean Jordan's already rotting body from where he had hidden it, and began stripping off her clothing, throwing it away after searching each piece for the £5 note. After checking the last item, her boots, and still not finding the note, he vented his anger and frustration on the corpse, stabbing it over and over with a knife and a large shard of glass from a nearby greenhouse.

He inflicted eighteen deep and slashing swipes on Jean's breasts, abdomen and vagina. So fierce was the attack that his knife sank a full eight inches into her body: it caused her stomach to blow open and the resulting stench made him vomit. But he continued to hack at Jean's body and attempted to cut off her head using a saw and a large piece of glass with a cutting edge. He had deliberately chosen this because glass was not a weapon associated with his previous attacks – another indication that, for all the perverted sexual pleasure he drew from mutilating his victim, a sharp and cool mind was always at work on ensuring the police did not catch him.

As a tool to sever a human head from its torso, the glass was, however, less than practical. Eventually, he abandoned the attempt and set off back to Bradford, Garden Lane and Sonia.

The pathology of necrophilia suggests that, while attacking and mutilating a corpse would provide a strong sexual charge, it might not deliver the full satisfaction of climaxing over a dying (as opposed to dead) body. This could well explain what happened later on the morning that Peter Sutcliffe drove back from Manchester.

Carol Wilkinson was on her way to work. She was twenty years old, and had lived almost all her life on the Ravenscliffe council estate, less than five miles from Garden Lane, Heaton, on Bradford's eastern edges and even closer to the premises of T. & W. H. Clark, where Peter Sutcliffe clocked on for work.

When she was four, Carol's mother and father had separated; her mother then married again, bringing a new adult into her young daughter's life. As Carol grew up, she rowed frequently with her stepfather, George Wilkinson. Home life became increasingly fraught, particularly after her sister – seven years older than Carol – moved out in 1967.

At the age of sixteen, Carol left school and got a job in Empire Stores, then a giant of the mail-order shopping trade, based in Bradford. The job didn't last and in 1974 she secured a position as a clerk in the wholesale department of another Bradford institution – Almond's Bakery. This offered the distinct advantage of being much closer to her house on Ravenscliffe.

Between 9 and 9.30 a.m. on the morning of Monday, 10 October 1977, Carol set off from home to walk to work. She had argued once again with her stepfather and her commute (as such journeys were now being fashionably termed) had been disrupted by a bus strike – one of an increasing number that year, as the British economy grew ever weaker. She had no choice but to walk, and she took a shortcut down a lonely lane across a field off Woodhall Road. It should not have been a dangerous journey: it was, after all, broad daylight and the lane ran close to the back of the bakery buildings.

Shortly before 10 a.m., a man taking the same shortcut found Carol lying face down in a pool of blood. She had been battered about the back of her head – with either a walling hammer or a rock – and partially stripped: her trousers and pants had been pulled down and her bra lifted up.

The incident had evidently happened just a few minutes earlier – indeed, there was some evidence that the man who stumbled on Carol's dying body had disturbed the attacker, causing him to run away.

By the time police and ambulance crews arrived, Carol was barely alive: she was rushed to hospital, where surgeons discovered multiple skull fractures and severe brain damage. After two days on a life-support machine, her doctors concluded that Carol's brain had ceased to function. The machine was switched off that morning: Carol died shortly afterwards.

The investigation of Carol's murder was overseen by one of West Yorkshire Police's most experienced detectives: Detective Superintendent Jim Hobson – the officer who had been in charge of the attack on Tracy Browne as well as the hunt for the killer of Irene Richardson and Jayne MacDonald. Despite the evident similarities between these attacks and the events that Monday morning, a decision was taken to exclude Carol Wilkinson's death from the growing list of Ripper victims. Once again, the obsessive belief that the Ripper targeted only prostitutes (Jayne MacDonald notwithstanding) drowned out the screamingly obvious evidence of pattern, criminal signature and MO.

Had the detectives kept a rather more open mind, they might well have discovered that a man called Peter William Sutcliffe – a man, we should remember, with a criminal record for attacking women and going equipped with a hammer – was known to have argued violently with Carol's stepfather. Ravenscliffe residents, who would later talk openly to the press, could have told them that in the summer of 1976 – just a year before Carol's murder

– Sutcliffe had carried out odd jobs for families on the estate. This, perhaps, is how he came to fall foul of George Wilkinson: what is certain is that at some point during that year Wilkinson threatened to beat up Sutcliffe – apparently for trying to pick up Carol. Not that this appeared to have stopped Sutcliffe hanging around the estate. In February 1977, residents reported his suspicious presence on Langdale Road – the street where the Wilkinsons lived – to the local police station.

Motive, means, opportunity – the holy trinity of any police investigation. Peter Sutcliffe had all three – as well as a criminal record for attacking women in exactly the way Carol Wilkinson was bludgeoned into fatal unconsciousness.

Within three weeks, two detective constables called at Number 6 Garden Lane, Heaton, and asked to speak with Sutcliffe. But they were not investigating the Wilkinson murder: instead, they were following up leads from the ongoing Jean Jordan case.

Jean's badly decomposed body had been discovered where Sutcliffe left her around noon on Monday, 10 October – at almost exactly the time when surgeons were fighting in vain to save Carol Wilkinson's life. Five days later, a fingertip search located her handbag a hundred yards further into the waste ground. The brand-new £5 Bank of England note was still in its hidden compartment.

The serial number on the note was AW51 121565. Manchester detectives traced it back to a consignment of bank notes sent to the Shipley and Bingley branches of the Midland Bank. The bank had distributed the money – a total of £17,500 – to firms throughout the local area: these, in turn, had used the cash in weekly pay packets for their employees.

It was – as Sutcliffe had feared – a piece of evidence that would, eventually, bring detectives to his door. Although the pool of potential suspects was huge – more than 8,000 men had received notes from the consignment, and there was no way of knowing which one had been given the one bearing serial number AW51 121565 – a combined team of officers from West Yorkshire and Manchester assiduously worked through each and every one. Which is what led them to the detached house on Garden Lane on the morning of 2 November 1977.

Both Peter and Sonia Sutcliffe were at home. The detectives asked first whether Sutcliffe still had any of the £5 notes from his wage packet: he told them he did not. Next they questioned the couple about Peter's movements on 1 October and 9 October. Peter told them he had been at home on the first date and holding the housewarming party on the second: Sonia corroborated this account. Neither of them mentioned the fact that, after the party, Sutcliffe had driven his parents home and not returned for several hours. Satisfied, the police left it at that. It would not be the last time officers visited 6 Garden Lane; nor would it be the last time the interviews in Sutcliffe's home failed to flag him up as the Ripper.

Nor was this the only blunder. By the time the two officers visited the Sutcliffes that November, the monumental investigation to track down the tyres that had left marks at the scenes of his previous attacks had finally been abandoned. It had been a vast and time-consuming exercise: for almost six months, officers had painstakingly examined the records of more than 30,000 vehicles that could potentially have had the tyres fitted. But after the attack on Maureen Long in July – and with the registration documents of 20,000 cars still to check – Detective

Superintendent Jim Hobson (once again the man at the top of the investigative chain) took the decision to shut down the exercise. It was simply too big a drain on West Yorkshire Police's already overstretched resources.

One of those 20,000 cars was Peter Sutcliffe's red Ford Corsair. On 2 November 1977, it was parked on, or close to, the driveway at Garden Lane. Not only did the two detectives not take the time to make a routine check of its tyres, but when they filed their report they stated that Sutcliffe did not own a vehicle.

By December, the police were no closer to catching the Ripper than they had been three years earlier. Nor, having excluded Carol Wilkinson from their list of victims, did their colleagues have any promising leads for her murder. It would be another eighteen months before a young and mentally handicapped man was charged with killing her. And it would take a further twenty-two years for this poor innocent to have his conviction quashed.

As Christmas approached, Peter Sutcliffe could count 1977 as a very satisfying year. In less than twelve months he had definitely murdered at least four – and most probably nine – women and attempted to kill one more. Nor was the year finished.

In late November or early December, another prostitute was attacked by a man in a multistorey car park in Doncaster. She survived the attack – and South Yorkshire Police has never named her, described her injuries or brought the man responsible to justice. What is known, however, is that the woman gave a clear description and produced a photofit: it showed a man around thirty-five years old, tall, of slim build with brushed-back dark hair and a beard and moustache. She also told police that she had seen the same man on another occasion, driving away from a Doncaster lorry park. The parallels with the murder of Barbara Young earlier in the year were striking – and so was the photofit. It matched closely those already adorning the walls of the Ripper inquiry offices at Millgarth police station in Leeds. But, although it was published in the local South Yorkshire press, it didn't come to the attention of the Ripper team. Another potentially vital witness had been missed.

Then, on Wednesday, 14 December, Sutcliffe struck again.

Around 8 p.m., Marilyn Moore was touting for business. She was twenty-five, the mother of two young children (neither of whom lived with her) and had been working the streets in London, Slough, Bradford and Leeds for six years, clocking up one conviction for soliciting.

Marilyn's regular 'beat' was the red-light district of Chapeltown. As she slowly walked down Gipton Avenue, she saw a car being driven in the slow and careful way that suggested a punter looking for a woman. As she passed into Spencer Place, the car passed by her. In anticipation that the driver would turn around and come back, she crossed the road and turned right on to Leopold Street. At the junction with Frankland Place, she saw the car parked at the kerb and a man standing beside the driver's door: he appeared to be waving to someone in a nearby house.

Marilyn got a good look at both the car – a dark-red saloon – and the man. He was aged about thirty, about five feet six inches tall, with dark wavy hair, and a full beard and a moustache that reminded her of Jason King, the secret agent hero of a then popular TV series.

Sutcliffe approached her and asked if she was 'doing business': they quickly agreed a price and her customer volunteered that he knew a 'right queer place' for sex on some spare ground at Scott Hall Street, about a mile and a half away. As they drove off, he told her that his name was Dave and the person he had been waving to was his girlfriend.

'Dave' suggested that they have sex on the back seat but when Marilyn got out of the front passenger door she found that the rear door was locked. As he came up behind her on the pretext of opening the door, he struck a sickening blow on the top of her head. Marilyn screamed loudly and with her hands attempted to protect her head from more damage: as she fell to the ground, frantically grabbing at her attacker's trousers, she felt further blows before collapsing into unconsciousness.

Marilyn Moore was saved by a dog heard barking nearby. As with Maureen Long in July and Jean Jordan in October, Sutcliffe was panicked into abandoning his attempted killing. He ran back to the car, slammed the door and gunned the motor so fiercely that the rear wheels locked into a skid. It left behind tyre tracks that matched those found at the scene of Irene Richardson's murder. The crime scene also had distinct similarities to the murder of Rosina Hilliard in 1974: there, too, the killer's desperation to get away caused him to spin his wheels, leaving deep gouges on the ground.

When Marilyn regained consciousness, she staggered towards the road to get to a telephone and help. When she reached the road, a couple saw her and the man ran to phone for an ambulance, and she was taken to Leeds Infirmary for emergency surgery. Surgeons found that she had been hit eight times with the hammer and had bruises on her hands where she had tried to protect her head. Only an intricate operation to relieve the pressure on her brain from a depressed fracture kept her breathing.

Due to the severity of her injuries, the police thought that Marilyn's description of her suspect might not be reliable. In fact, her photofit impressions were a startlingly good likeness and matched every one of those prepared by Sutcliffe's other victims – including those for which he would never face justice. Among that list were the names of Tracy Browne and Debbie Schlesinger.

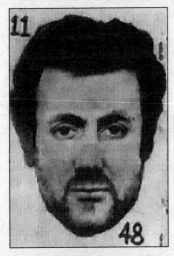

The confusion seemed to sum up a year in which Peter Sutcliffe had attacked and murdered with increasing regularity – and one in which the shortcomings and blunders of police investigations left him free to carry on killing. It was a pattern that would continue from the very start of 1978.

Photofit of Marilyn Moore attacker

FIFTEEN

HOT AND COLD IN YORKSHIRE

Nora Browne marched up the steps into Keighley police station and asked to speak with a detective. When the photofit of Marilyn Moore's attacker was published, her daughter, Tracy, had recognised it instantly as the man who had smashed a hammer into her head on the moors above Silsden two and a half years earlier. Now mother and daughter tried to persuade the young constable on the front desk to listen. They were not successful.

The uniformed officer looked them up and down and dismissed their pleas to be heard with a flippant and remarkably callous response: 'We're all having fun and games today, aren't we?'

Had that constable taken Tracy seriously, West Yorkshire Police might have avoided the succession of mistakes it would make throughout the coming year – and the Ripper might have been caught before continuing his bloody reign of terror.

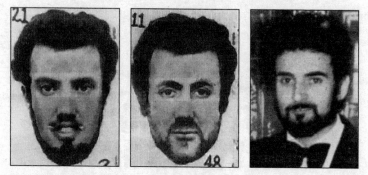

Tracy Browne, 1975/ Marilyn Moore, 1977/ Sutcliffe, 1974

As the bitterly cold month of January 1978 wore on, the investigators hunting for him had begun to wonder if their quarry had gone to ground. As far as they were aware, no new victims had been reported: could the killer have been scared into inactivity by the failed attempt on Marilyn Moore and the possibility that she might be able to identify him? They could not have known that, even as they speculated, another young woman was about to die.

Yvonne Anne Pearson was reported missing on Sunday, 22 January. She had left her terraced home in Heaton – just a few hundred yards away from Garden Lane – the previous evening, entrusting the care of her two young children to a babysitter; Colette was aged two, Lorraine just five months. It was a Saturday night and the slightly built twenty-one-year-old platinum blonde had two things on her mind: a few drinks in the local pub, followed by the prospect of earning some money on the streets of Manningham's red-light district. At 9.30 p.m., she left the Flying Dutchman on Leeds Road. She would not be seen alive again.

Yvonne knew the dangers of her business only too well.

One of her friends had recently been attacked while servicing a punter in a London hotel, and she had also been on drinking terms with Tina Atkinson in the months before her murder in April 1977. Nor was it only clients threatening Yvonne: she had already served one term of imprisonment for prostitution and had recently been arrested again. She had been summoned to appear before Bradford magistrates on 26 January, and the likelihood of being sent back to jail was extremely high. But with money in short supply – and despite confiding in a neighbour that it 'would be just my luck to get knocked on the head' – she made her way towards Lumb Lane and the heart of Bradford's vice area.

That Saturday night, Peter Sutcliffe helped his parents move into a new home in the centre of Bingley. His brother, Mick, and his father, John, suggested a drink, but Peter – apparently anxious to get home to Sonia – turned them down.

He did not, however, return to Garden Lane. Instead, he took the main road from Bingley to Bradford and was soon cruising through Manningham. He quickly spotted Yvonne Pearson and pulled up a few yards ahead of her. She walked up to his car and they agreed on a price of £5. Sutcliffe drove to a stretch of waste ground behind Drummond's Mill – where his father worked – and they climbed out of his vehicle. Within seconds, Sutcliffe hit Yvonne repeatedly on the back of her head with a either a lump of masonry or with a heavy walling hammer, which he had slyly taken from under his car seat.

But before he could continue, another car pulled up alongside his. Sutcliffe hurriedly pulled Yvonne's limp body into the cover of an old discarded sofa, and, since his victim was gurgling, grabbed handfuls of horsehair from it, which he stuffed into her mouth. As he pushed the wadding deep down her throat, he pinched her nose closed. After a while, he released his grip to see if she was still making a noise: she was, so he grabbed and squeezed it tight once more.

Finally, the other car pulled away and off the derelict ground. Alone with his victim at last, he pulled down her trousers, bared her breasts, and started kicking her in the head and body. Next, he jumped down on her chest with the weight of both feet until her ribs cracked. Finally, he hid Yvonne Pearson's corpse by covering it with soil, rubble and turf, before pulling the old sofa on top of the pile.

When news of Yvonne's disappearance became public, newspapers speculated that she was latest prostitute to be claimed by the serial killer prowling the red-light districts of Bradford and Leeds. But anxious as ever not to risk contaminating their already overwhelming investigation, police played down the likelihood of Yvonne Pearson being a Ripper victim.

Yvonne's body would lie, undetected, in the filth and rubble of her makeshift grave for another two months. By the time she was found, Peter Sutcliffe had struck again.

Helen and Rita Rytka were twins. The daughters of an Italian mother and Jamaican father, both worked as prostitutes in Huddersfield's small red-light area, and had worked out a system by which each would keep a careful eye on the other as they serviced the men who picked them up for sex.

Tuesday, 31 January was a bleak and snowy night. Despite the weather, both girls were out working their 'beat' amid the railway arches and timber yards of Great Northern Street. At 9.25 p.m., Sutcliffe was cruising the area: he spotted Helen on her way back to the place where she was due to rendezvous with her sister. This was the system the twins had worked out: every twenty minutes, they met up at the public lavatories. Helen had a few minutes to spare before Rita was due and Sutcliffe persuaded her to get into his car. They drove to Garrod's Timber Yard near the railway, a common haunt of prostitutes and their clients.

He suggested they have sex on the back seat and, as Helen began climbing in through the rear passenger door, he swung his hammer. For once his aim was inaccurate: the blow caught the roof of the car and then only grazed Helen.

When she said, 'What was that?' he replied, 'Just a small sample of one of these', and then hit her again on the head with the hammer: she collapsed on the ground and began making a loud moaning noise. But Sutcliffe suddenly realised that he was in full view of two taxi drivers parked nearby: they had not yet noticed what was happening, but that was likely to change if Helen continued to moan.

He grabbed her by the hair and dragged her to the end of the wood yard. Although she was no longer making a noise, he could see that she wasn't yet dead: her eyes were open and she had raised her hands to ward off further blows. He climbed on top of her struggling body and covered her mouth with his hand: he told her to keep quiet and she would be all right. He then had sex with her as she lay bleeding to death.

Eventually, the taxi drivers left. Sutcliffe got up and went to retrieve the hammer. As he moved away, Helen staggered to her feet and attempted to escape. As she ran across the snowy ground, Sutcliffe hit her several more times on the back of her head. Then he took a kitchen knife from the car and stabbed her repeatedly through the heart and lungs.

Finally satisfied, he hid her corpse in a patch of undergrowth and drove back to Garden Lane: here he sponged Helen's blood from his shoes and the knife, before carefully replacing it in the kitchen drawer.

Rita Rytka was, understandably, alarmed when her sister did not show up at their rendezvous – and even more terrified when there was no sign of her the next day. But she was also frightened of the police and how they would treat an eighteen-year-old sex worker. As a result, she did not report Helen missing until Thursday, 2 February. A police dog found her body the following day behind a stack of timber and concealed beneath a sheet of corrugated asbestos – just as Judith Roberts had been discovered five and a half years earlier in lonely Comberford Lane, Wigginton. As with Gloria Booth, Helen Rytka's clothes were scattered over a wide area and – another key similarity – she was naked apart from her bra and black polo-neck jumper.

In the immediate aftermath of Helen's murder, the national press turned its attention to the spate of killings. The tabloid phrase 'The Yorkshire Ripper' made its first appearance: for the next three years, it would be repeated with growing frequency. The pressure was now growing ever more intense on the men leading what journalists dubbed 'Britain's biggest manhunt'. George Oldfield took the strategic decision to use the media interest to appeal for help from both the public and the Ripper himself.

Immediately after the discovery of the body in the timber yard, Oldfield appeared live on Jimmy Young's mid-morning BBC radio show – then the most listened-to programme on the national airwaves. He told listeners that he was certain someone in Yorkshire was shielding the killer – or at least had suspicions that had not been reported to police. And he coined a phrase that would forever be associated with the investigation.

> The Ripper is someone's neighbour and he is someone's husband or son.

Shortly after this dramatic appearance, Oldfield used a local television documentary to speak directly to the man he was hunting. Speaking slowly and with apparent confidence, he said:

> We are getting nearer and nearer to you and it is only a matter of time before you are caught. In your own interests and in the interests of the relatives and friends of past victims; in the interests of your own relatives and friends; and in the interests of any potential future victims, it is now time for you to come forward and give yourself up.
>
> The net is closing. I am anxious that we catch you before you have time to add another death to the appalling catalogue that you already have to your credit.

It was a bravura performance from a man who – whatever the failings of the investigation he led – was genuinely haunted by the serial murderer roaming the streets of Yorkshire with apparent impunity. Unfortunately, it fell on deaf ears.

By Oldfield's own count, the Ripper had killed six prostitutes. This did not include Yvonne Pearson, whose body still lay rotting and undetected behind Drummond's Mill in Manningham. Nor did it take account of the succession of earlier attacks and murders on women – many of them with no connection to the vice trade – up and down the country. As West Yorkshire Police

Chief Constable Ronald Gregory reorganised the investigation team, forming it into the Prostitute Murder Squad, these were firmly ruled out of the burgeoning inquiry. Even had a national intelligence system been functioning that winter of 1978, Oldfield's team was convinced the immutable element of the Ripper's MO was an obsession with killing women who worked the streets.

Ironically, this decision could – indeed should – have yielded vital evidence. The new Prostitute Murder Squad began undercover operations to record the number plates of cars kerb-crawling in the red-light districts of Leeds, Bradford and Huddersfield. The intelligence thus gained would be used as justification subsequently to visit and question the drivers in their homes.

It is a mark of men's grim and relentless determination to buy sexual services from the desperate women forced by poverty or cruel circumstance to prostitute themselves that these covert patrols were quickly swamped by the sheer number of vehicles. So great was this flow of callous traffic that the police were forced to abandon the time-consuming practice of physically writing the number plates down in their notebooks and to dictate them instead into pocket cassette recorders.

It was, to some extent, an operation born of desperation. And yet it would throw up Peter Sutcliffe's name and lead to new visits by detectives to Number 6 Garden Lane. But these, like the interview following Jean Jordan's murder, were destined to be bungled.

Before then, however, Oldfield's team had a new body to contend with. On Sunday, 26 March, Yvonne Pearson's rotting body was found on wasteland off Lumb Lane in Bradford. A passer-by noticed an arm sticking out from under an old sofa. He gingerly crept closer to what he believed must be a discarded tailor's dummy: the strong smell of putrid flesh quickly chased that assumption from his mind.

When they arrived, the police faced several puzzles. Since the dead woman's arm was sticking out, how could the body not have been discovered earlier? Then there was the evidence of putrefaction: this clearly indicated that she had been dead for several months: yet a copy of the *Daily Mirror*, dated 21 February, was tucked under one of her arms: the killer must have returned to the scene of his crime. It also looked as if it had been deliberately placed there as some form of bizarre 'staging' of the crime scene.

But the biggest question was whether this was a Yorkshire Ripper murder. The post-mortem revealed massive head wounds, but Home Office pathologist Professor David Gee's examination led him to believe they had been caused by a boulder, not a hammer. Additionally, although the victim's clothing had been arranged in typical Ripper fashion – her bra and sweater pulled up to expose her breasts, her trousers dragged down – there weren't any of the stab wounds that marked his other assumed killings. As a result, the police initially discounted Yvonne Pearson as a Ripper victim. Only later would they include her in his catalogue of murders and attacks.

But in the patient and thorough notes filed away in the files of the Bradford coroner's office there was one other crucial piece of information. It was the conclusion that the murders of Yvonne Pearson and Carol Wilkinson were linked: whoever had murdered one had also killed the other. It was a remarkable finding – formal and official – and yet West Yorkshire Police would somehow either overlook or ignore it. The result would – eighteen months later – be the conviction of an innocent man for Carol's death.

But in any event, by the time Yvonne Pearson's body was discovered, West Yorkshire Police had received the first in a series of missives that would, ultimately, completely misdirect the entire Ripper investigation. On Thursday, 9 March 1978, a letter arrived at Millgarth: addressed to 'Chief Constable George Oldfield' (he was, in fact, Assistant Chief Constable) at 'Central Police Station, Leeds', it had been posted the day before in Sunderland.

Dear Sir

I am sorry I cannot give my name for obvious reasons. I am the Ripper. I've been dubbed a maniac by the Press but not by you, you call me clever and I am. You and your mates haven't a clue. That photo in the paper gave me fits and that bit about killing myself, no chance. I've got things to do. My purpose to rid the streets of them sluts. My one regret is that young lassie McDonald, did not know cause changed routine that nite.

Up to number 8 now you say 7 but remember Preston '75, get about you know. You were right I travel a bit. You probably look for me in Sunderland, don't bother, I am not daft, just posted letter there on one of my trips. Not a bad place compared with Chapeltown and Manningham and other places. Warn whores to keep off streets cause I feel it coming on again.

Sorry about young lassie.
Yours respectfully
Jack the Ripper

Might write again later I not sure last one really deserved
it. Whores getting younger each time. Old slut next time
I hope. Huddersfield never again, too small close call last
one.

The letter, with its absence of punctuation and erratic spelling,
bore all the hallmarks of a crank: certainly, Oldfield's initial
instinct was to view it as the product of a deranged mind with
no connection to the Ripper. But two elements gave him pause
for thought. The first was that it fitted the profile that had been
assigned to the serial killer – a man obsessed with attacking
prostitutes. The second was the reference to 'Preston '75': there
had indeed been a murder there in that year, which had – briefly
– been considered as a possible case for Oldfield's squad. But the
killing of Joan Harrison – brutal though it was – had ultimately
been ruled out as a possible Ripper murder: because of this no
one had publicly linked it with the manhunt being run from
Millgarth. Oldfield checked with his colleagues in Sunderland
whether the handwriting matched any known local oddballs: it
didn't and there were no fingerprints on either letter or envelope.
He decided to put it to one side for the moment.

Five days later, a second missive was posted from Sunderland:
it was clearly the same handwriting and once again the author
made claims of responsibility. But this time he posted his note
to the Manchester office of the *Daily Mirror*.

Dear Sir

I have already written to Chief Constable [sic] George Oldfield 'a man I respect' concerning the recent Ripper murders. I told him and I am telling you to warn them whores I'll strike again and soon when heat cools off. About the MacDonald lassie, I didn't know that she was decent and I am sorry I changed my routine that night.

Up to number 8 now you say seven but remember Preston '75. Easy picking them up don't even have to try you think they're learn but they don't. Most are young lassies, next time try older one I hope. Police haven't a clue yet and I don't leave any I am very clever and don't look for me up there in Sunderland cause I not stupid just passed through the place not a bad place compared with Chapeltown and Manningham. Can't walk the streets for them whores. Don't forget warn them I feel it coming on again. If I get chance sorry about lassie I didn't know.

Yours respectfully

Jack the Ripper

Might write again after another week gone maybe Liverpool or even Manchester again. To hot here in Yorkshire. Bye. I have given advance warning so its yours and their fault.

The newspaper was persuaded not to publish the letter and Oldfield still harboured doubts about the sanity of its writer. It joined the previous note in a securely locked filing cabinet. But, however much the detective suspected they were the work of a deranged fantasist, they would, in twelve months, come to dictate the course of the Ripper investigation – and to send it on a fatal wild goose chase.

In the meantime, Peter Sutcliffe continued to add to his grim tally of victims.

Vera Millward was not a well woman. She was forty, the mother of seven children and had undergone three major operations in 1976 and 1977. She had only one lung and suffered from chronic stomach pains; yet she eked out a miserable living as a prostitute working the run-down streets of Moss Side and Hulme – two of the roughest council estates in Manchester.

On Tuesdays and Thursdays, she had a regular client who would usually park outside her flat in Greenham Avenue and flash his car headlights. On the night of Tuesday, 16 May, he didn't show up; Vera decided instead to try her luck with the steady procession of cars that kerb-crawled through the area. Just before 11 p.m., she encountered Peter Sutcliffe. She climbed into his red Ford Corsair.

They drove for about two and a half miles to the Manchester Royal Infirmary and a quiet spot in a parking compound regularly used by the local prostitutes to service clients.

After getting out of the car, Sutcliffe struck Vera three times on the back of the head. He then undressed her in what, by now, was his regular fashion, before slashing her so viciously across the stomach that her intestines spewed out. He then stabbed her repeatedly in the back, plunging the knife in and out of the same wound. Next he punctured her right eyelid. During this ordeal Vera screamed for help; her desperate pleas were heard by a man taking his son to the hospital: he thought it was a patient inside having a nightmare and ignored them.

As Vera Millward's life ebbed away, Sutcliffe dragged her twelve feet across the car park and dumped her on a rubbish pile by a chain-link fence. He positioned the corpse, carefully laying Vera face down with her arms folded beneath her, legs straight and her shoes placed neatly on her body. He then climbed back into the Corsair and drove off into the night.

The body was found shortly after eight the next morning by workers arriving at the hospital to tend its gardens. While unloading tools from the back of one of their vans, they spotted what looked like a tailor's dummy lying near a temporary fence. When one of the men walked over to take a closer look, he was horrified to realise that it was a dead woman.

Police took impressions of tyre tracks found nearby: these matched the murder scenes of both Irene Richardson and Marilyn Moore. Together with the distinctive injuries inflicted, they were unequivocal evidence that the Yorkshire Ripper had crossed the Pennines once more and killed in Manchester for a second time. Vera Millward's name was added to the growing mountain being climbed by Oldfield and his team in Leeds.

The Ripper investigation had, by this stage, completely outgrown West Yorkshire Police's abilities and resources. Nor was this surprising: not only had it become Britain's biggest – and longest-lasting – manhunt, but the nature of its quarry was something completely new to most detectives. Here was a man who evidently killed for the sheer pleasure to be found in death, and who did so seemingly at random. Complex and ambitious enquiries – like the one to trace the tyres and the cars they fitted – had been attempted but eventually abandoned. The running cost of the investigation had now reached more than £1.5 million just for overtime, transport and additional office facilities: this was in addition to wages for the several hundred detectives assigned exclusively to Ripper duties.

There were also less tangible – but equally serious – knock-on effects. The overall area crime rate had risen 17 per cent since the hunt for the serial killer had begun, and fewer 'ordinary' criminals were being caught. Morale was ebbing away fast: police officers were resigning from the force in unprecedented numbers because of the unbearable demands of the Ripper investigation on them. Something needed to change.

Ronald Gregory came from three generations of police officers. He began his own career as a beat constable in 1941 and had been West Yorkshire Chief Constable since 1969. Now faced with a murder spree of (in his own words) 'epic proportions', and convinced that without a retooling of the massive investigative effort the Ripper would carry on killing with impunity, he set up a new elite group of the most experienced senior detectives in the region. Although it would still be under the overall command of George Oldfield, he appointed Detective Chief Superintendent John Domaille head of the super-unit. To emphasise the implicit change, Domaille's team was given its own offices, set apart from the Ripper incident room in Millgarth. The plaque on the squad's door read 'Special Homicide Investigation Team': in the fevered atmosphere of panic, overwork and recrimination it was – unsurprisingly – referred to as 'the SHIT Squad'.

Domaille had been the senior investigating officer on Patricia Atkinson's murder. He had come to West Yorkshire some years earlier from Devon and Cornwall Police and settled his family in Wakefield. He felt the burden placed on him by Gregory acutely: it was – plainly – the most important job of his career to date. But he also had very personal reasons for it to consume his every waking thought: his twenty-one-year-old daughter was a trainee nurse at Leeds General Infirmary, and she shared a flat with other student nurses in Chapeltown – the heart of Ripper territory. Like any responsible father, he worried constantly for her safety.

The task at hand, though, was not made easier by the traditional Yorkshire resentment of 'an outsider' being brought in – especially since Domaille was charged with reviewing the way the inquiry had operated, with the hope of discovering how and why it had failed. Some of the most senior officers inside West Yorkshire Police saw his appointment as a snub to George Oldfield – a man to whom, for all his inability to catch the Ripper, they were intensely loyal. Nonetheless, Domaille set about a root and branch examination of the nine known murders as well as those that, though very similar, had been rejected by the Ripper Squad.

As a result, in June 1978, details of all suspected Ripper attacks were published in a confidential criminal intelligence special bulletin. The number of murders attributed to the serial killer rose to ten, with the 1975 Preston prostitute case being (incorrectly, as it happened) added: four attempted murders – Anna Rogulskyj, Olive Smelt, Maureen Long and Marilyn Moore (though not poor Tracy Browne or Marcella Claxton) were also included. For the first time, West Yorkshire Police faced up to the terrifying possibility that there could be many more victims: more importantly, the bulletin was circulated to all police forces throughout the country. This should have spurred detectives in Derbyshire, Leicestershire, Staffordshire, the Met and Essex to re-examine their own unsolved cases for any similarities – particularly in MO or criminal signature. There is no evidence that any did.

Domaille's work also produced the next – potentially vital – lead. On 19 June 1978, fixed observation points were set up in the red-light districts of Leeds, Manchester, Sheffield and Hull. Officers watched for cars crawling up and down the streets, their occupants clearly searching for prostitutes, and sent details of the number plates back to base. Desk-bound officers then fed the results into the Police National Computer at Hendon: if the same vehicle was identified as having been seen in two of the separate areas where observations were in progress, the car's owner was marked down for a visit from Ripper Squad detectives.

Peter Sutcliffe's red Ford Corsair was duly noted as having been spotted in the Chapeltown area of Leeds and the Manningham area of Bradford, and on 13 August police once again arrived at Number 6 Garden Lane. The detective who interviewed him was the same officer who had seen him during the £5 note enquiry and he knew Sutcliffe was a lorry driver. This time Sutcliffe denied having visited Leeds or any other West Yorkshire towns at night in the relevant period. When told that his Corsair had been recorded there, Sutcliffe explained that he had bought a grey Sunbeam Rapier in May and was exclusively driving that vehicle: for good measure, he said that he had sold the Corsair at the start of August.

Both of those statements were strictly true (though the exact date Sutcliffe disposed of the Ford remains open to question). The same interviewing officer later visited the new owner of the red Ford Corsair: he confirmed that he had fitted four new tyres upon acquiring it. Another line of cross-enquiry petered out.

By now, Peter Sutcliffe's name had cropped up several times and he had been the subject of a series of interviews. Despite this, no one appears to have compared the details of his convictions with the profile of the man being sought for the Ripper murders – much less compared his heavily bearded face with the identikits that a succession of his victims had prepared. Had they done so, much pain – and more deaths – could have been avoided.

But how effective was the enormous effort being expended on basic police legwork? In September 1978, it emerged that a number of detectives had not been completing some enquiries allocated to them correctly: after an internal audit team checked a sample of just 10 per cent of the completed enquiries, finding glaring omissions and errors, two detectives resigned from the force and a further thirteen were subjected to disciplinary action. It did not bode well.

Nor was West Yorkshire Police any nearer to closing in on its man. Despite the bravado of his radio appeal, George Oldfield had no more clue as to the likely profile of the Ripper – the key to finding him – than he had at the beginning of the year.

He had, though, formulated a number of theories that he took for evaluation to Dr Stephen Shaw, a psychiatrist at Stanley Royd Hospital in Wakefield. Perhaps, the Assistant Chief Constable suggested, the Ripper was suffering from general paralysis of the insane (GPI) – the third and invariably final stage of syphilis infection? If he had contracted the disease from a prostitute, might this explain his desire to kill them?

Dr Shaw indicated that GPI was a highly unlikely diagnosis, since sufferers most usually experienced symptoms of dementia – premature old age – not consistent with being able to undertake a prolonged and remarkably cunning series of murders. Nor did he support Oldfield's alternative theory of schizophrenia: if the Ripper was a schizophrenic, his behaviour would (as had been the case with Sonia Sutcliffe) have attracted attention, and he would almost certainly be receiving some form of medical treatment as a result. All in all, Oldfield's genuinely valiant attempt at psychoanalysing his quarry had led – like every other police effort – nowhere.

By November 1978, Oldfield and Domaille were facing a new puzzle: the Ripper appeared to have gone quiet. There had been no murders since Vera Millward was found in May: why would so prolific a serial killer suddenly call a halt to his career?

In the pages of the *Yorkshire Post*, Dr Stephen Shaw offered his thoughts. The Ripper was, in his clinical opinion, an over-controlled aggressive psychopath; a man who would usually appear quiet, who would look and act normally until subjected to some form of pressure. This could then trigger a new murderous attack.

But Dr Shaw also offered the possibility that the Ripper had simply grown out of the personality disorder that had led him to kill.

We know for a fact that at the age of about 35 personality disorders can mature and sometimes settle down forever. That could happen with this man, and we might never hear of him again. I don't want to tempt fate but it is a possibility.

Though Dr Shaw could not have known it, at precisely the time he was sharing his opinions with *Yorkshire Post* readers, a traumatic event occurred in Peter Sutcliffe's life. On 8 November 1978, his mother, Kathleen, died: after four years battling with angina, she finally succumbed to a myocardial infarction. Her funeral took place six days later on 14 November.

There is no question that Kathleen's passing hit Sutcliffe hard.

He had always been intensely close to her in childhood and had remained so even after his marriage to Sonia. His brother, Michael, would later tell journalists:

> There was no doubt that Peter was closer to her than any of us. He was heartbroken when she died: it really upset him.

A fortnight after Kathleen Sutcliffe was interred, another young woman was attacked. On Tuesday, 28 November, an eighteen-year-old addressograph operator (an addressograph was a pre-computer-age machine for stamping addresses on envelopes) was walking through Bradford in the gloom of the early evening. She found herself being followed along the street by a man who suddenly grabbed her by the hair. In the ensuing struggle, she managed to throw a brick at him and he ran off. She had, however, got a good look at her attacker and was able to describe him clearly: 'Male, thirty years old, slim build; dark straggly hair below the shoulders; a mandarin moustache and a goatee beard.' Detectives helped her assemble a photofit of the man who, quite plainly, resembled the serial killer being sought for the Ripper murders. Despite this, the attack was not brought into the Ripper investigations and another opportunity for photofit comparison was lost.

As 1978 drew to an end, the bitterest winter for more than a decade was waiting in the wings. And the all-consuming manhunt for the Yorkshire Ripper was about to take a completely wrong turn. It was a mistake that would allow Peter Sutcliffe to roam free, killing at will for another two years. And it would also falsely condemn a young and vulnerable man to half a lifetime in prison for one of the Ripper's murders.

SIXTEEN
'I'M JACK'

The murder of poor, sick Vera Millward marked a fundamental change in the Ripper series. By the official account of his crimes, Peter Sutcliffe would kill at least four more women – in all probability the total would be nine – as well as attempting to dispatch another six. But never again would he attack a prostitute. His targets in 1979 and 1980 would all be what George Oldfield thought of as 'innocent' victims.

The start of 1979 saw the heaviest snow in Bradford for thirty years. This was promptly followed by a national lorry drivers' strike: together the weather and industrial action – the first signs of the Winter of Discontent – gave Sutcliffe an extended Christmas holiday. The heavy snowfalls eased off after a week – though they would return throughout the ensuing months, frequently blanketing much of Britain until late spring – allowing T. & W. H. Clark to resume its pattern of nationwide deliveries.

Sutcliffe was one of the firm's most conscientious drivers – an apparently model employee who kept immaculate logs and repair records. To his workmates he seemed something of a loner, but unlike the stereotype of a truck driver he didn't swear or speak crudely about women at work, much less display any inclination towards violence. True, he christened his lorry 'Wee Willie', but this was a source of amusement rather than cause for suspicion.

In short, Peter Sutcliffe was well liked both by his bosses and by his colleagues. He was celebrated for his ability to rope-and-sheet large and often difficult loads; and he was also the driver to whom others turned for advice whenever they had to make a delivery to an unfamiliar town. Sutcliffe seemed to have *A–Z* street maps for every possible destination.

The nature of his delivery duties meant that it was perfectly normal for Sutcliffe to be away from home three nights a week, returning during the afternoon of the fourth day; this would prove to be a significant factor in understanding a succession of (still unsolved) attacks on unaccompanied women throughout Britain during 1979 and 1980.

One of his regular deliveries was to the LEP transport depot just off the A2 at Charlton, in London. Sutcliffe knew the area well, having lived in neighbouring Deptford when Sonia was at teacher training college in the early 1970s. The records of his work journeys have never been released by West Yorkshire Police, but it is entirely conceivable that he was in London when Lynda Farrow was murdered on Monday, 19 January 1979.

Lynda was twenty-nine; a mother of two children – one aged eleven, the other eight – that January, she was four months into her third pregnancy. She worked as a croupier at the International Sporting Club, a popular West End gambling spot, and finished her shift early that afternoon. After a shopping trip with her mother, at 2.40 p.m., she returned alone to her home in Whitehall Road, Woodford Green, East London.

As she got there, it appears the phone was ringing. Lynda rushed to answer it, leaving the front door ajar: her killer took the opportunity to follow her inside. Two schoolgirls passing by heard a shriek before the door was slammed shut.

Twenty minutes later, her daughters arrived home. A lunchtime snowstorm had closed their school early and their unexpected return almost certainly disturbed the killer, forcing him to abandon his attack. The girls knocked repeatedly on the front door, and getting no reply they then looked through the letter box: they saw their mother's body lying face down on the floor in a pool of blood.

The way in which Lynda had died was distinctive and familiar. She had been brutally battered before being stabbed repeatedly. Her killer had then knelt on her back and tried to sever her head with a deliberate sawing action using a serrated knife (identical, as it would turn out, to one of the weapons produced as an exhibit at Peter Sutcliffe's trial). Outside the house, footprints in the snow led to the front door: they were made by heavily ridged size 7 wellington boots.

Detectives from the Metropolitan Police noted the similarities between Lynda's murder and that of Eve Stratford, five miles away in Leyton four years earlier, and that of Kay O'Connor in Colchester in 1974: unsurprisingly, they linked all three cases.

But with little or no contact between the forces in London, West Yorkshire and Manchester, they failed to connect the scene-of-crime evidence in Woodford Green with the Ripper killings. Had they done so, they would have seen that the man who attacked Jean Jordan and mutilated her body had tried to saw off her head, and size 7 wellington boots featured in several of the attacks being investigated by George Oldfield's men.

There were also sightings of a suspect in the Farrow case – a man running up Whitehall Road from Forest Road towards where police believed the killer had parked his car: to any detective even faintly familiar with the Ripper attacks these would distinctly have rung bells. Eyewitnesses reported seeing a man in his thirties, around five feet nine inches tall, with deep-set eye sockets. They also described his distinctive hairstyle: a dark, neat Afro, curly and seemingly flecked with grey, completed by dark sideburns to the bottoms of his ears. While this wasn't quite the full beard of the Ripper photofits, it was snowing so heavily that the true facial picture could easily have been slightly obscured. Certainly, a photofit of Lynda's killer, drawn up by the Met on Thursday, 25 January (though not published in the local newspapers until the following Friday, 2 February), bears an uncanny resemblance to Sutcliffe; and if the sideburns are extended to join into a beard, the picture is remarkably close to the succession of identikit images by then pasted on the walls of Millgarth police station.

Even the vehicle believed to have been used for the killer's getaway was familiar: a white Ford Cortina (easily mistaken for a Corsair) with a black vinyl roof. While Peter Sutcliffe had sold his almost identical car in July 1977, subsequent official investigations would reveal that 'he retained possession of it for some time after that date'. The coincidences are simply too frequent to dismiss.

Photo fit of man seen running up Whitehall Road

Suspect with moustache and beard drawn in like Sutcliffe's

Sutcliffe's 1981 arrest photo

Hampered as they were by the absence of a national intelligence system, the Metropolitan Police might as well have been operating in a different country from the embattled detectives of the Ripper Squad, 200 miles away in Yorkshire. There was simply no way to transfer or share information that could assist both investigations. Still, the man who led the inquiry into Lynda Farrow's murder did get one thing right about her killer: as the case wore on with no sign of a breakthrough – it remains unsolved to this day – he warned:

We are dealing with an extremely sick and dangerous man.
He will get progressively more gruesome and macabre.

But the lack of joined-up policing was not simply the product of geography. The following month, an attack in Harrogate – less than fifteen miles from West Yorkshire Police HQ in Leeds, but under the completely separate jurisdiction of North Yorkshire Police – exemplified the problem.

In the early hours of Sunday, 18 February, a sixteen-year-old student was hit from behind with an all-too-familiar blunt instrument. She survived, though suffering from severe head injuries she was not able to give a description of her attacker as she had not seen him.

What happened next was straight out of the Keystone Cops school of investigation. North Yorkshire Police decided that the young woman had injured herself by falling on the icy pavement, and that therefore no crime had taken place. They maintained this incredible fiction even after Home Office pathologist (and consulting Ripper expert) Professor David Gee examined the victim at Leeds General Infirmary and discovered deep and serious skull damage. He noted that 'there was one linear laceration on the left side of the top of the head two and a half inches long and on the right side of the top of the head two inches long. A third curved laceration at the back of the head was about one inch long.'

It would take several years for the North Yorkshire force to concede that these could not have been caused by an accidental fall, and that the student had indeed suffered a vicious attack. But still no connection was made to the unprecedented and enormously high-profile hunt for Britain's most notorious smasher of the backs of women's skulls being conducted by the Ripper teams.

Would it have made much difference if the two neighbouring forces had managed to work together effectively? The evidence of what happened just two weeks later on the Ripper detectives' own doorstep makes this doubtful at best.

On the evening of Friday, 2 March 1979, Ann Rooney was walking through the grounds of Horsforth College. Ann was twenty-two, originally from Ireland, and a student at the institution: it was less than three miles from Millgarth police station. Suddenly, she was struck three times on the back of her head; luckily, her would-be killer was disturbed by other students and ran off before he could inflict any further injuries.

Ann survived the attack and was able to give Leeds detectives a clear description of the man who had hit her: he was in his late twenties, around five feet ten inches tall, with a seemingly broad build (though this was possibly due to the fact that he was wearing a loose, thick jacket on that cold night). But once again it was the face that should have rung bells: dark, curly hair was framed by a droopy moustache and a beard.

Even more tellingly, Ann had noticed the man before he attacked her, sitting in a dark-coloured car. She was able to identify this as a Sunbeam Rapier – identical to the one sitting on the drive at Sutcliffe's home, just a few miles away in Heaton.

That vehicle had been flagged numerous times driving through the red-light districts of Leeds and Bradford: it had also been spotted in Manchester's Moss Side vice area just ten days before Ann Rooney was attacked. The Police National Computer records showed it to be one of only three Sunbeam Rapiers recorded in all three high-profile 'Ripper' areas. This, together with the previous flagging of his Ford Corsair in Chapeltown and Manningham, should have made Peter Sutcliffe a clear suspect. Yet he would not be interviewed for another four months – and even then, his significance would be missed.

Ann Rooney was carefully examined by surgeons at the hospital. They discovered that the attack had left very distinctive semicircular wounds in her skull, which had come from a round hammer. Despite this catalogue of similarities to the Ripper attacks, Oldfield's detectives refused to accept it as a new case on the bizarre grounds that the injuries had been made by a hammer of a slightly different size from that used in other Yorkshire Ripper attacks. Since he had, by then, quite plainly used a variety of hammers (and particularly given the facial and vehicle identification), the decision made no sense whatsoever – a conclusion confirmed when, many years later, Peter Sutcliffe would grudgingly admit attempting to murder the young student.

In large part, the refusal of the Ripper Squad to entertain the Ann Rooney attack was due to the continuing assumption that their quarry was obsessed with prostitutes. Since Ann was a student, not a 'vice girl', and her ordeal took place well away from the red-light district, police logic insisted that she could not be a new victim. It was an entirely misguided belief, but one that would shortly be reinforced by a new letter from the north-east of England.

The two previous pieces of correspondence – one addressed to George Oldfield, the other sent to the *Daily Mirror* – had been locked away in a drawer for the past year because the detective suspected they were the work of a crank. But on Saturday, 24 March, a third note arrived. It was in the same handwriting (and semi-literate spelling) as its predecessors, and like them had been posted in Sunderland.

Dear Officer

Sorry I havn't written, about a year to be exact, but I hav'nt been up north for quite a while. I was'nt kidding last time I wrote saying the whore would be older this time and maybe I'd strike in Manchester for a change, you should have took heed. That bit about her being in hospital, funny the lady mentioned something about being in hospital before I stopped her whoring ways. The lady won't worry about hospitals now will she.

I bet you be wondering how come I hav'nt been to work for ages, well I would have been if it hadnt been for your cursered coppers I had the lady just where I wanted her and was about to strike when one of you cursing police cars stopped right outside the lane, he must have been a dumb copper cause he didnt say anything, he didnt know how close he was to catching me. Tell you the truth I thought I was collared, the lady said don't worry about the coppers, little did she know that bloody copper saved her neck.

That was last month, so I don't know when I will get back on the job but I know it wont be Chapeltown too bloody hot there maybe Bradfords Manningham. Might write again if up north.

Jack the Ripper

PS Did you get letter I sent to Daily Mirror in Manchester.

The reference to a murder in Manchester clearly meant the killing of Vera Millward. Oldfield now began to take the letters seriously: the writer appeared to know that Millward had recently been a patient at the same hospital in whose car park she was attacked: the detective believed (wrongly, as it turned out) that this information had not been published anywhere. Therefore, if the letter writer knew it, he must be her killer. The Ripper Squad's attention began to shift north-eastwards towards Sunderland.

But ten days later, the killer struck again in West Yorkshire. On the night of Wednesday, 4 April, a nineteen-year-old clerk called Josephine (Jo) Whitaker went to visit her grandparents at their home on Huddersfield Road, Halifax. She had wanted to show them the new silver watch she had just bought for £60. Jo's grandmother had been at a church party across the road and had not returned home until late: conscious of the long and dark walk back to the home Jo shared with her mother, stepfather and two younger brothers, she invited her granddaughter to stay the night. But Jo had to be up in good time the next day to get to her job at the Halifax Building Society: she insisted on walking back and left at about 11.40 p.m. She took a familiar route through Savile Park and across it to Ivy Street where she lived.

That night, Peter Sutcliffe had been out drinking with Trevor Birdsall. Shortly after closing time, he dropped off his friend and set off towards Halifax in his grey Sunbeam Rapier. Before long, he arrived at Savile Park: he spotted Jo Whitaker, walking alone.

He quickly parked, tucked a hammer and giant rusty Philips-head screwdriver into his pocket, and began to follow her. Within a few minutes, he caught up to her, and asked her if she had far to go: Jo explained that she had been at her grandmother's and that it was quite a walk home.

As they started to walk across the field, and were about thirty to forty yards from the main road, out of the range of the street lamps, Sutcliffe asked her the time. When she told him, he pronounced himself mightily impressed by her good eyesight at being able to see the nearby clock tower. He lagged behind a little, pretending to look at the clock, but in reality removing a weapon from his jacket: he then hit Jo from behind with his ball-peen hammer and knocked her to the ground. As she made a low moaning noise, he hit her again.

Sutcliffe then noticed someone coming along the pavement where they had been walking a couple of minutes earlier. He dragged Jo's dying body thirty feet into the darkness, away from the road. As he crouched over the body, he was horrified to hear voices close behind him. He turned and saw two figures hurrying across the field, and watched as they passed close by him. A man walking past the park at the time of the murder would subsequently tell the police that he had heard 'the type of noise that makes your hair stand on end'.

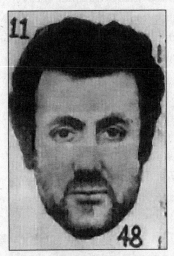

Witness photofit of man sought

Jo was still moaning loudly when Sutcliffe pulled her clothing back, turned her over, and proceeded to stab her twenty-one times with the screwdriver in the chest and stomach, and six times in the right leg. He also thrust the screwdriver into her vagina – over and over again, in the same wound.

Jo's body was discovered at first light the next morning. Scenes of crime officers discovered that her skull had been fractured from ear to ear: they also found clear size 7 wellington boot prints near the corpse.

Although George Oldfield initially cautioned reporters against assuming that the Ripper had killed again, he and the team at Millgarth knew from the outset that Jo Whitaker was the serial killer's latest victim. Given that Jo had no connection with prostitution or the red-light district, her murder should have given Oldfield cause to reconsider the overriding assumption that the Yorkshire Ripper was focused on 'vice girls'. But just five weeks later, a new missive from his correspondent in Sunderland overtook any possible reassessment of the investigation's direction. It was an audio cassette tape: on it a soft Geordie voice mocked and taunted the detective.

> I'm Jack. I see you are still having no luck catching me. I have the greatest respect for you, George, but Lord, you are no nearer to catching me than four years ago when I started. I reckon your boys are letting you down, George …

The voice droned on for a few more minutes before signing off with an insouciant warning.

> Well, I'll keep on going for a while yet. I can't see myself getting nicked just yet. Even if you do get near I'll probably top myself first. Well, it's been nice talking to you George. Yours, Jack the Ripper.

Oldfield and his senior officers agonised over the tape: should they suppress it or make it public? In the end, they opted for openness. A televised press conference was held at 2 p.m. on 26 June: in it, Oldfield played the tape and sat uncomfortably while the voice mocked his efforts. He then told the assembled media that this was the break the investigation had been waiting for.

Before ... we have been looking for *a man* [Oldfield's emphasis]. There are literally millions and we didn't know where he came from. But now that we can localise the area the field is narrowed appreciably, as I'm sure you must agree.

For the next eighteen months, the Sunderland connection would dominate all aspects of the Ripper inquiry. Scientific voice analysis would narrow down the speaker's accent to the Wearside mining village of Castletown, three miles from Sunderland itself. Forensic analysis of the envelope revealed that the man who had licked it – and who was, therefore, presumably the sender – was of B blood group and (unlike Peter Sutcliffe) a secretor. An eighteen-page report would be produced by West Yorkshire Police, outlining for neighbouring forces the criteria for including any future attack within the Ripper series of crimes. This 'points for elimination' section would be the inflexible rule by which all and any murders or attempted murders were judged: the fifth and final qualification instructed that if a suspect's 'accent is dissimilar to a North Eastern (Geordie) accent' then he could not be a Ripper suspect. It was a tragic over-reliance on what would – eventually – turn out to be a cruel hoax.

It is, of course, easy to apply the judgement of hindsight and criticise the Ripper team for putting so much reliance on this single lead; indeed, George Oldfield would subsequently be heavily censured for his decision. But even as the focus of attention turned towards the north-east, detectives were warned that they were barking up the wrong tree. Tracy Browne had already tried – unsuccessfully – to tell West Yorkshire Police that the man who attacked her matched exactly the photofits provided by other confirmed Ripper victims: now she tried to convince them that the Geordie connection was a red herring.

> George Oldfield came round and asked me to listen to the Geordie tape. I said: 'Look – he's not a Geordie, he's a Yorkshireman. I can tell the difference between a Yorkshire accent and a Geordie accent.' But it was like banging my head against a brick wall. I felt 'I don't know whether I'm coming or going': do the police know whether they're coming or going?

With the search focused in entirely the wrong location, Peter Sutcliffe was left free to carry on killing.

On the evening of Saturday, 9 June, a thirty-eight-year-old woman with psychiatric and alcohol problems was found drunk and wandering on the inner ring road in Leeds. Her name was Marion Spence, and a passing motorist took her to Millgarth police station, where she was detained for her own safety.

She was seen by a doctor and social worker who declared that she was not certifiably insane: she was released from custody at 10.30 p.m. and sent off to stagger two miles to her lodgings in a hostel for destitute women on Meanwood Road. That she was highly vulnerable and that her journey took her through the heart of 'Ripper Country' did not appear to occur to the police.

Shortly after 6.30 p.m. the following evening, a thirteen-year-old boy out walking his two dogs found Marion's naked body in long grass behind a derelict warehouse formerly known as Grannelli's Ice Cream Factory in Middle Fold, Mabgate. The location was just 300 yards from the police station, the time of death very shortly after she was sent off into the night. She appeared to have been strangled – possibly with a garrotte – after which her attacker had piled her clothes neatly on top of her corpse. There was also evidence of stab wounds on her body. Despite all of these distinctive elements to the crime, West Yorkshire Police ruled out any connection with it being a Yorkshire Ripper case: it didn't fit the now inflexible criteria.

Quite how rigid these had become – and how dysfunctional the entire Ripper inquiry now was – came into sharp focus on Sunday, 29 July 1979. That afternoon two young detectives – DC Andy Laptew and DC Graham Greenwood – called at Number 6 Garden Lane, Heaton. They were following up an 'action' – a slip of paper generated by the observation teams in the red-light districts: it was handed to them at random, with only the most basic of supporting information.

P.W. Sutcliffe, lorry driver, triple area sighting.

Decoded, this told them that Sutcliffe's car had been spotted in all three of the vice areas – Manningham in Bradford, Chapeltown in Leeds and the areas of Manchester where Jean Jordan and Vera Millward worked the streets. It did not, however, tell them that Peter William Sutcliffe had already been interviewed on four previous occasions by their colleagues, nor that he worked for a firm whose name had cropped up in the abortive £5 note enquiry.

Instead, as they rang the bell that summer afternoon, they knew only that this was yet another, almost certainly fruitless, follow-up call – Laptew had already made hundreds of similar visits to other possible suspects – and that the Ripper was, according to the bosses at Millgarth:

Literate and of reasonable intelligence. It is known that in the past he has worn wellington boots and industrial protective, or army-type, boots, both of which were size seven. There are defects in his upper teeth which are natural, not false and which can be identified. His blood group is B and he is a known secretor. He is known to have been in possession of a motor vehicle.

It was not, in truth, much to go on – and in one crucial regard (the secretor information) completely wrong. The follow-ups were not a popular duty, having never yielded anything of apparent value. Laptew did not, therefore, have any great expectations when he arrived at Garden Lane.

From the outset, though, he felt there was something wrong. Both Peter and Sonia Sutcliffe were at home and said they were willing to answer the detectives' questions. But getting information proved to be a painfully slow process: Sutcliffe, in particular, took such a long time to respond to each enquiry that Laptew would later describe the interview as 'like pulling teeth'.

Sutcliffe did, though, deny that he used prostitutes: 'I don't have anything to do with them' was his firm answer to that question. He explained away the sightings of his car in the red-light district as either routine journeys to work or shopping trips with his wife. Since the detectives had not been provided with the actual times at which his vehicle had been logged they were unable to challenge this bare-faced lie. Nor had they been given crucial information about his criminal record.

When I made an enquiry with the records office, all I got
was a note saying he had a conviction for going equipped
for theft. It did not say that the conviction was going
equipped for theft with a hammer.

Sutcliffe was also happy to give a sample of his handwriting
for comparison to the Sunderland letters: it did not, of course,
match. But as the two-hour visit wore on, Laptew became
increasingly suspicious. Sutcliffe's demeanour was, frankly, odd,
and while the explanations for the cross-area sightings of his car
were plausible, it felt like a coincidence too far. His boot size
was similar to the intelligence sheet on the Ripper and Sutcliffe
clearly had a gap in his front teeth.

Above all, though, there was his overall facial appearance: the
colour, shape and texture of his beard and moustache strongly
resembled the photofit of Marilyn Moore's attacker.

I had bad feelings about the man. He had too many
uncanny links with what we knew. His shoe size fitted the
suspect's shoe size, there was a gap in his teeth, and the
thing that struck me more than anything was the striking
resemblance to the Marilyn Moore photofit. Both my
colleague and myself, when we left the house, looked at
each other and said: we're not happy with this man. There
was something sinister about him, something weird; and
there's always your own particular irrational feeling – your
gut feeling, if you like – about a person.

Out of sight of their interviewees, Laptew and Greenwood
conferred: they were tempted to arrest Sutcliffe on the spot and

take him back to the police station for more formal questioning. But they were all too aware of an official order that no Ripper suspects were to be hauled in for interview without the express permission of the Assistant Chief Constable. They decided instead to submit a detailed report that would spell out their intuitive suspicions about Peter William Sutcliffe.

That report – submitted on 2 August 1979 – stated baldly: 'The reporting officers are not satisfied with this man.' Laptew expected it to be acted upon, but, as days and then weeks passed with no sign of any interest, he bypassed his immediate boss and took his concerns to the man in charge of the Ripper investigations.

By mid-summer 1979, command had passed from George Oldfield – who had suffered a heart attack – to Detective Superintendent Dick Holland, deputy head of CID for the western district of the force. Holland had come up with Oldfield through the ranks of the old West Riding Constabulary and was widely seen as the Assistant Chief Constable's protégé. A tough, no-nonsense giant of a man – he turned out regularly for West Yorkshire Police rugby team – he was unusual for this time and career in that he neither smoked nor drank. Such was his reputation as a detective that Laptew (in his own words) 'revered him like a God'. He was about to discover that deities created by man often have feet of clay.

Laptew outlined to Holland his unease about Sutcliffe and finished off by drawing his superior's attention to the similarity of his suspect to the Marilyn Moore photofit: it seemed to enrage the new Ripper chief. Laptew would later recall his shock at the vehemence of Holland's response.

He said: 'Anybody who mentions photofits to me will draw uniform and do traffic for the rest of their career.' He just bit my head off.

Shortly afterwards, Holland wrote the single word 'File' in green ink on top of Laptew's report. Given the chaotic state of the Ripper Squad's filing – hundreds of cardboard boxes containing tens of thousands of pieces of paper – it was essentially consigning the intelligence to the dustbin. There it would lie, untouched and unnoticed, until – in the aftermath of Sutcliffe's conviction – it would mysteriously disappear.

Peter Sutcliffe could not have known how close he came to being arrested that July afternoon. He was, though, acutely aware that he had been identified as a person of interest because his cars had been frequently observed quartering the red-light districts for prostitutes. Once again, he took the logical action of selling the Sunbeam Rapier he had used in several attacks. But if this demonstrated his rational approach to crime – a far cry from the hopelessly God-driven schizophrenic he would later claim to have been – he was not ready to stop killing.

Six weeks after Laptew's visit to Garden Lane, the Yorkshire Ripper struck again. The official account of Sutcliffe's crimes shows that at 1 a.m. on Sunday, 2 September 1979, he murdered Barbara Leach, a young student at Bradford University. But that weekend saw two murders, both bearing all the hallmarks of the Ripper: while Barbara Leach would be recorded as one of his victims, 200 miles away the death of another young woman would be discounted by West Yorkshire detectives and would go unsolved.

Alison Morris was twenty-five years old and a university

lecturer, living in the small Essex village of Ramsey. On Saturday, 1 September, she left her home in Wrabness Road for an early-evening walk to the nearby River Stour: later that evening she was due for dinner at her parents' home. At 6.30 p.m., she was walking down a lane through some woods when a man came up behind her and stabbed her repeatedly in the chest with a single-bladed knife.

Alison's father discovered her body an hour later. Essex Police quickly began a murder investigation, and its senior investigating officer told the press:

> We must conclude that the attack was made by a mentally deranged person for some sort of sexual gratification. It is more than likely that he may attack again. He is obviously a man whom both the police and public must do everything they can to remove from society. The sooner the better.

Initially, the detectives considered the possibility that Alison had been killed by the Yorkshire Ripper. Since West Yorkshire Police had issued its intelligence bulletin on the man it sought, other forces were finally aware of the possibility that murders on their patch could be the work of a travelling criminal. And there were solid reasons to open this line of enquiry in the Morris case – not least a sighting of a possible suspect who bore a strong similarity to the bearded Ripper.

The brutal killing of Barbara Leach six and a half hours later in Bradford killed that angle stone-dead. Detectives simply assumed that it would be most unlikely – if not impossible – for the Ripper to travel the 200 miles between the two crime scenes in such a short time. It was – at best – a crude and unscientific conclusion with no empirical support.

Barbara Leach had come to Bradford from her hometown of Kettering. She was twenty years old and living in student digs close to the university. That Saturday night, she went with friends to the Mannville Arms pub on Great Horton Road: they left at 12.45 a.m. on the Sunday morning.

Sutcliffe was driving through the area and was watching nearby as the group walked away from the pub. He saw Barbara separate from her friends; he quickly drove past her and turned left into Ash Grove. As he opened the door to get out of the car, she was walking towards him. He let her walk past him before attacking her with a hammer from behind, and then dragged her body into a nearby backyard.

After pushing up her shirt and bra to expose her breasts and undoing her jeans and partly pulling them down, he stabbed her eight times with the same screwdriver that he had used on Josephine Whitaker. He then positioned her corpse in a distorted jack-knife position behind a low wall and covered her body with an old piece of carpet. For good measure he placed some stones on top of the small, sad heap.

When Barbara's body was found just before 4 o'clock that Sunday afternoon, the Ripper Squad was grimly sure that their quarry had killed again. But had he also struck in Essex?

By this time, Peter Sutcliffe was driving a powerful 3.5-litre Rover: it would easily have carried him from the scene of Alison Morris's death in Ramsey to Great Horton Road, Bradford, in time to attack Barbara Leach. After all, he had back in April travelled 260 miles before murdering Josephine Whitaker.

Nor was that part of Essex unknown to Sutcliffe. T. & W. H. Clark regularly made deliveries in the area, and Ramsey village is just three miles from Harwich – a town Sutcliffe had regularly travelled to on behalf of the haulage firm. Some years later, a couple who had run a business near Ramsey told West Yorkshire Police that they remembered a man matching Sutcliffe's description stopping to ask directions: this man was driving a large, dark-blue delivery lorry with a Yorkshire address emblazoned on its side.

Against this admittedly circumstantial case was the fact that Alison Morris had not been killed in classic Ripper style. But a more careful comparative examination reveals that her murder closely resembled the fatal attack on Debbie Schlesinger the previous year. In both cases, the girls had been stabbed through the heart without any interference to their clothing. If – as at least one very senior West Yorkshire detective would come to believe – Debbie was one of Sutcliffe's victims, then it is very likely that he also took the life of Alison Morris.

After Barbara Leach's murder, West Yorkshire Police embarked on a high-profile publicity campaign: newspapers and advertising billboards reproduced one of the Sunderland letters while a special phone line played the 'I'm Jack' tape on a continuous loop.

HELP US STOP THE RIPPER FROM KILLING AGAIN. LOOK AT HIS HANDWRITING. LISTEN TO HIS VOICE. IF YOU RECOGNISE EITHER, REPORT IT TO YOUR LOCAL POLICE.

The campaign reflected the police's conviction that their quarry had a 'Geordie' accent and was fixated on prostitutes (despite his most recent victims having no connection whatsoever to the vice trade). It missed completely the fact that Peter Sutcliffe, a distinctively bearded lorry driver, with a Yorkshire accent clearly recalled by Tracy Browne, was the subject of a heavily annotated card in the Ripper inquiry major incident filing carousel – it had been updated thirteen times in recent years – as well as the telling detail that he had been interviewed on nine separate occasions. Even Sutcliffe's workmates had taken, jokingly, to calling him 'The Ripper' because of the persistent police interest in him. But the obsession with the voice on the Sunderland tape blinded West Yorkshire Police to the obvious.

John Stainthorpe was an old-school, no-nonsense Yorkshire detective who knew the obvious when it stared him in the face. On Thursday, 11 October 1979, it did just that.

Yvonne Mysliwiec was a twenty-one-year-old reporter for the *Ilkley Gazette*. She lived in the quiet, refined town on the moors between Leeds and Silsden, and supplemented her wages by working as a barmaid every Thursday night. That October night, as she was crossing the footbridge over the railway station, she was attacked from behind: a man smashed a blunt instrument – probably a hammer – into the back of her skull. Only the arrival of a passenger from the station interrupted her attacker and saved her life. The man – described as in his thirties, dark and swarthy with crinkly hair – ran off into the dark.

John Stainthorpe was then a detective superintendent: when the case was assigned to him, he clearly saw the similarities to the manhunt being run from Millgarth.

It was clearly, in my view, another Ripper attack. Stalking the victim from behind, using a ball-peen hammer. Certainly all my team – I had about 60 officers there – were left in no doubt. I said that if we find this man we find the Ripper. But senior officers from the Ripper Squad didn't think this was another Ripper attack and I was given the job of investigating it as a non-Ripper attempted murder.

But as in previously discounted murders or attempted murders, the reason for denying that the Ripper had struck again – and in a respectable middle-class enclave twenty-five miles from the nearest red-light district – was driven as much by politics as by good, sensible policing. As an officer who had given all his life to the job, Stainthorpe grudgingly accepted the realpolitik.

I can well understand the reason for trying to placate the public and saying this is unlikely to be the Ripper because all it would have done would be to create more pressure. And we were already a sinking ship, believe you me: we were in very deep trouble at that time.

It would take almost two decades for West Yorkshire Police to be convinced that Peter Sutcliffe tried to kill Yvonne Mysliwiec. And even then this information would be suppressed.

This pattern of excluding from their enquiries murders which bore all the hallmarks of the Yorkshire Ripper continued to the end of the year.

On Friday, 30 November, a twenty-four-year-old restaurant manager was on her way back into London after visiting friends in Essex. Sally Shepherd lived in Peckham, south-east London, and after buying a takeaway curry she caught the last bus of the night from New Cross. It stopped at Clayton Road, Peckham, a little after midnight and Sally set off to walk the few hundred yards to her home in Friary Road. She never made it.

Somewhere along the silent streets she was stalked and then struck on the back of the head with a blunt instrument – again, most probably a hammer. Her attacker then dragged her semi-conscious body through a hole in a wire-mesh fence surrounding a yard being used as a temporary gypsy site at the back of Peckham police station. He stripped off her boots and some of her clothes, and mutilated her genitalia. Finally, he stamped up and down on her chest, caving in her ribs.

There were clear similarities between Sally's murder and the Ripper killing of Yvonne Pearson in January 1978. The Metropolitan Police also recognised the likely motivation of her murderer; the senior investigating officer told the press:

> This is the worst murder I have dealt with in twenty-six years. She suffered horrific injuries, including massive head wounds caused by a blunt instrument. This heinous crime defies normal logic. There was no need to inflict the terrible injuries she suffered. I believe we are hunting for a sex maniac who is extremely unbalanced.

The crime scene was also less than one mile from the junction with the A2 at New Cross Road: this was the road that Sutcliffe regularly travelled to make deliveries to the LEP depot at Charlton. But despite all the similarities of MO, and the clear evidence that Sutcliffe's work could have given him ample opportunity to attack Sally Shepherd, no attempt has ever been made to establish whether he was responsible. Sally's death remains unsolved to this day.

But, however shocking the incompetence and wilful blindness that prevented a proper investigation of the attacks on Sally, Yvonne Mysliwiec and all their predecessors going back almost thirteen years, what happened just two weeks later was simply unforgivable.

As 1979 drew to a close, it was almost two years since Carol Wilkinson had been bludgeoned to death on her way to work at Almond's Bakery in Bradford. For almost all of that period, no progress had been made in finding her killer. But around the time that Josephine Whitaker was murdered, West Yorkshire Police suddenly swooped on the home of a young man who lived close to the Wilkinson family on the Ravenscliffe Estate.

Anthony Steel was twenty-two but had the mental age of a young child. His IQ was measured at 65 – deep within the range that was then officially termed 'mentally retarded or handicapped'. There was absolutely nothing to connect him to Carol's death other than the slight suspicion of his mother-in-law about a key ring Anthony had given to his wife as a present.

Despite the inconvenient fact that there was no evidence that this key ring had ever belonged to Carol Wilkinson, detectives took the confused and vulnerable young man in for questioning. He would not leave custody for the next twenty-four years.

Over a period of two days, Anthony Steel was interviewed no fewer than seven times. There were no tape recordings of these interviews; nor – despite his mental handicap – was he provided with either a solicitor or a supportive adult. At some point, he signed a confession, written for him by the police: he was then charged with murder.

His case came to trial in December 1979. The only evidence against him was the confession, which he had – after finally being allowed to see a lawyer – withdrawn. Nonetheless, on Thursday, 13 December, a jury convicted him of murdering Carol Wilkinson and the judge imposed the mandatory life sentence.

It was a travesty of justice – and far from the only such case affecting West Yorkshire Police during the 1970s. That Anthony Steel was a mentally subnormal young man, who was led to confess to a crime he hadn't committed by detectives who did not consider his vulnerability, was finally recognised in 2003. In June that year, the Court of Appeal (Criminal Division) quashed his conviction as unsafe: the Chief Constable of West Yorkshire issued a public apology and the Home Office subsequently paid him £100,000 to compensate for his ordeal. He died four years later.

But if Anthony Steel did not kill Carol Wilkinson, who did?

The most likely candidate was – and remains – Peter Sutcliffe. His home was just three miles from the bakery (and his place of work even closer). The nature of the attack and the injuries that killed Carol matched almost exactly the criminal signature of the Yorkshire Ripper. He had, on the morning that she was attacked, just come back from mutilating Jean Jordan's rotting corpse in Bradford: he was angry and frustrated at being unable to find the £5 note he had given her. It is no great leap of investigative effort to place him at the scene of Carol's murder, primed and ready to attack; indeed, it was a line of enquiry West Yorkshire Police should have followed between 1977 and 1979.

Instead, they managed to convict an entirely innocent man, robbing him of the best years of his adult life. It was depressingly symbolic of all the failures that dogged the Ripper investigation throughout the 1970s: a further manifestation, too, of the closed minds and hubris that had sent two other innocent men – Andrew Evans and Stephen Downing – to prison for crimes almost certainly carried out by Peter Sutcliffe.

And, as the decade ended, those mistakes would continue – and the Ripper would keep killing.

SEVENTEEN

'WE DO NOT BELIEVE THIS IS THE WORK OF THE YORKSHIRE RIPPER'

At the start of 1980, Peter Sutcliffe was, to all outward appearances, the very model of respectability. Sonia was now well established as a teacher, the couple owned their own home in a good part of Bradford and he was very highly regarded at T. & W. H. Clark.

The jibes from his workmates that he must be the Yorkshire Ripper had subsided for two reasons. The first was that the succession of police visits had ceased; the second was that Clark's had sacked all their drivers, save one: Sutcliffe.

The firm had suffered from repeated thieving: goods regularly – and quite literally – disappeared from the back of its lorries. The only driver who had apparently resisted temptation was Peter Sutcliffe. The company's owner, Tom Clark, would later tell reporters:

He could have made quite a bit of money for himself, but he never got involved in the fiddles.

So impressed were the management with their driver's honesty that he was chosen to be the company's poster boy. A photograph of Sutcliffe, hair combed and beard neatly trimmed, behind the wheel of 'Wee Willie' was used as the centrepiece of a promotional brochure. A much-enlarged version of the picture was also displayed in the entrance of the company's premises.

Throughout the winter months, Sutcliffe certainly seems to have kept a low profile and a clean nose. There were no new reported murders or attacks for the Ripper Squad to investigate. Nor, in the official account of his crimes, would the Ripper strike again until late in the summer. But that official version is wrong in several crucial regards.

The spring bank holiday in 1980 fell on Monday, 26 May. Later that week, Maria Szurma asked Sutcliffe to take a washing machine and a few other items to her elder daughter. Marianne still lived in Alperton, near Wembley, but because he could hardly use a Clark's lorry, Sutcliffe hired a van. With Sonia in the front and her parents sitting on chairs in the back, the Sutcliffes and Szurmas travelled down to London: they stayed overnight in Alperton and also made a visit to Sonia's uncle, who also lived not too far away. It increased Sutcliffe's already encyclopaedic knowledge of the local area.

A few weeks later, Sutcliffe was once again on family duties in Alperton. Marianne and her family were going away for a few days and Sutcliffe readily agreed to house-sit for them. Since Sonia was working, he took his brother, Mick, with him: the pair appear to have used the trip as an excuse to slip the leash of domestic responsibilities, frequently visiting the then thriving vice scene in Soho. Here they picked up women and drove to a park near Alperton to continue the nights' pleasures.

Patricia (Patsy) Morris disappeared during the sunny afternoon of Monday, 16 June. Patsy was fourteen and a pupil at the Feltham Comprehensive. That day, she faced an afternoon of double history – a subject for which she evidently had little fondness, since she had previously missed six classes. And so she bunked off school. A witness recalled seeing her soon after noon near her home. Another witness saw a girl who might have been Patsy crouching at a bus stop on the Hounslow Heath side of Staines Road, just west of the Hussar public house between 12.20 p.m. and 12.40 p.m. Those were the last two sightings of her alive.

On the morning of Wednesday, 18 June, scores of police began a massive search of Hounslow Heath: as evening fell, a dog handler discovered Patsy's body lying face down in undergrowth, ten yards from a path through one of the small woods close to Heathrow Airport. She was half naked and her clothing had been positioned in what should by then have been a very familiar manner – pushed upwards over the top half of her body. Her tights and the two pairs of knickers she was (for some unknown reason) wearing had been pulled down over her ankles. A second pair of tights, one leg missing from the gusset downwards, was tied around Patsy's leg and wound upwards until it was knotted four times around her neck: it was, quite plainly, some form of ligature.

An identical pair of one-legged tights was wrapped three times around both wrists in front of her body and then over her breasts. Although her knickers had been pulled down – strongly suggesting a sexual motive for the killing – there was no sign of sexual assault or evidence of rape. Whoever murdered Patsy Morris had found satisfaction without penetration.

Although attacks on women – even deaths – were not unknown in the area, the killing of Patsy Morris was highly unusual: previous sexual assaults and murders on or around the heath had invariably involved the full rape of the victim. But the crime scene did present distinct similarities to the 1975 murder of Eve Stratford: she, like Patsy, was found with her wrists tied behind her back using one of her stockings, while the other leg was tied around her ankle. And the evidently deliberate – and distinctively elaborate – staging of the corpse was eerily reminiscent of many of the Ripper's murders.

Could Patsy Morris have been Peter Sutcliffe's first victim of 1980? There were certainly similarities of criminal signature and her body was discovered just twelve miles from Alperton, where Sutcliffe was staying. In any normal investigation, this coincidence of MO and opportunity would have merited – at the very least – a cross-comparison to establish whether this was a Ripper attack. But then the Ripper inquiry was very far from normal.

This was brought home by the events of Wednesday, 25 June 1980. With no apparent new attacks or murders to investigate – and therefore no new leads – the team in Millgarth was pinning its hopes on catching its quarry by monitoring cars entering the red-light districts. Observation points were set up throughout the West Yorkshire force area, with the intention that vehicle number plates would be sent back to base and checked for previous sightings.

At 11.30 p.m., a brown Rover 3.5-litre saloon sped erratically past one of the observation points on Grosvenor Road, Manningham: it was exceeding the speed limit and the way it was swerving across the road strongly suggested either the driver was drunk or the vehicle was stolen. The two uniformed constables started the engine of their unmarked car and set off in pursuit.

What followed reinforced their suspicions. For the next two miles, the police gave chase to the Rover through the residential streets at speeds of up to 80 miles per hour. They finally caught up with it when the driver pulled up outside 6 Garden Lane, Heaton.

Peter Sutcliffe had spent the evening drinking heavily in the Royal Standard pub on Manningham Lane. When the constables confronted him as he climbed out of the car, he was both drunk and aggressive. A loud argument ensued – waking his neighbours – before Sutcliffe finally agreed to be breathalysed: the test, inevitably, showed him to be well over the limit and he was arrested, taken to the nearest police station and charged with driving while intoxicated.

Because Sutcliffe had been spotted in a red-light district, one of the officers sent a formal memo referring his name to the Ripper Squad. Despite the fact that the lorry driver had previously been interviewed on several occasions, the team in Millgarth breezily advised that he had been eliminated from their enquiries: the reason given was that his handwriting did not match that on the letters sent from Sunderland. Sutcliffe was simply told that he would, at some point, be summoned to appear in court and that he was certain to lose his licence.

It was – at best – a tragic missed opportunity. It would leave the Yorkshire Ripper free to prey on women for the next six months.

This brush with the law had two effects on Sutcliffe. After a period of relative calm, he once again began striking regularly: but conscious of how close he had come to detection, he also deliberately altered his MO.

On the night of Wednesday, 20 August, Marguerite Walls was working late at the education department in Pudsey, Leeds. Miss Walls was forty-seven and known to her colleagues as a dedicated and diligent civil servant. She was about to take ten days' holiday leave and was determined to tie up all loose ends in her files.

She left the office at 10.30 p.m. and set out on the short walk through well-lit streets to her home in nearby Farsley. At the same time, Peter Sutcliffe was driving through the area on his way to Chapeltown. He spotted Marguerite Walls walking towards him, parked his car and set off on foot to overtake her.

As Marguerite walked past the imposing home of a local magistrate, Sutcliffe jumped out from behind a fence, shouting, 'Filthy prostitute.' He smashed his hammer repeatedly into the back of her skull. She did not fall to the ground as he had expected but instead began to scream: he grabbed her by the throat and looped a length of rope around her neck. Then, tightening the ligature as he went, he dragged her up the driveway and into a high-walled garden. There, while kneeling on her chest, he garrotted her with the rope. After she was dead, he ripped at her clothes, tearing them from her body before scattering them around the garden. Before leaving, he partly covered her corpse with a pile of grass clippings and leaves and, after checking that the street was quiet, drove off.

Two gardeners found Marguerite Walls' body the next morning. A post-mortem later that day revealed two deep injuries to her skull – both consistent with a hammer attack – and three broken ribs. There was also clear evidence of sexual interference: the pathologist noted three scratches – probably made by fingernails – on the outside of her vagina.

The murder of another woman in Leeds, and the blows to the back of her skull from a hammer, unsurprisingly led the press to ask pointedly whether the Ripper had struck once more. Remarkably, the man heading up the hunt for Marguerite Walls' killer was quick to refute the suggestion. Detective Chief Superintendent Jim Hobson announced:

> We do not believe this is the work of the Yorkshire Ripper.
> My feelings are that it is a local man who did this murder. I
> have a team of detectives at Miss Walls' house looking for
> addresses of male and female friends. She had boyfriends
> in the past but that was twenty-odd years ago. She was
> a very private person who would always go home after
> finishing work.

Hobson's comments were uncomfortably similar to his public pronouncements after the attack on Tracy Browne in Silsden five years earlier. Then, too, he had been convinced the attacker would be 'a local man' and had followed the familiar routines of appealing for information only in the surrounding towns and villages. They had not produced any results.

What drove Hobson's thinking – and it was a decision over which he agonised – was that, while there were obvious Ripper-like elements in the Marguerite Walls case, to the best of his knowledge, the serial killer had never before used a ligature. This, in itself, was an indictment of the utterly inadequate systems for sharing intelligence between forces. There had, of course, been previous ligature killings – ones that closely matched the circumstances of Marguerite Walls' death – but because they were outside the West Yorkshire Police area they were never factored into the equation. It would take an accidental arrest – and a thoroughly botched initial investigation – six months later to alert the squad at Millgarth to the simple fact that the Ripper had changed his MO.

That he had deliberately done so was clear one month later. On Wednesday, 24 September, a thirty-four-year-old doctor from Singapore was attacked in the middle-class Leeds suburb of Headingley. Upadhya Bandara was a postgraduate student at the university: she had won a scholarship from the World Health Organization to come to Leeds for a course at the Nuffield Centre. That evening she was making the long walk back to her digs after visiting friends: at 10.30 p.m., as she walked past a Kentucky Fried Chicken shop, she noticed a man inside staring at her. She increased her pace and turned into Chapel Lane, an alley that cut through to the main Cardigan Road.

Seconds later, Peter Sutcliffe smashed his hammer into her head: he hit her twice, knocking her unconscious. He then looped a length of blue-and-pink-plaited nylon rope around her neck and dragged her down the road. Realising that her shoes were making a dragging noise that could attract unwanted attention, he pulled them off and threw them, together with her handbag, over a nearby wall.

Before he could resume his attack, he was disturbed by the sound of footsteps: a woman whose house backed onto the alley had heard the noise and came out to investigate. She also called the police. Sutcliffe barely had time to sprint away before a patrol car arrived and found Dr Bandara lying on the ground. She was, mercifully, still alive and as she regained consciousness was able to give a very clear description of the man who had been watching her by KFC, and who was, presumably, the attacker. He was in his mid-thirties, five feet six inches tall, with black hair and a full beard and moustache.

Once again, the Ripper Squad refused to accept that this was the work of the man they had been seeking for five long years. Despite the remarkable similarity between the description given by Dr Bandara and the photofits adorning the walls of the incident room – and the fact that a hammer had once again been smashed into the back of a young woman's skull – the use of the ligature persuaded the Ripper Squad that this could not be the work of 'their man'.

As with the murder of Marguerite Walls, the detectives chose to believe the highly improbable instead of the most obvious. Improbable because, if this wasn't a Ripper case, it meant that there must be two identical-looking men attacking their victims with a hammer.

To describe this as incompetent would be generous. The truth was that the Ripper investigation was overloaded, overworked and – as John Stainthorpe had noted after the attempted murder of Yvonne Mysliwiec the previous year – 'a sinking ship'. Little wonder, then, that if a case could be rejected, it was.

There was, though, a price to be paid: it is one that Maureen Lea has been paying for thirty-four years.

That autumn, Maureen was twenty and in the third year of an arts course at Leeds Polytechnic. On the evening of Saturday, 25 October – exactly one month after the attack on Upadhya Bandara – she was walking through Headingley not far from the strip of shops and the KFC where Sutcliffe had lurked before pouncing. Since the area was 'respectable' – in other words, nowhere near the red-light district – and because West Yorkshire Police had explicitly ruled it out as a Ripper location in the aftermath of the Bandara case, students were not overly concerned about the possibility of encountering Britain's most hunted serial killer.

Around 10.50 p.m., Maureen was walking along Hillary Place, on the grounds of Leeds University. She became aware of a man behind her. He called out, 'Hey, you, don't I know you?'

Thinking it was a friend, she stopped and turned round. When the man came closer, she realised that she didn't know him: she made her excuses and started to walk away. Then she sensed something dangerous and started to run: as she picked up pace, she heard his footsteps coming faster and faster behind her. Suddenly, she felt herself being grabbed from behind and repeatedly hit on the back of the head. She collapsed to the ground and lost consciousness. As she lay there, her attacker pushed two sharpened screwdrivers into her spine. But the sound of approaching voices disturbed him and he ran off, leaving Maureen bleeding out on the cold, hard street.

Maureen Lea was lucky: she survived what was unquestionably an attempted murder. But – just as with Marguerite Walls and Upadhya Bandara – West Yorkshire Police refused to accept that she had been attacked by the Ripper. Unlike those two cases, however, Maureen would never be given the psychological satisfaction of an admission by the police that they were wrong. As we shall see, this was – and remains – a cruel and still painful additional burden for her to carry.

If the men in charge of the Yorkshire Ripper investigation

were wilfully closing their minds to the clear evidence that their quarry had changed his MO, they now at last abandoned the assumption that he only targeted prostitutes. The observation posts were removed from the red-light districts and the public was – finally – warned that no woman was safe.

But old attitudes and prejudices die hard in police stations – especially in incident rooms like those at Millgarth, which are completely overwhelmed by the magnitude of their task. Which explains how, just two weeks later, the Ripper Squad initially failed to recognise the next attack by Peter Sutcliffe.

At 7.30 p.m. on Wednesday, 5 November, Theresa Sykes stepped out from the flat where she lived with her boyfriend and baby son in Willwood Avenue, Huddersfield: the sixteen-year-old walked to a grocery shop on the main road to buy a packet of cigarettes and then set off back home.

Sutcliffe had been watching her from inside a telephone kiosk and followed her: as she came close to home, passing within 200 yards of the local police station, she saw him appear from the evening shadows. She had time to notice his long, thin face and neatly trimmed beard before he disappeared down a nearby ginnel. Suddenly, he reappeared: he caught up with her and struck her on the head from behind with a metal hammer. She turned as she fell and tried to grab the weapon.

Theresa's desperate screams were heard by neighbours and by her boyfriend, Jim Furey: a fitness fanatic, he raced out of the flat. Sutcliffe took off, with Furey in hot pursuit, running through the residential streets before finally hiding beneath a hedge in a nearby front garden. The Ripper crouched there until his pursuer gave up and he felt it was safe to crawl out. It was as close as he had ever come to being caught in the act.

Theresa Sykes had had a very narrow escape: Sutcliffe's hammer had badly damaged her skull, leaving a familiar half-moon-shaped scar: she would spend the next five weeks in a specialist neurosurgical unit at Chapel Allerton Hospital in Leeds – but the teenager lived to tell her tale and describe her attacker.

That description, however, contained one small inaccuracy: she recalled the colour of her would-be killer's beard and moustache as ginger: this was enough for the Ripper Squad to decide that, since the man they were seeking had a black beard, Theresa could not be one of his victims. One of the detectives assigned to the case gave an unequivocal statement to reporters.

> I am convinced a local man was involved ... All this talk that Theresa may have been attacked by the Ripper is making it more difficult to catch her assailant.

This was, of course, nonsense, and even some of the Ripper Squad detectives argued strongly that the attempt on Theresa's life should be added to their growing list of cases. They perhaps realised what their senior officers did not: that the artificial light of a street lamp would make the attacker's facial hair take on an orange tint. Eventually, too, they would be proved right and the chaotic, overwhelmed and disastrous Ripper investigation would be shaken up on the orders of Prime Minister Margaret Thatcher. But it would take the death of another young woman for that to come to pass.

Monday, 17 November was miserable. It had rained for much of the day and the evening was cold, wet and unpleasant. As night fell, Peter Sutcliffe made his last delivery of the day, to Kirkstall Forge in Leeds, before returning to Clark's depot around 7 p.m. He should have gone straight to Garden Lane, where Sonia was waiting in front of the television for her husband to come home. Instead, he slipped into a public phone box and told her that he was in Gloucester making a delivery and would not be back till very late. It was not a completely unexpected call: since his arrest for drink-driving, Peter had often worked late – ostensibly to bring in money before the court case that would inevitably lead to his losing his job.

Having provided himself with some breathing space, Sutcliffe climbed into the Rover and made for Headingley: by 9.30 p.m., he was sitting in his car outside the Arndale Centre, a quarter of a mile from where he had attacked Dr Bandara seven weeks earlier.

His choice of killing ground was significant: Headingley was a long way from the red-light district of Chapeltown and no prostitutes walked its respectable streets. The woman he would choose as a victim that night would be selected solely on the criterion of opportunity, not – as he would come to claim – because he was on a divine mission to rid the world of sex workers. He settled down in his car outside Kentucky Fried Chicken, eating a takeaway and watching the passing foot traffic.

Jacqueline Hill was twenty, a student in the third year of her English degree at Leeds University; that night, she had attended a probation officers' seminar in the city centre before catching the bus home. She got off at the stop opposite the Arndale Centre, crossed the road and turned up Alma Road to walk the hundred yards to her hall of residence.

Waiting in the shadows, Sutcliffe spotted her and quickly gunned the Rover into life. He drove up Alma Road, overtaking

Jacqueline, and waited for her to walk past. After she did, he got out of the car and began to follow her: he then smashed his hammer into the back of her skull.

Seconds later, he heard footsteps approaching: he quickly hoisted his victim into a standing position before dragging her approximately thirty yards onto some spare land behind the Arndale. There he pulled her clothes off and, with his yellow-handled screwdriver, stabbed her repeatedly in the chest and once in the eye.

When he had finished, he left, headed back to his car and drove home, apparently forgetting that Jacqueline's handbag and glasses still lay on the pavement where he had first attacked her.

A short time later, an Iranian student found the bag as he walked to his digs in Lupton Court: he took it home to show to his five flatmates, one of whom was a former chief inspector of the Hong Kong Police. He, in turn, was alarmed to see that nothing had been taken from the bag – and that there were fresh spots of blood on it. The police were called.

It was some time before two officers arrived at the flat, and only after insistent demands by the Iranian student did they agree to make a brief search by torchlight of the area where the handbag had been found. Jacqueline was lying, still alive, less than thirty yards away: the officers did not see her. Twenty minutes later, they were called away to respond to a burglar alarm going off.

Jacqueline Hill's body was not discovered until 10 a.m. the next day. Home Office pathologist David Gee examined it in situ and quickly saw that it bore all the hallmarks of a Ripper attack. The young girl's bra had been pulled up to expose her breasts and there were obvious head injuries. Later that morning, he began a post-mortem.

In the meantime, news of the murder had leaked out and speculation grew that the Yorkshire Ripper had struck again. But at a bad-tempered press conference that afternoon, West Yorkshire Police once again denied that the attack had been the work of Britain's most notorious serial killer. Detective Superintendent Alf Finlay insisted there was nothing to link Jacqueline's murder with the Ripper: his statement was greeted with disbelief and outright hostility by reporters. After an hour of savage questioning – the first time the press had turned on West Yorkshire's detectives – Finlay was close to losing his temper and announced that he would not speak to the media again unless or until new evidence emerged.

Across Leeds, David Gee's autopsy was finding just such evidence. The blows to Jacqueline's skull had been made by a ball-peen hammer: conclusive proof – if it were needed – that the Ripper had killed once more. On the morning of Wednesday, 17 November, Assistant Chief Constable George Oldfield made the news public and official.

And the public was outraged. The Ripper inquiry had clearly failed: the body of a young student in a leafy middle-class enclave was the latest testimony to that. Chief Constable Ronald Gregory had also managed to pour oil on the flames of outrage by glibly dismissing criticism of the officers who had failed to discover Jacqueline's body just a few hours after the attack; finding a bloodstained handbag in Leeds, he suggested, was nothing terribly out of the ordinary.

For the next three nights, feminists marched through Leeds under the banner of Women Against Violence Against Women.

Fights broke out with police when they protested outside a cinema showing the erotic crime thriller *Dressed to Kill*. Nor could the West Yorkshire force seem to grasp the mood of public anger: when Gregory's men issued advice that women should not go out alone at night, it was roundly attacked as a curfew and an attempt to shift the responsibility for keeping the streets safe from police to civilians.

But West Yorkshire Police's most significant foe – other than the serial killer they seemed unlikely ever to catch – was 200 miles south of Leeds. Margaret Thatcher summoned Home Secretary William Whitelaw to 10 Downing Street and read him the riot act. She was so angry at the evident failures of the Ripper Squad that she had decided to go straight up to Leeds and take personal charge of the investigation. Only Whitelaw's sage counsel that if – or when – the Ripper struck again she would become the lightning rod for public fury held her back.

But something clearly had to be done. Under the arcane rules of what passes for a constitution in Britain, chief constables are independent of national government: Gregory himself was therefore untouchable. But there was a means of reining him in and forcing a rethink of the disastrous state of affairs: Her Majesty's Inspectorate of Constabulary could be brought in to get a grip on the investigation. Lawrence Byford, HMIC's man in the north and a trained lawyer (as well as a former chief constable for Lincolnshire), was given the task.

When he arrived at the Millgarth incident room, he was appalled by the low morale and atmosphere of despair among the detectives.

> From the top to the bottom, they were mentally exhausted.
> By then it had become the largest, the most significant,
> the most demanding criminal case in British history and I
> don't think the police service and the forces involved were
> geared up to take on such a long, hard, difficult inquiry
> that affected the health and well-being of so many officers.

If anything, Byford's comments understated the case. A core
group of a hundred officers formed the nucleus of the Ripper
Squad. They had worked nearly two and a quarter million
man-hours; 250,000 people had been interviewed, each of them
recorded on a small white card in the central names index that
sat in the middle of the incident room. At least 157,000 cars
had been checked, 28,600 formal statements taken and 27,000
house-to-house enquiry visits carried out. Yet, as Christmas
approached, there were still more than 600 'actions' – follow-
up enquiries – outstanding from the Josephine Whitaker murder
in April 1979. At least 1,500 such tasks were waiting to be dealt
with from the killing of Barbara Leach in September 1979 and
there was a backlog of 36,000 documents waiting to be filed. It
was, in short, chaos.

But far more serious even than the organisational dysfunction
was the stubborn adherence of West Yorkshire Police's most
senior officers to theories that were palpably wrong and which
had steered the Ripper investigation up disastrous blind alleys.
The first had been the unshakeable belief that he only attacked
prostitutes: the second was the overwhelming credence still given
to the letters and tape sent to George Oldfield from Sunderland.

For more than a year, the scientists who had isolated the
accent on the tape had privately told Oldfield and Jim Hobson

303

that, since all the men in and around the village of Castletown had been interviewed and eliminated (along with tens of thousands of others from the surrounding areas), the police should no longer rely on it. The academics were ignored.

Finally, on 3 December 1980, one of them voiced his warning publicly. In an article in the *Yorkshire Post* that morning, Jack Windsor Lewis completely destroyed the credibility of the tape as an evidential tool. The story went national within minutes and West Yorkshire Police was once again besieged by angry journalists. Faced with the politically impossible prospect of admitting they had spent millions of pounds on a wild goose chase, the Ripper chiefs refused to acknowledge their mistake. Hobson – who had just supplanted Oldfield at the head of the squad and been elevated to the temporary rank of Assistant Chief Constable – clung grimly to the conviction that the man with the Geordie accent was the Yorkshire Ripper.

For some time, individual newspapers had offered a reward for information that led to the arrest of the serial killer. In the aftermath of Jacqueline Hill's murder, the sum on offer rose from £30,000 to £50,000. However well intentioned, the increase led to a new mountain of paperwork for the police: members of the public sent in 8,000 letters, 7,000 of them anonymously.

One of the envelopes was posted by Peter Sutcliffe's sometime best friend, Trevor Birdsall. On Tuesday, 25 November, he (anonymously) handwrote the following note:

TO WHOM IT MAY CONCERN
I am writing to inform you that I have very good reason to believe I now [sic] the man you are looking for in the 'Ripper Case'.

It is an incident which happened within the last 5 years. I cannot give any date or place or details without myself been [sic] known to the ripper or you if this is the man.

It is only until recently that something came to my notice, and now a lot of things fit into place.

I can only tell you one or two things which fit, for example. This man as [sic] had dealings with prostitutes and always had a thing about them. Also he is a long distance lorry driver, connecting engineering items etc. I am sure if you check up on dates etc you may find something.

His name and address is

PETER SUTCLIFFE   CLARKE [sic] TRANS.
6 GARDEN LANE   SHIPLEY
HEATON, BRADFORD.

The following day, Birdsall's girlfriend nagged him into taking the matter further. At 10.10 p.m., they turned up, together, at Bradford Police headquarters and spoke to a young constable manning the front desk. Without revealing that he had already sent an anonymous letter, Birdsall recounted the story of being with Sutcliffe on the night Olive Smelt was attacked in August 1975.

The constable forwarded a note of the conversation to the incident room at Millgarth. Here a detective marked it down for 'action to trace/interview Sutcliffe'. It was a mark of the exhaustion of every member of the Ripper Squad that the officer failed to recognise the name – despite the fact that he had interviewed Peter Sutcliffe eleven months earlier.

Had that detective not been so worn down, or the system so

EIGHTEEN

THE ACCIDENTAL ARREST

In the middle of January 1981, Peter Sutcliffe was due to appear before Bradford magistrates, on the drink-driving charge. It was a date he never kept: at the time he should have been arraigned, he was sitting in a cell in Armley Gaol, awaiting trial for rather more serious offences. He was, though, also carefully plotting a potential way out of his predicament.

The weeks since the murder of Jacqueline Hill had seen a frenzy of activity in the hunt to catch him. Margaret Thatcher's fury at the apparent incompetence of West Yorkshire Police was recorded in an internal governmental note (eventually declassified in 2010).

The Prime Minister said that the local police had so far failed totally in their enquiries into a series of murders which constituted the most appalling kind of violence against women. It was now a question of public confidence.

There were doubts whether the investigation was being conducted as effectively as it might be, and something needed to be done to restore the faith of the public in the performance of the police.

That 'something' turned out to be the formation of what was quickly dubbed 'The Ripper Super Squad'. Jim Hobson was to be in nominal charge, but five new and highly experienced men from outside West Yorkshire Police were to sit alongside him. Scotland Yard sent its head of the criminal intelligence branch, Commander Ron Harvey. He was joined by David Gerty, a former senior Yard detective and now Assistant Chief Constable in the West Midlands; Andrew Sloan, national coordinator of regional crime squads; Leslie Emment, Deputy Chief Constable of Thames Valley (reputedly, one of the brightest men anywhere in British policing); and Professor Stuart Kind, one of the country's top forensic scientists.

Quite how much influence these five experts could or would bring to bear on Hobson was debatable. While the press greeted news of the shake-up positively – 'Six Against the Ripper: Police bring in best brains to lead the hunt' was a typical headline – the newly appointed Assistant Chief Constable was initially reluctant to accept that mistakes might have been made throughout the five-year manhunt. In interviews with reporters, he rejected the idea that West Yorkshire Police could already have interviewed – but failed to recognise – their quarry, or that his identity could lie buried somewhere in the mountain of paperwork that clogged the arteries of Millgarth police station.

The first sign of real change came with a decision to re-examine cases that had previously been rejected as part of the

Ripper series. Among these were the attacks on Theresa Sykes in early November 1980 and Yvonne Mysliwiec a year earlier.

The second came in an internal – and never publicised – acceptance that, far from being a resident of Sunderland and its hinterland, the Ripper was almost certainly from West Yorkshire. A file note from 10 December 1980 advised investigators that their quarry probably:

- Lives in or near Bradford, possibly in the Manningham or Shipley area;
- selects target towns which are different from the previous two incidents;
- goes out and if unsuccessful in finding a victim in the target town, he looks for one on the way home.
- It follows that the next incident is unlikely to be in Leeds and, on the principle of maximum variety, it is likely to be in Huddersfield or Manchester or, in default, Bradford.

This document showed that, for the first time, the Ripper Squad was learning the lessons of both criminal and geographic profiling. In fact, only one detail of the prediction was wrong – the location of his next strike.

On Friday, 2 January 1981, Peter Sutcliffe left his home in Garden Lane, Heaton, just after 4 p.m. He told Sonia that he was going to collect the key of his sister's car, which, he said, had broken down. But he didn't drive to Maureen Sutcliffe's house in Bingley: instead, he went to a scrap yard near Mirfield, just outside Leeds. Here he picked up two number plates from a Skoda saloon that had been written off after an accident.

Five hours later, he rang Sonia from a service station to claim that he was now having car troubles himself. It was, of course, another lie: the Ripper was buying himself time to go hunting.

Using a roll of black electrical tape, he fixed the stolen number plates over those on his Rover: an hour later, he was cruising around the Havelock Square red-light district of Sheffield. This was thirty miles from home and new territory for him to locate a victim.

His first attempt at a pick-up was a nineteen-year-old prostitute called Denise Hall. He pulled up and asked her if she was 'doing business'. As she bent down to negotiate a price, something in his eyes frightened her: she mumbled a brief 'Sorry' and walked away.

Olivia Reivers was walking along Broomhall Street when she saw the Rover. Olivia was twenty-four, had been a prostitute for four years and was well known to the Sheffield vice squad.

> I was walking along the pavement when it stopped. The driver asked me if I was doing business and I said I was. I told him it was £10 with a rubber. He said it was OK.

Sutcliffe drove them to Melbourne Avenue, half a mile away. He parked up in the driveway of the Light Trades House and turned off the engine. When Olivia asked for the cash up front, he gave her a £10 note, and she took out a condom. Sutcliffe then asked her if they could talk for a while before having sex. He told her his name was Dave and that he had just had an argument with his wife. Eventually, he removed his car coat, placed it on the back seat and asked her to get into the back of the car.

Olivia's decision to refuse this request almost certainly saved her life. She insisted on staying in the front passenger seat and removed her panties while Sutcliffe unzipped his flies and lowered himself onto her. He tried for ten minutes but could not achieve an erection. He zipped himself up and began telling Olivia about his marital problems.

Suddenly, a police car with its headlights full on turned into the drive and parked nose-to-nose with the Rover.

PC Robert Hydes was a probationary constable; Sergeant Robert Ring had been with South Yorkshire Police for twenty-six years. That night, the older man was due to demonstrate, for his junior colleague's benefit, the correct procedure for dealing with street prostitution in Sheffield's red-light district. They set off from Hammerton Road station at 10 p.m. and half an hour later spotted Sutcliffe's car parked up in the driveway of the Light Trades House. Since this was known to be a place where prostitutes took their punters, the officers drove quietly up beside the suspect vehicle.

Hydes climbed out of the patrol car and approached the Rover. Inside, Sutcliffe hissed at Olivia Reivers: 'Leave it to me. You're my girlfriend.' He wound down the window, told the young constable the absurd and flimsy lie and gave his name as Peter Williams: for good measure he also provided a false address. In the meantime, Sergeant Ring went round the back of the car: he noted down the number plates and sent through a radio request to the station for a check with the Police National Computer.

As they waited inside his car, Sutcliffe asked Olivia, 'Can't you make a run for it?' She shrugged and said, 'No, I can't.' She realised that, as a known local prostitute, there was little chance of escaping a night at the police station.

When Ring discovered that the number plates belonged to a Skoda, rather than the Rover, he stepped back up to the car, removed the ignition keys from the steering column and informed both occupants that they were under arrest on suspicion of theft. Both officers then escorted Olivia to the patrol car, leaving Sutcliffe alone in the Rover. He quickly sized up the situation and seized his only opportunity to hide the tools of his trade. Grabbing the ball-peen hammer and single-bladed knife he had concealed under his car seat, he announced that he was 'bursting for a pee' and headed out of site behind a stone porch. Next to it was an oil storage tank: Sutcliffe hid both weapons behind it and returned to his car. He had another knife inside his jacket but neither Ring nor Hydes searched him; instead, they bundled him into the patrol car next to Olivia and drove the pair back to the station. Without realising it, they had arrested the Yorkshire Ripper, completely by accident.

When they got to the police station, Sutcliffe asked to use the toilet again. Bizarrely, since he had apparently just peed, this request was not queried. Nor was he searched or supervised. Safely inside the cubicle, he took the knife from his jacket and dropped it in the water cistern. In the side pocket of his coat was the length of cord he had used in the strangulation of Marguerite Walls and the attempted strangulation of Upadhya Bandara: it would be several hours before this was discovered, together with some very strange undergarments.

There would be a pattern to what ensued over the next forty-eight hours. Sutcliffe would be calm, courteous and apparently helpful, though he would try for much of it to sell a succession of interviewing officers a series of cock-and-bull stories. The police would continue with the remarkably lackadaisical approach that had characterised the handling of the man in their custody.

Sutcliffe began, that Friday, with a limited admission: he had stolen the number plates from a scrap yard at Cooper Bridge near Mirfield because in less than two weeks' time he was due in court on drink-driving charges. Since his car's insurance had just run out and he was certain to lose his licence, he had decided it wasn't worth renewing his insurance cover. Less than three hours later, his cover story unchallenged, the Ripper was sleeping soundly in a cell at Hammerton Road.

Because the theft of the number plates had occurred in West Yorkshire Police's area, the desk sergeant in Sheffield began calling round the neighbouring force's divisional stations to see which one wanted to handle the case. Finally, an officer in Dewsbury agreed to send someone to collect the suspect just as soon as the day shift arrived at 6 a.m.

The value of the theft was just 50 pence and, until a month earlier, would have been dealt with by a swift and routine charging, followed by the granting of police bail. But the mishandling of the Jacqueline Hill case – and in particular the much-criticised failure to find her body during the first search – had led Ronald Gregory to issue new operating orders. Any man found with a prostitute in suspicious circumstances was to be held and referred to the Ripper Squad for checks. As three West Yorkshire officers travelled down to Sheffield to collect Sutcliffe, the duty officer at Dewsbury passed his name up to the incident room in Leeds.

At 8.59 a.m. on Saturday, 3 January, Sutcliffe was booked in at Dewsbury. He was strip-searched and taken to a basement interview room. Evidently rested, and perfectly calm, he told the interviewing officers that he was a lorry driver from Bradford and volunteered the information that he had been interviewed at least twice by the Ripper Squad: once as part of the £5 note enquiry, and on other occasions because his car had been spotted in red-light areas.

One of the officers took careful note: he had already spotted Sutcliffe's dark hair and beard and the gap between his teeth. At 10.00 a.m., another call was made to the Ripper incident room, suggesting that someone from Millgarth should come down to interview Peter Sutcliffe. At around the same time, Sonia Sutcliffe was notified that her husband was in police custody being questioned about the theft of number plates.

At noon, Detective Sergeant Desmond O'Boyle arrived at Dewsbury. Formerly a detective in the Bradford division, he had been attached to the Ripper Squad for some time and, over the previous two hours, had taken the trouble to familiarise himself with the information contained on Sutcliffe's card in the giant index file carousel at Millgarth. He noted that the man had been interviewed nine times: nonetheless, at this stage, O'Boyle didn't think that Sutcliffe was any more a likely suspect for the Ripper murders than many others he had already checked out.

O'Boyle began by introducing himself as a member of the Ripper Squad. He started questioning Sutcliffe about his interests, home and social life and employment history. Throughout, the bearded lorry driver was pleasant and cooperative. On the subject of what he was doing in Sheffield, though, Sutcliffe began to spin an elaborate fiction. He had left his home at about 4 p.m. to look for spare parts for his car. He found a plate that had fallen off the Skoda, and pulled the other off the wreck. Since his insurance had run out the previous night, and he was due on a breathalyser charge, he thought he could use the plates for a few days.

The only point at which Sutcliffe seemed concerned and reluctant to cooperate was when he was asked to give a blood sample. 'What', he asked, 'if it's the same as the one you're wanting?'

Even given the fact that he knew O'Boyle was from the Ripper Squad, it was an odd response; it prompted the detective to ask outright: 'Are you the Ripper?' Sutcliffe insisted that he was not.

O'BOYLE: Well, what have you to fear?
SUTCLIFFE: Oh, all right then. Will you let me know the result of the blood test as soon as you get it?

Sutcliffe then cooperated with the police doctor and gave a blood sample. It revealed that he belonged to the rare B group – the same as the Ripper.

It is, perhaps, a measure of Sutcliffe's ability to control his fear and remain apparently helpful that, by 5.30 p.m., O'Boyle came to the conclusion that the man sitting calmly in front of him was unlikely to be the Yorkshire Ripper. He was ready to recommend that Sutcliffe be released. But the senior officer at Dewsbury was less convinced. Something in Chief Superintendent John Clark's bones told him that this man was a major suspect in the Ripper case.

O'Boyle returned to the interview room and began to ask rather more probing questions. For a start, what had led Sutcliffe to Sheffield?

Sutcliffe came up with another barely credible story: he had been approached by three young men who offered him £10 to give them a lift to Rotherham and then on to Sheffield. When he dropped the last one off, he had put the Skoda number plates over those of his Rover and begun driving home, but a woman had flagged him down, and thinking she was in trouble, he stopped. She had then asked whether he wanted 'business'.

SUTCLIFFE: I was surprised. I did not know she was a prostitute. I thought about things and realised I had £10 burning a hole in my pocket, and thought I might as well use it. The first girl had disappeared, so I drove on and saw another girl and stopped. She asked me if I wanted business. She got into the car and told me where to drive. I paid her £10. I did not want sex – I just wanted to talk about my problems at home. I did not want sex at all.

O'Boyle noted down this transparent nonsense and moved on to questions about the occasions when Sutcliffe's various vehicles had been logged in red-light areas in Leeds, Bradford and Manchester. As he had done when originally interviewed during the £5 enquiry, Sutcliffe denied ever having been to Manchester. But now he claimed that on the day in question his car had broken down in Bradford city centre and he had left it in the car park at Bradford Central Library. 'Someone must have used it to go to Manchester and put it back on that spot,' he suggested to the detective.

Next, O'Boyle asked where he had been on the night that Jacqueline Hill was murdered. Sutcliffe said that he thought he was with his wife at home. When the detective informed him that Sonia would be interviewed the following morning,

Sutcliffe appealed to him not to tell his wife that he had been arrested with a prostitute. It was a plea that fell on deaf ears.

> *O'BOYLE:* You got yourself into this. As far as I'm concerned I think you are a regular punter.
> *SUTCLIFFE:* I am not. I've never been with another woman.
> *O'BOYLE:* Your car has been seen in the red-light districts of Leeds and Manchester and last night you were caught in a car with a prostitute in Sheffield and you paid her £10. I don't believe these are coincidences.
> *SUTCLIFFE:* It is true – I am not a punter.

Meanwhile, the night shift had begun again at Hammerton Road police station in Sheffield. At 10 p.m., Sergeant Ring came back on duty and remembered that during the previous night's arrest Sutcliffe had left his car and gone out of sight to urinate. He decided to go back to the Light Trades House and have another look around. One hour later, as he shone his torch behind the oil tank, he discovered Sutcliffe's discarded hammer and knife.

A quick call back to the station ensured that a photographer was sent out to take pictures of the weapons at the scene. Another call was made to Dewsbury: in turn, news of the discovery was sent up to Detective Superintendent Dick Holland, the most senior Ripper Squad officer on duty. Holland ordered that an officer be stationed in Sutcliffe's cell overnight; he then prepared himself to meet Sonia the following morning.

At 9.30 a.m., Holland, O'Boyle, DCI George Smith and DC Jenny Crawford-Brown arrived at Number 6 Garden Lane.

They searched the house and a workshop in the back of the garage. They found ball-peen hammers, a hacksaw and a screwdriver as well as lengths of rope, women's underwear and a leather apron. Oddly, although the hammers and screwdrivers were destined to become exhibits at the Old Bailey, the rope, underwear and apron were never mentioned again.

The detectives then took Sonia for questioning at Bradford Police headquarters. Inside the station, Sonia began the lengthy process of helping the police build up a personal profile of her husband and their married life. But it was her account of his movements over the last two months that would prove crucial. She had given him an alibi on at least three previous occasions: this time would be different.

At Dewsbury, Peter Sutcliffe's day had started at 8 a.m. with coffee and toast. Then, almost sixteen hours of detailed interviews began.

His new interrogators were Detective Inspector John Boyle and Detective Sergeant Peter Smith. Dick Holland had specifically ordered the more junior officer to be present: Smith was one of the longest-serving Ripper Squad detectives and had an encyclopaedic knowledge of all the attacks. Systematically and patiently, the two men worked through a list of general questions: each was designed to close off possible avenues of escape for their suspect. Still Sutcliffe appeared friendly, articulate, calm and cooperative: he made no request for bail, and nor did he ask to see a solicitor.

After lunch, the questioning changed: now the detectives focused on Sutcliffe's whereabouts for the dates of the Yorkshire Ripper killings and attempted murders. Where was he at 8 p.m. on 5 November 1980, when Theresa Sykes was attacked?

Sutcliffe said that he was home, having arrived there no later than 8 p.m.

Fifteen miles way, in Bradford, Sonia Sutcliffe had given a different account. She told her interviewers that she distinctly remembered her husband walking through the kitchen door at 10.00 p.m.

Back in Dewsbury, Boyle and Smith asked about the night of 17 November 1980, when Jacqueline Hill was murdered. Sutcliffe told them he was at home with Sonia.

BOYLE: Every time you have been seen, you always seem to have the same alibi – that you were at home with your wife. I find that rather strange. How can you be sure that's where you were?

SUTCLIFFE: I'm always at home every night when I'm not on an overnight stay.

Not until Boyle shifted his attack to the events in Sheffield the previous night did Sutcliffe's façade of quiet confidence begin to crack.

BOYLE: I understand you were interviewed yesterday by DS O'Boyle about your movements during last Friday afternoon and evening up until the time you were arrested at Sheffield.

SUTCLIFFE: Yes, I've told him what happened.

BOYLE: I am not concerned with the allegation of theft of car number plates. I want to speak to you about a more serious matter, concerning your reason for going to Sheffield that night.

SUTCLIFFE: I've told him all about that night.

BOYLE: I've spoken to Sergeant O'Boyle and I am not satisfied with your account of that night.

SUTCLIFFE: What do you mean?

BOYLE: Why did you go to Sheffield that night?

SUTCLIFFE: I gave three people a lift to Rotherham and Sheffield from Bradford. They stopped me on the M606 and offered me £10 to take them home, so I did.

BOYLE: I don't believe that. I believe you went to Sheffield on Friday night with the sole purpose of picking up a prostitute.

SUTCLIFFE: That's not true. It was only after I got to Sheffield and had declined an offer to go with a prostitute that I decided to use the money I got from the hitch-hikers and go with one.

BOYLE: When you were arrested in Sheffield you had a prostitute in your car, which had false plates on it. I believe you put them on to conceal the identity of your vehicle in the event of it being seen in a prostitute area.

SUTCLIFFE: No, that's not true. To be honest with you, I've been so depressed that I put them on because I was thinking of committing a crime with the car.

BOYLE: I believe the crime you were going to commit was to harm a prostitute.

SUTCLIFFE: No, that's not true.

But when the detective got to the part about Sutcliffe going to urinate beside the oil storage tank, it became clear that the police had found his hammer and knife. With his Ripper tools of the trade discovered, Peter Sutcliffe knew, finally, that the game was up.

> BOYLE: Do you recall that before you were put in a police car at Sheffield you left your car and went to the side of a house?
>
> SUTCLIFFE: Yes, I went to urinate against the wall.
>
> BOYLE: I think you went for another purpose.

When there was no response to this from Sutcliffe, Boyle pressed him harder.

> BOYLE: Do you understand what I am saying? I think you are in trouble – serious trouble.
>
> SUTCLIFFE: I think you have been leading up to it.
>
> BOYLE: Leading up to what?
>
> SUTCLIFFE: The Yorkshire Ripper.
>
> BOYLE: What about the Yorkshire Ripper?
>
> SUTCLIFFE: Well, it's me.
>
> BOYLE: Peter, before you say anything further I must tell you that you are not obliged to say anything unless you wish to do so but what you say may be put in writing and given in evidence. Do you understand?
>
> SUTCLIFFE: Yes, I understand.
>
> BOYLE: If you wish you may have a solicitor present on your behalf.
>
> SUTCLIFFE: No, I don't need one. I just want to tell you what I've done. I'm glad it's all over. I would have killed that girl in Sheffield if I hadn't been caught, but I'd like to tell my wife myself. I don't want her to hear about it from

anyone else. It's her I'm thinking about, and my family. I'm not bothered about myself.

With his man on the ropes, Boyle carefully made sure there could be no escape.

BOYLE: You didn't go to the side of the house to urinate, did you?

SUTCLIFFE: No, I knew what you were leading up to. You've found the hammer and the knife, haven't you?

BOYLE: Yes, we have. Where did you put them?

SUTCLIFFE: When they took the girl to the Panda car I nipped out and put them near the house in the corner. I was panicking; I was hoping to get bail from there and get a taxi back and to pick them up. Then I would have been in the clear.

BOYLE: Tell me, if you are the so-called Ripper, how many women have you killed?

SUTCLIFFE: Eleven, but I haven't done that one at Preston. I've been to Preston but I haven't done that one.

BOYLE: Are you the author of the letters and the tape-recording posted from Sunderland to the police and the press from a man admitting to be the Ripper?

SUTCLIFFE: No, I am not. While ever that was going on I felt safe. I'm not a Geordie. I was born at Shipley.

BOYLE: Have you any idea who sent the letters and the tape?

SUTCLIFFE: No, it's no one connected with me. I've no idea who sent them.

A little while later, Boyle asked Sutcliffe if he knew all the names of his victims.

> *SUTCLIFFE:* Yes, I know them all.
> *BOYLE:* Do you keep any press cuttings of them or make any records?
> *SUTCLIFFE:* No, they are all in my brain reminding me of the beast I am.
> *BOYLE:* You say you have killed eleven women. Just take your time and think about how many there are.
> *SUTCLIFFE:* It's twelve, not eleven. Just thinking about them all reminds me what a monster I am. I know I would have gone on and on but now I'm glad I've been caught, and I just want to unload the burden.

Over the next fifteen hours and forty-five minutes, Sutcliffe dictated a detailed statement of confession to twelve of the Yorkshire Ripper crimes with which he would ultimately be charged. In a calm and unemotional voice, he gave a chilling and accurate description of the attacks and murders, including information that only the killer would have known and which had been kept secret from all but the most senior officers.

He described trying to cut off Jean Jordan's head with a hacksaw; he detailed the way he had stuffed horse hair from an old settee down Yvonne Pearson's throat to keep her quiet. He also revealed where he had discarded the weapons used to kill Josephine Whitaker and Barbara Leach; he even drew a picture of the walling hammer he had used to kill Yvonne Pearson.

But, although the Ripper appeared to be making a clean breast of his crimes, in reality he was carefully calibrating his responses and auditing the version of his killing spree. He claimed that the event that had started his attacks had been the encounter with Wilma McCann.

SUTCLIFFE: I didn't mean to kill her at first, but she was mocking me. After that it just grew and grew until I became a beast.

He made no mention of the attempted murders of Anna Rogulskyj or Olive Smelt and vehemently denied strangling Marguerite Walls with a ligature. (He would later admit the omissions, saying in the case of Miss Walls that he feared confessing to it 'might open up lots of new lines of enquiry that were nothing to do with me [and that I chose] just to deal with the ones that have been attributed to me'.)

In this, he should unquestionably have been correct. The MO in Marguerite Walls' murder was not only distinctive but also very similar to a catalogue of unsolved attacks up and down the country. Additionally, the strip-search that had relieved Sutcliffe of his clothes had uncovered a piece of blue-and-red-plaited nylon cord about three feet long in his jacket pocket. This rope had two knots at each end and two additional knots a few inches apart near the middle: it was, plainly, a garrotte. The search of his house, garage and car had located further very similar pieces of rope, including one about four feet long, hidden in his bedside cabinet.

The combination of all this evidence should have led to a nationwide examination of all murders and attempted murders in which a ligature had been used. In the heat and excitement of his confession – however partial it might be – no such search took place.

THE ACCIDENTAL ARREST

Instead, at 9 a.m. on Sunday, 4 January, Chief Constable Ronald Gregory, Assistant Chief Constable George Oldfield and Acting Assistant Chief Constable Jim Hobson held a filmed press conference.

Steering just the right side of the law of contempt (which, after charges have been laid, precludes any statement being made that might affect the chances of a fair trial), they nonetheless clearly indicated that the Yorkshire Ripper had at last been caught. A beaming Gregory announced to a phalanx of reporters, photographers and television cameras:

> We are absolutely delighted with developments at this stage. Absolutely delighted. Really delighted. George is delighted as well.

In the avalanche of newsprint and broadcasting that followed, and in off-the-record interviews given to journalists as they prepared lengthy background articles for after the trial, there was one vital piece of information about Peter Sutcliffe's confession that was overlooked.

Throughout almost a day and a night of dictating his statement. he never once mentioned hearing voices or being on a divinely ordered mission to rid the streets of prostitutes. He said nothing that could, in any way, have indicated that he was suffering from paranoid schizophrenia or was in the grip of delusions. All that would come much later.

There was a reason for this startling omission, and it was simple. Peter William Sutcliffe, the Yorkshire Ripper, was not mad but bad.

NINETEEN

COVER-UP

In 2012, a request was submitted to the National Archives – the vast repository of all government papers, dating back hundreds of years, located in the leafy West London suburb of Kew. The application, made under the Freedom of Information Act, sought access to the case papers for the trial of Peter William Sutcliffe.

Those 'case papers' are the most complete and official record of all the proceedings against the Yorkshire Ripper, from his original arraignment at Dewsbury magistrate's court to the trial at the Old Bailey. They also include the documents generated within the Home Office relating to Sutcliffe's prosecution and the commissions of inquiry that reported in 1982. Each stage of that judicial process was paid for by British taxpayers, who also foot the bill for maintaining the National Archives.

Despite this, reference J 82/4193, as the FOI submission was logged, was refused. A terse note on the Archives' files states that the entire record is closed until 1 January 2045 – almost sixty-four years after a jury found Sutcliffe guilty of mass murder. The only reasons cited for this official secrecy were the vague catch-all 'health and safety' and an exemption on the grounds that the documents contained 'personal information'.

British governments have a lamentable addiction to secrecy, and the Ripper records are far from the only case papers to be withheld from the scrutiny of those who paid for their preparation. But there is another – and very particular – reason for the Sutcliffe files to be locked away in official vaults: the decision to block public access to them is simply the latest incident in a long line of cover-ups about the Ripper – a shameful succession that began in the months after his conviction.

The farcical proceedings at the Old Bailey – a fiasco that began with the Attorney General accepting Sutcliffe's claims of insanity and then being forced to prove the precise opposite – ended on 22 May 1981. That afternoon, the Yorkshire Ripper was transported from the Old Bailey to Parkhurst Prison to begin his twenty life sentences.

The same day, Colin Sampson, Assistant Chief Constable of West Yorkshire Police, began an internal inquiry into the evident failures of his force throughout the Ripper inquiry. Simultaneously, and on the direct orders of Home Secretary William Whitelaw, Lawrence Byford began a separate investigation into the Ripper affair.

These two parallel examinations were aimed at uncovering what had, so plainly, gone wrong. Both were detailed and rigorous: Byford's team – and there were many members of it – would spend five months grilling senior detectives and junior officers alike.

The costs of his in-depth study (and of Sampson's more rudimentary analysis) were all borne by the public purse: British taxpayers had footed the bill for the police manhunt and were now charged for the privilege of two official examinations of its failure. And yet both the Sampson and the Byford inquiry reports were to be kept secret. As we shall see, some of their most important sections remain under lock and key today.

Sampson delivered his findings to Chief Constable Ronald Gregory in October 1981. In over 200 closely typed pages, he laid out the details of the investigations into each murder and attempted murder for which Peter Sutcliffe had been convicted. He concluded that the deaths of the last six victims could have been prevented if West Yorkshire Police had been more efficient in collating the mass of information early in the series of killings.

The force, Sampson ruefully conceded, missed every clue that pointed to Peter Sutcliffe, firstly because those clues were lost in their filing systems, and subsequently because they did not fit the profile drawn from the Sunderland tape recording and letters. He noted that the Ripper incident room was saturated with reports and could not cope with the mass of information and that this resulted in detectives being sent on enquiries without knowledge of what had happened in previous interviews.

Faced with such a devastating condemnation of his force – all the more potent since it was written by an insider – Ronald Gregory ordered the suppression of the Sampson Report. But the reason for this secrecy was not simply an attempt to avoid embarrassment: the key lay in two very brief sections towards the end of the document. The first was headed 'Other Similar Attacks'.

A number of similar attacks on women since 1966 in West Yorkshire remain undetected. Sutcliffe has now been interviewed about these and other cases which occurred elsewhere in the country, but has denied responsibility.

In and of itself this was an explosive revelation. After years of failing to link the Yorkshire Ripper to a succession of murders or attempted murders, West Yorkshire Police had now, apparently, rushed to ask Sutcliffe whether he would like to confess to them. Since the detectives knew that his original confession statement had been carefully calibrated to admit only to cases with which he had publicly been linked, the effort was – at best – naïve. Nor was the claim wholly truthful.

In the months following Sutcliffe's arrest, Detective Sergeant Desmond O'Boyle had been pursuing enquiries into at least two of these mysterious unsolved cases. He had done so on that most intangible of investigative qualities – a hunch: it led him to John Tomey.

The years had not been kind to Tomey. The attack by his taxi passenger on Cockhill Moor near Oxenhope in 1967 had left deep indentations in his skull. He had been unable to return to work and had not married. O'Boyle read his file and spotted the similarity between Tomey's ordeal and the proven Ripper attacks: the blows that had rained down on the back of the taxi driver's head appeared to have been made by a ball-peen hammer. He also noted that the description of Tomey's attacker matched that of Peter Sutcliffe: a local man with a West Yorkshire accent, in his mid-twenties (as Sutcliffe was in 1966), around five feet eight inches tall, with darkish skin, dark hair and a distinctive full set of moustache and beard.

When the detective interviewed John Tomey that early winter of 1981, he became convinced that he had uncovered another Ripper victim.

The discovery also led him back to the murder of Fred Craven in April 1966 in Bingley. Carefully piecing together the evidence from the old case files, O'Boyle realised that the most likely suspect was Peter William Sutcliffe. Nor, as it turned out, was he alone: immediately after the arrest in January 1981, Fred Craven's son, Ronald, had taken the trouble to ring up George Oldfield and ask whether his father could have been a Ripper victim. Oldfield had brusquely said he was too busy handling Sutcliffe's confession to speak; he promised to call back – but never did.

O'Boyle believed firmly that Sutcliffe should be interviewed about the Craven and Tomey cases. He put this as a formal recommendation to Acting Assistant Chief Constable Jim Hobson. The suggestion was rejected: Hobson insisted that the Ripper only attacked women.

The second, potentially devastating, revelation in the Sampson Report was headed 'Description and Photofits of Suspects'.

During the inquiry at least 77 photofit pictures and four artists' impressions were compiled from descriptions given by witnesses and victims. 41 photofits related to either unknown men whom women reported had been violent to them, or who had been seen in the area of the crimes but not at relevant times. 26 related to men who had been seen in the area of the crimes about the relevant times; five of men seen with victims on relevant dates; two of men seen with a woman, possibly the victim; and the remaining three produced by the two survivors, [Marcella] Claxton and [Marilyn] Moore.

Here, in the leaden prose of a career police manager, was evidence that the Ripper Squad had been given a large number of photofits from a succession of cases other than those for which Sutcliffe would be convicted. It begged the question of what had been done with them: that question would remain an official secret.

Gregory's decision to suppress the Sampson Report was based substantially on the revelations about other unsolved attacks – inside West Yorkshire and all over Britain – and the photofit evidence that linked them to the Yorkshire Ripper.

Only when the Chief Constable sold his memoirs to the *Mail on Sunday* in June 1983 was a much-redacted version of the document made public by West Yorkshire Police Authority – the semi-elected body of local councillors that notionally exercised some sort of supervision over Gregory's force. It led to a flurry of headlines that focused exclusively on the devastating criticisms of the Ripper inquiry: references to the unsolved cold cases went unremarked.

While Sampson's report sat on Ronald Gregory's desk, Lawrence Byford was putting the finishing touches to his account of the Yorkshire Ripper story. His remit was wider than the internal police inquiry and his team had been tasked with drawing up a series of recommendations for future major murder inquiries. These were, by Home Office fiat, to be communicated to every chief constable in Britain with the firm expectation that they would be acted upon.

But – initially, at least – Byford believed that his inquiry should be shown to the very people who had paid for it: the public. He wrote, privately, to a colleague:

> I have made the point very strongly to the Home Office that the cost of conducting the inquiry and preparing the report cannot be justified by what has happened so far and that the publication of the report, albeit in an expurgated version, will be necessary ...

But before he could deliver his 156 pages of findings, something (or someone) appears to have changed his mind. The report, he later wrote to the same colleague, would now only be shown to those with a need to know – and that did not include the taxpayers who funded it.

> I need hardly point out that any leakage of information would, even at this stage, prove highly embarrassing to the Home Secretary. I am as conscious as anyone for the need of the [police] Service to learn the valuable lessons contained in the report, and am anxious that the report should be circulated so far as is consistent with the need for these lessons to be got across to serving officers.
>
> At the same time, I am aware of the inherent dangers which the release of material from the report would involve for the morale of the West Yorkshire force and the Police Service, as well as for the Home Secretary, whose handling of the issue has been so helpful to the Service generally.

And so it proved. Byford sent his report the Home Office, which promptly locked it away from public scrutiny. Other than William Whitelaw's brief and bland announcement to the House of Commons on 19 January 1982 – a typically emollient assurance by the Home Secretary that lessons would be learned and that MPS (and, by extension, the public) could rest assured that such a fiasco would never happen again – the very expensive forensic examination of the Ripper's crimes would remain officially secret until June 2006. Even then, when a Freedom of Information request winkled it out of Whitehall, the report would be heavily redacted.

What was it that Byford had found that demanded such protection? What was so potentially explosive that the public could not be trusted for twenty-four years? He certainly reached a damning conclusion about what had happened to the report made by Detective Constable Andy Laptew of his interview with Peter Sutcliffe in August 1979 and which recommended further investigation of the occupant of 6 Garden Lane, Heaton.

> Despite the most probing investigation it has not been possible to trace what happened to Constable Laptew's report after he submitted it. Detective Superintendent Holland is adamant that it was not attached to the papers which he marked 'File' … in spite of the fact that the report is referred to on the completed action …
>
> I cannot help concluding that one or other of the senior officers involved in these events is now loath to accept responsibility for what, in effect, was a serious error of judgement.

But the need for suppression could not be just the revelation of West Yorkshire Police's failings, or even the apparent duplicity of a senior officer in answering questions about Laptew's perceptive call for Sutcliffe to be targeted. That story emerged within months of the Ripper trial – not through any leak by Laptew – and caused Laptew's police career to stall permanently. In fact, the sorry catalogue of police errors was dissected repeatedly and publicly from the moment the Ripper's trial ended. There had to be something much more damning.

There was.

Tucked away in his conclusions, Byford warned the Home Secretary:

There is a curious and unexplained lull of Sutcliffe's criminal activities and there is the possibility that he carried out other attacks on prostitutes and unaccompanied women during that period ...

We feel it is highly improbable that the crimes in respect of which Sutcliffe has been charged and convicted are the only ones attributed to him. This feeling reinforced by examining the details of a number of assaults on women since 1969 which, in some ways, clearly fall into the established pattern of Sutcliffe's overall modus operandi ...

It is my firm conclusion that between 1969 and 1980 Sutcliffe was probably responsible for many attacks on women, which he has not admitted, not only in West Yorkshire and Manchester but also in other parts of the country ...

I hasten to add that I feel sure that the senior police officers in the areas concerned are also mindful of this possibility but, in order to ensure full account is taken of all information available, I have arranged for an effective liaison to take place.

'Many attacks'; 'other parts of the country'. What, and where, were these? Who were the victims? And what, exactly, was the 'effective liaison' Byford had set in motion?

In May 1982, Sutcliffe applied to the Court of Appeal for a review of his trial. He once again claimed that his convictions for the thirteen murders should be reduced to manslaughter on the grounds of diminished responsibility. The learned judges sitting in the Victorian sub-fusc of London's Royal Courts of Justice rejected his appeal.

In the wake of that decision, police forces from across Britain queued up to interview the Ripper about unsolved attacks and killings in their areas. Among them was Derbyshire Police: its detectives believed that Sutcliffe was the prime suspect for the murder of Barbara Mayo in October 1970. But, true to form, West Yorkshire Police was determined to keep the lid on any future investigations.

Keith Hellawell was one of Britain's most able and intelligent police officers. Born in 1942 into the mining communities around Dewsbury, he had left school at the age of fifteen and spent the first four years of his working life down the pit. But he had always wanted to be a policeman and, in 1962, was accepted (on his second attempt) into the old West Riding county force.

Before long he was marked out for the nascent 'fast-track' programme, aimed at identifying future leaders. He passed a series of exams with flying colours, launched one of Britain's first dedicated drugs squads, and in his spare time studied for degrees in social policy and law. By 1983, he had risen to the rank of assistant chief constable in West Yorkshire Police, and was handed the poisoned chalice of handling inquiries into the extensive series of murders and attacks that were suspected to have been the work of the Yorkshire Ripper. He later, in his memoirs, recounted the way in which he was assigned this task.[5]

> Other police forces with outstanding murders of young women approached us to ask us if they could interview him [Sutcliffe] about their crimes. Colin Sampson, smarting from the criticism we had received at the hands of the media and conscious that (due largely to political pressure) we had interviewed Sutcliffe for only a short time, and would be embarrassed if he admitted further crimes to someone from elsewhere, asked me to take on this responsibility. 'Make sure that if he admits any further crimes, he admits them to you alone,' Colin instructed me.

Hellawell went about his task carefully and forensically. He put together a team of detectives to help him examine unsolved cases from all over Britain. One of them was Detective Inspector John Boyle, one of the officers who had helped secure Sutcliffe's original confession. What Hellawell's team uncovered must have shocked them.

> There were seventy-eight unsolved murders and attempted murders potentially committed by Sutcliffe. By a process of elimination we reduced the number to twenty-two

---

[5] Keith Hellawell, *The Outsider*, HarperCollins, London, 2002

possible offences, twelve within our force area, the remainder outside.

Of the West Yorkshire cases, Hellawell would write in his memoirs after retiring from the police, he was certain that Tracy Browne, Ann Rooney and Yvonne Mysliwiec had been attacked by the Yorkshire Ripper. He could not, at that point, list any further names for the simple reason that West Yorkshire Police had refused to allow him access to his own papers on the grounds that they were 'confidential'.

It was an unprecedented rebuff – and one that was driven, above all, by a determination to keep secret the extent of Peter Sutcliffe's crimes. More than any other police officer, Hellawell knew where the Ripper's unsolved bodies were buried: he knew because from 1983 onwards he spent ten years researching the cases and interviewing Sutcliffe.

> He was housed in Parkhurst prison on the Isle of Wight, which necessitated a long drive to Southampton and a ferry crossing. I travelled with Detective Inspector John Boyle ... and our mood was sombre when we approached the gaol for the first time.
>
> It was a cold, grey, dark winter's morning and the Victorian entrance looked like Bleak House. We were received by the Governor ... who told us that Sutcliffe was not under any medication and had been trouble-free.

Over the ensuing decade, Hellawell met regularly – and secretly – with Sutcliffe. Patiently, the detective picked away at the Ripper's defences until he won two confessions: Sutcliffe admitted to the attacks on Tracy Browne in 1975 and Ann Rooney in 1979.

Hellawell had done exactly as his former boss, Colin Sampson, had instructed. He had secured confessions from the Yorkshire Ripper and ensured that they were made solely to West Yorkshire Police. By the time Sutcliffe ended their meetings, Hellawell had also been promoted to the force's Chief Constable. All in all, this should have led to new charges being laid: it didn't.

'Not in the public interest' is a peculiarly English weasel-phrase. Nowhere – not in statute nor in common law – is there a definition of what it means. It is, instead, a power taken by government to itself with absolutely no oversight or mechanism for challenge. Quite what the public is, or should be interested in, and the method by which this is determined, is at the complete discretion of those in power. And, as Lewis Carroll's absurdly fantastical Humpty Dumpty wryly noted, 'When I use a word it means what I choose it to mean – neither more nor less.'

In 1993, Barbara Mills QC, the (unelected) Director of Public Prosecutions, decided the words meant that Peter Sutcliffe should not be charged with any further offences. No matter that he had confessed to two (out of a possible twenty-two) murderous attacks, it was 'not in the public interest' to prosecute him.

Why? What possible reason could there be for failing to bring to justice – and into the sanitising light of public understanding – one of Britain's worst serial killers? Money? Of course such prosecutions are expensive, but – as we shall shortly see – when it comes to Peter Sutcliffe, successive governments have been remarkably generous with public funds.

There is, simply, no legitimate reason to bury these cases. Which means, by a process of deduction, there is an *illegitimate* reason. Even in a country where secrecy (and its assistance in the preservation of power) is endemic, the Yorkshire Ripper saga stands out by the dogged official determination to cover up the extent and depth of his crimes.

Firstly, there is Keith Hellawell's patiently reinvestigated list of twenty-two unsolved cases. The murders and attempted murders listed in this book were first detailed by Hellawell during his employment with West Yorkshire Police. From the local murder of Fred Craven in 1966, through the Midlands and London killings of the 1970s and back to the succession of failed attacks in West Riding, all were examined by Hellawell and his team.

Throughout the twelve months in which this book was written, a succession of Freedom of Information requests were made to police forces across the country. From Derbyshire Police we sought access to information about Wendy Sewell's murder. From the Metropolitan Police we asked a series of questions about the unsolved cases across London; from Staffordshire we requested information about the death of Judith Roberts; Cheshire Police were contacted about Jackie Ansell-Lamb. And to West Yorkshire Police we addressed detailed requests for facts about the miscarriage of justice that wrongly caused Anthony Steel to lose more than twenty years of his life in prison for the killing of Carol Wilkinson. Above all, we asked for access to Keith Hellawell's list of twenty-two likely Ripper cases, and to the long-suppressed photofits identified by Colin Sampson and Lawrence Byford.

We also asked the Home Office for access to the suppressed

sections of the Byford Report. These refer to the thirteen cases Byford knew of that were most likely the work of Peter Sutcliffe. They also include all the photofits that the Ripper Squad had and which, as we know from leaks over the past twenty years, clearly show a resemblance between Sutcliffe and the unsolved cases.

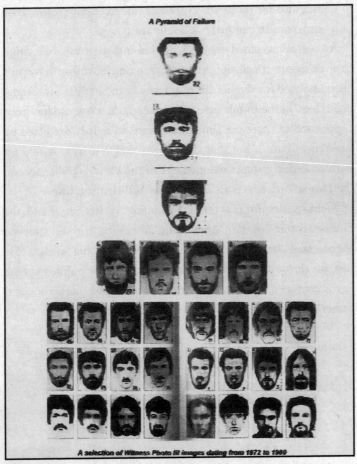

Included are two photographs of Peter Sutcliffe, taken in 1969 and 1981

In each and every case our requests were refused. Frequently, these refusals were unlawfully late – weeks or months past the deadline for responses; more often than not, they cited a need for 'confidentiality'.

Whose privacy is being protected? The victims'? Unlikely: in the murder cases we have cited there remains no confidentiality to guard, and for those who survived, the need for closure that only information can bring is debilitating.

As we approached the end of our investigation, we came to a different conclusion. The secrecy and cover-up have not been imposed for the benefit of those whom Sutcliffe attacked – much less 'in the public interest'. Instead, the evidence has been suppressed to spare the 'embarrassment' so rightly predicted by Lawrence Byford: but that shame (for shame it is) is bound up with a need to protect the interests of the various police forces, the Home Office, and above all Peter William Sutcliffe.

Because, despite the verdict of a jury of his peers and the finding of the Court of Appeal, the Yorkshire Ripper achieved the pleasing outcome he had once predicted to Sonia Sutcliffe. He has, for thirty years, been featherbedded at great public expense in the cosy and supportive environment of a psychiatric hospital rather than the punitive regime of a high-security prison.

TWENTY
AFTERMATH

At precisely 10 o'clock every Monday morning, the peace of the comfortable commuter-belt town of Crowthorne is shattered by the eerie wail of an air-raid siren. The alternating high and low notes are unchanged from the signal introduced at the start of World War Two: they howl through the quiet Berkshire countryside until the all-clear sounds at 10.05 a.m. This is how Broadmoor Hospital begins its working week.

The siren is no more than a test of the system for alerting the local population when a patient escapes the hospital's high walls and strict security. Breakouts from Broadmoor are rare in the extreme. The last time the siren sounded in anger was 1991: since then, its drone has largely faded into a familiar and unthreatening routine.

The hospital itself is a complex collection of red-brick buildings. They began life in 1863 as a criminal lunatic asylum and have been used ever since to house some of the most dangerous men in Britain. Among them is Peter William Sutcliffe, the Yorkshire Ripper.

The process by which Sutcliffe arrived at Broadmoor – and, indeed, by which he remains there – is symptomatic of the secrecy that has shrouded his career of crime ever since the Old Bailey trial concluded. The care and sensitivity shown to this mass killer are in marked contrast to the way in which many of his victims have been treated.

Broadmoor is not a prison. Despite its seventeen-foot-high walls and very visible security cameras, inside its layout and regime are deliberately those of a hospital. The 210 men who live within it are not referred to as prisoners or inmates, but as patients. There are no grim galleries or overcrowded cells – the way ordinary criminals are housed in conventional penal establishments: instead most live in single rooms that, while guarded by serious locks, are a far less retributive, much more comfortable environment in which to be confined. As its director of nursing, Jimmy Noak, admitted when challenged in 2011 about the ethics of treating Britain's most violent offenders with such kindness:

> It's not fair, but what is the alternative? If these people committed crimes because they were suffering from an acute mental illness then they should be in hospital.

Noak is surely right: a humane and enlightened society tries to help those afflicted by mental illness, not grind them into submission. The question, though, is whether Peter Sutcliffe was mentally ill when he murdered and maimed his victims.

Two courts have decided that he was not. First, the Old Bailey trial determined that he was not insane and was therefore not able to claim the protection of a defence of diminished responsibility. Then the Court of Appeal upheld this view. Both hearings were open: both decisions were made in public.

By contrast, the decision to alter those rulings was made in secret and with no attempt at explanation. In March 1984, Sutcliffe was simply transferred from Parkhurst to Broadmoor under Section 47 of the Mental Health Act – the law that allows a prison to decide that an inmate is sufficiently ill to warrant treatment in hospital. He has remained there ever since: he is one of only a handful of offenders in Britain who are subject to a 'whole-life tariff' – bureaucracy-speak for someone who will be held behind bars until he (or she) dies.

How did this happen? Was it simply the case that the professional opinion of psychiatrists ultimately prevailed over the judgments of the legal system? And if so, does this not demonstrate that this country has a civilised response to mental illness even in those who commit the most heinous of crimes?

The answer is that we cannot know: the process and reasoning behind Peter Sutcliffe's move to more congenial surroundings are – officially – secret. But even if the benign explanation of a caring penal system is correct, it raises many more fundamental and deeply disturbing questions.

Why did Sutcliffe not mention the 'voices from God' anywhere in his extraordinarily lengthy confession? Why did he wait until his meeting with Dr Hugo Milne in March 1981 to reveal this divine mission to kill prostitutes? What interpretation should be placed on his statement to Sonia that he would persuade the psychiatrist that he was mad and would, as a result, be sent to 'a loony bin'?

How much reliance should the doctors have placed on Sutcliffe's pronouncements that he heard a voice telling him to kill? Milne and his fellow practitioners admitted they had only the Ripper's word to go on.

Ultimately, the most important question of all is what drove this man to kill. If his story about God speaking to him was no more than an opportunistic exploitation of the psychiatrists, sex – in the form of necrophilia – is the most likely motivation. It is certainly supported by the evidence of what he did to several of his victims; and there is also the very odd item of clothing he was found to be wearing on the night he was arrested.

When South Yorkshire Police officers strip-searched him, they discovered that his underpants were in his coat pocket, and that beneath his trousers he sported a specially adapted garment consisting of two sleeves of a jumper crudely sewn together upside down and pulled up to the waist with a leg to go in each arm; in the middle was a gap exposing his genitals.

It was obvious to the officers who saw this that the bizarre arrangement would have afforded Sutcliffe quick and easy access to his penis when his trousers were unzipped: this would enable him to masturbate over his victims while simultaneously killing them – a textbook description of the necrophilic urge.

This remarkable item should have been shown to each and every psychiatrist who examined Sutcliffe and who swallowed his self-presentation of paranoid schizophrenia. Before reaching such an important diagnosis, they surely should have questioned him about the meaning and purpose of his carefully crafted undergarments. They did not.

This was not, though, their fault. From the moment it was taken from Sutcliffe, bagged, tagged and placed in an evidence locker, no mention was ever made about this garment. It was not shown to the doctors during their consultations with the Ripper;

First picture of a murderer's outfit

BY DAVID BRUCE

THIS is the 'killing kit' of Yorkshire Ripper Peter Sutcliffe – never before seen by the public.

The YEP has obtained an exclusive picture of the bizarre, home-made outfit which Sutcliffe was wearing when he was arrested 22 years ago.

A book published earlier this year and based on Home Office documents made the first-ever reference to the crudely-made 'jumper' which Sutcliffe wore as an undergarment.

Michael Bilton's book *Wicked Beyond Belief* reveals that when arrested, Sutcliffe was wearing a V-neck jumper worn upside down over his legs which allowed him to expose himself when carrying out his attacks.

The Old Bailey jury that tried Sutcliffe never knew about his killing kit. And photographs of the crudely-made garment have never been seen before.

A former detective held on to the item for 20 years – before handing it back to police chiefs.

Turn to Page Two

● GRUESOME FINDS: Peter Sutcliffe's crudely-made 'killing kit', above, which the Yorkshire Ripper, top left, was wearing when police arrested him 22 years ago. And left, a photograph of a stash of tools found by officers at the Ripper's home

Extract from *Yorkshire Evening Post*, Saturday, 20 February 2003, which revealed Sutcliffe's specially adapted garment

nor was it entered into evidence at his subsequent trial. Worse, West Yorkshire Police ordered it to be destroyed. Only the secret intervention of an exhibits officer saved it. Today it remains locked away – undiscussed and unexamined. Yet it could and should provide the most important clue in the mystery of many of the unsolved murders and attacks between 1966 and 1981.

Since Peter Sutcliffe will never be released, there is a legitimate viewpoint that questions why it matters exactly how many people the Yorkshire Ripper attacked or killed. The argument lays out the impeccable logic that being convicted in twenty of the cases is recognition enough of the evil that he did: what possible benefit could accrue from pursuing – at great public cost – further charges against him?

It is, on the surface, an appealing line of reasoning. But, as is so often the case, we should beware elegantly simple solutions.

On the most fundamental and prosaic level there is a question of cost. Official statistics show that the average annual cost of keeping a man locked up in the regular prison system is £37,163. The price tag for keeping that same prisoner inside Broadmoor is almost ten times that figure – an average of £325,000 per year.

This disparity is, of course, primarily due to the cost of the medical regime. As Professor Tony Maden – one of Britain's most eminent psychiatrists – points out, the most effective way of managing mentally ill criminals is pharmaceutical.

> The main features of schizophrenia are delusions – false beliefs about the world: so, for example, believing that other people are persecuting them. And it is also characterised by hallucinations – hearing voices.
>
> Most of the serious violence I've seen associated with schizophrenia has arisen primarily from extreme fear on the part of the individual who carries out the violent act. So they would see it as a form of self-protection. Totally misguided and irrational, but nevertheless that emotion is very real to the individual.
>
> The delusions, the hallucinations will go away if you give people drugs.

Maden is now professor of forensic psychiatry at Imperial College, London, but between 2001 and 2012 he was head of the Dangerous Severe Personality Unit at Broadmoor. A year after he left, he publicly stated that the Yorkshire Ripper did not belong at the special hospital.

> My understanding of Sutcliffe is that he is no longer acutely mentally ill in a way that would require hospitalisation.

It was a view that was – bizarrely – apparently shared by Sutcliffe's own lawyer. In 2009, Saimo Chahal brought unsuccessful legal proceedings against the Home Office for keeping his client locked up indefinitely. He demanded – in the name of the Ripper's human rights – that a final release date be fixed and that Sutcliffe be moved back into the regular prison system.

If Peter Sutcliffe is, indeed, not mad, there is no moral or ethical reason for him to be spared new investigations into the extent of his murders and attempts. What's more, police forces now have the technology to provide forensic support for such enquiries. DNA testing is now routine and – from the attack on Anna Rogulskyj onwards – West Yorkshire Police recovered crime scene samples. They also have the Ripper's unique under-wear, which will still retain recoverable DNA evidence.

True, Sutcliffe's condition as a 'non-secretor' means that these samples will not provide cast-iron proof. But by the same token, if material recovered from the scenes of the unsolved crimes shows that the suspect was a non-secretor of B blood group, because of its relative rarity this in itself would be strongly indicative of the Ripper having committed the crimes.

Nor is it only West Yorkshire Police who has samples to work with. Although every one of the forces whose unsolved murders and attacks are detailed in this book refused to provide information about what evidence they have retained, contemporary press accounts of the Barbara Mayo and Wendy Sewell cases in Derbyshire and several of those in London make mention of material being taken away for examination.

If the unholy trinity of a criminal's pattern of offending is 'means, motive, opportunity', the same must apply to the responsibility of those paid to run the criminal justice system. In 2014, as courts up and down Britain heard cases of historical child sexual abuse, the new Director of Public Prosecutions went on record to acknowledge this and to redefine the doctrine of 'public interest'. Alison Saunders stressed that 'a sense of justice for the victim' should be the overriding concern.

I want potential victims of crime to know that it doesn't matter how long ago a crime is alleged to have been committed, we will take it seriously and we will take the views of the victims, or their families where appropriate, into account when deciding if we should prosecute.

Of course, where the most serious offences are being alleged, it is nearly always in the public interest to prosecute, and the evidential test remains the same – only those cases where there is sufficient evidence will be considered for prosecution.

But whereas previously we have thought that the passage of time in certain cases lessened the public interest in prosecuting, that is not the case anymore. We will consider cases in the same way be they 30 days or 30 years old. I am determined that victims of these crimes get their day in court, where appropriate.

The forgotten and secret victims of the Yorkshire Ripper – the survivors and the families of the dead – want that day in court. Maureen Lea, attacked in Leeds in October 1980, can speak for the first group. She has lived ever since with the pain of her physical injuries and the hurt of never being acknowledged.

Being a victim of Peter Sutcliffe makes you part of a pretty exclusive club, one that you don't want to be part of. When I see his face on television or in the newspapers I am catapulted back to that horrific time and I do still have nightmares. I have been diagnosed with long-term post-traumatic stress disorder but I've learned to live with that.

Thirty years is a long time, but I've finally reached the conclusion whereby we could utilise the media interest in the Sutcliffe story to raise money for Victim Support.

That Maureen Lea was definitely a Ripper victim was confirmed in 2002, when West Yorkshire Police publicly stated that it was in a position to charge Sutcliffe with her attempted murder and the killing of Debbie Schlesinger. Yet since then no action has been taken.

Then there are the families of those who died. Irene Vidler, daughter of Sutcliffe's probable first victim, Fred Craven, in 1966, describes the agony of not knowing who killed her father.

It just seems incredible that, in a small place like Bingley where a murder was a phenomenal event in 1966, that the same method of killing my dad was used as was used to kill those women. Nothing has been proved and the police say that there is nothing to be gained by looking into it again, but we haven't got closure.

Her views are echoed by Elsie Cowen, sister of Gloria Booth. Gloria was murdered in West London in 1971.

She died on the Saturday night and it was the Sunday night when they came to tell my mam. It was a terrible time.

No one wants to hear their child has died but the way it happened was horrible.

I hadn't realised how bad the murder had been. The things he had done to her were horrific.

I am convinced that the Ripper did this. Reading the pathologist's report the similarities between her death and how Peter Sutcliffe killed his victims, it all makes sense.

We want the police to look into the case again to see whether there is more evidence that can give our family closure. The years have gone by and you think they are never going to get anybody for it. This has been going on for years and years. It would be nice if someone could just say, 'Yes it was him.'

Gladys Hayes, the mother of Lynda Farrow, murdered in 1979, has a very pressing need for her child's death to be re-investigated.

I wasn't there to help her when she needed me and that awful thought has haunted me since the day it happened. I'm not getting any younger and it is my greatest wish that I find out what happened to my daughter before I pass away.

But there are other victims, too: three men who lost the best years of their lives, rotting in prison cells for crimes they did not commit.

Andrew James Evans served twenty-five years after being wrongly convicted of the murder of Judith Roberts in 1972; Stephen Downing was falsely condemned to twenty-seven years behind bars for the 1973 killing of Wendy Sewell; and Anthony Steel was locked away for twenty-five years after being railroaded into a bogus confession about the death of Carol Wilkinson in 1977.

All three were innocent of crimes whose most likely culprit was – and remains – Peter Sutcliffe. In all three cases, the police forces involved – Staffordshire, Derbyshire and West Yorkshire – say publicly that the murders remain open and unsolved, but that they are undertaking no new investigations to solve them.

Anthony Steel went to his grave in 2007 without seeing the real killer brought to court. His brother-in-law, Don Emmott, speaks for all the families affected by these miscarriages of justice.

I want to see the investigation reopened and for the police to come and see me. Details show that it was Sutcliffe that killed Carol Wilkinson.

We need to get justice – for Anthony and for the family of Carol.

These hidden victims of the Yorkshire Ripper – the men and women he killed with impunity, the families of the dead, and the unacknowledged survivors – have been kept silent too long. Their voices have not been heard: their plight has been ignored.

It is time – long past time – for justice to be done, and for it to be seen to be done. It is time for Peter William Sutcliffe to face prosecution for the full catalogue of his crimes. Only then will all the ghosts of the Yorkshire Ripper finally be laid to rest.

THE YORKSHIRE RIPPER: THE SECRET MURDERS

APPENDIX 1: *MODUS OPERANDI* IN CONFIRMED ATTACKS AND KILLINGS

(MURDERS IN CAPITALS; ATTEMPTED MURDERS IN LOWER CASE)

NAME	YEAR	HAMMER $	STABBED	LIGATURE	BODY POSED	BODY MOVED	BODY COVERED	STRIPPED	BITE MARK	BOOT USED	SEMEN	CONVERSATION	DISTURBED
ANNA ROGULSKYJ	1975	✓	✓		N/A	N/A	N/A	N/A			✓	✓	✓
OLIVE SMELT	1975	✓	✓		N/A	N/A	N/A	N/A			N/A	✓	✓
WILMA MCCANN	1975	✓	✓		✓							✓	
EMILY JACKSON	1976	✓	✓					✓		✓	✓	✓	✓
MARCELLA CLAXTON	1976	✓			N/A	N/A	N/A	N/A			✓ ?	✓	
IRENE RICHARDSON	1977	✓	✓				✓	✓				✓	
PATRICIA ATKINSON	1977	✓	✓			✓	✓	✓				✓	
JAYNE MACDONALD	1977	✓	✓			✓	✓	✓					
MAUREEN LONG	1977	✓	✓			✓	✓	✓				✓	
JEAN JORDAN	1977	✓	✓			✓	✓	✓		✓		✓	✓
MARILYN MOORE	1977	✓			N/A	N/A	N/A	N/A				✓	✓
YVONNE PEARSON	1978	✓				✓	✓	✓		✓		✓	
HELEN RYTKA	1978	✓	✓			✓	✓	✓				✓	
VERA MILLWARD	1978	✓	✓			✓	✓	✓				✓	

JOSEPHINE WHITAKER	1979	✓	✓		✓	✓		✓	✓			✓	
BARBARA LEACH	1979	✓	✓			✓	✓	✓					
MARGUERITE WALLS	1980	✓		✓		✓	✓	✓		✓			
UPADHYA BANDARA	1980	✓		✓	N/A	✓	N/A	N/A					✓
THERESA SYKES	1980	✓			N/A	N/A	N/A	N/A					✓
JACQUELINE HILL	1980	✓	✓			✓		✓					

§ OR OTHER BLUNT INSTRUMENT

APPENDIX 2: MODUS OPERANDI IN SUSPECTED ATTACKS AND KILLINGS

(MURDERS IN CAPITALS; ATTEMPTED MURDERS IN LOWER CASE)

NAME	YEAR	HAMMER &	STABBED	LIGATURE	BODY POSED	BODY MOVED	BODY COVERED	STRIPPED	BITE MARK	BOOT USED	SEMEN	CONVERSATION	DISTURBED
FRED CRAVEN	1966	✓								✓			
JOHN TOMEY	1966	✓			N/A	N/A	N/A	N/A			N/A	✓	✓
MARY JUDGE	1967	✓						✓					
LUCY TINSLOP			✓	✓									
JACQUIE ANSELL-LAMB	1970			✓	✓	✓	✓	✓					
BARBARA MAYO	1970	✓	✓		✓	✓	✓	✓					
GLORIA BOOTH	1970	✓		✓	✓	✓		✓	✓		✓		
JUDITH ROBERTS	1972	✓			✓		✓	✓					
WENDY SEWELL	1973	✓		✓	✓	✓		✓		✓		✓	✓
ROSINA HILLIARD	1974	✓		✓									
KAY O'CONNOR	1974					✓	✓	✓		✓			
CAROLINE ALLEN	1974	✓				✓	✓	✓				✓	
GLORIA WOOD	1974	✓			N/A	N/A	N/A	N/A			N/A	✓	✓
EVE STRATFORD	1975		✓		✓			✓				✓	

Name	Year												
TRACEY BROWNE*	1975	✓		N/A	N/A	N/A	N/A		N/A			✓	✓
LYNNE WEEDON	1975	✓			✓	N/A	✓						✓
ROSEMARY STEAD	1976	✓			N/A	N/A	N/A	N/A	N/A				✓
MAUREEN HOGAN	1976	✓	✓		N/A	N/A	N/A	N/A	N/A				
BARBARA YOUNG	1977	✓											
DEBBIE SCHLESINGER	1977		✓					✓					✓
ELIZABETH PARAVICINI	1977	✓		✓			✓	✓	✓				
CAROL WILKINSON	1977	✓		✓			✓						✓
LYNDA FARROW	1979	✓					✓	N/A	✓	✓			
ANN ROONEY*	1979	✓		N/A	N/A	N/A	N/A	N/A	N/A				✓
MARION SPENCE	1979		✓	✓	✓		✓						
ALISON MORRIS	1979	✓											
YVONNE MYSLIWIEC	1979	✓	✓		N/A	N/A	N/A	N/A	N/A				✓
SALLY SHEPHERD	1979	✓	✓		✓	✓	✓			✓			
PATRICIA MORRIS	1980		✓	✓	✓	N/A	N/A		N/A				
MAUREEN LEA	1980	✓	✓		N/A	N/A	N/A	N/A	N/A			✓	

§ OR OTHER BLUNT INSTRUMENT
* ADMITTED BY SUTCLIFFE AFTER HIS CONVICTION

A NOTE ON PHOTOFITS

Throughout this book we have reproduced police photofit pictures, made by survivors of (or witnesses to) unsolved historic attacks that match the Yorkshire Ripper's *modus operandi*. Even a cursory glance shows them to resemble Peter Sutcliffe very closely.

Readers may, however, wonder at the poor quality of these reproduced images. There is a reason for this.

These photofits were originally published by the police. After Sutcliffe's conviction they were included in Sir Lawrence Byford's official report on the failures of the Ripper investigation.

The section of the Byford Report which contains them has never been made public. Even when the majority of Byford's enquiry was published, more than twenty years after Sutcliffe's conviction, the Home Office withheld the photofits.

We have repeatedly requested them under the Freedom of Information Act. The Home Office, supported by West Yorkshire Police, has refused our requests, claiming that publishing the images 'would constitute a disclosure of the linkage of Peter Sutcliffe to the crimes that he has not been publicly linked to, and therefore to other potential victims who have right to privacy'.

Nothing encapsulates more clearly than this the cynical determination to cover-up the true extent of the Yorkshire Ripper's crimes.

We believe that these photofits show quite clearly that the prime suspect in these cases strongly resembled Peter Sutcliffe, and that this supports the other evidence we have uncovered.

That is why have included them within this book, even though they are of lower technical quality than they would have been if the Home Office and police had released the originals.